CLIFF RICHARD

The Biography

*To my Dad and Mum, Gordon and Ivy Turner,
with thanks for all their love and encouragement,
and to the memory of George Hoffman*

Cliff Richard

The Biography

STEVE TURNER

A LION BOOK

Oxford · Batavia · Sydney

Published by
Lion Publishing plc
Sandy Lane West, Oxford, England
ISBN 0 7459 2249 X
Albatross Books Pty Ltd
PO Box 320, Sutherland, NSW 2232, Australia
ISBN 0 7324 0534 3

First edition 1993

A catalogue record for this book is available
from the British Library

Printed and bound in Great Britain
by HarperCollins Manufacturing, Glasgow

Cover photo of Cliff Richard: Paul Cox
Cover photo of Steve Turner: Michael Putland

Contents

Introduction

I was nine years old when I first became aware of Cliff Richard. I can remember hearing 'Living Doll' on the radio—the 'wireless' as we then called it—and have a clear memory of children singing 'Travellin' Light' on the way back home from junior school.

At that age I didn't know anything about Cliff having 'softened up' his sound. I had no knowledge of Little Richard, Jerry Lee Lewis, Chuck Berry and Gene Vincent because I hadn't heard Uncle Mac play their records on 'Children's Favourites', one of the few BBC wireless shows in those days to play pop records. All I knew was that Cliff wasn't like the Perry Como and Alma Cogan sound that seemed to dominate pop through my childhood, and I liked what I heard.

I also liked what I saw. I wanted a striped shirt like Cliff's ('too jazzy,' said Mum). I wanted pink socks ('girls clothes,' said Mum). Most of all I wanted a hairstyle which swept back at the sides and tumbled forward at the front ('you're having a short back and sides and that's it,' said Mum).

I'd like to be able to say that I have all Cliff's early singles in mint condition, but the fact is that in those days my parents had a gramophone that only played 78 rpm records. My first Cliff purchase (other than a comb in a grey plastic case bearing his image and signature) was the sheet music to 'Please Don't Tease'. It cost two shillings and I only bought it for the photograph on the cover.

It's easy to look back and see what a 'nice' boy Cliff really was, but at the time, to someone not yet in his teens, he seemed like forbidden fruit. The only people I knew who dressed in such outrageous colours and wore their hair without a clean parting were Teddy boys, Rockers and the boys who operated the bumper cars at fairgrounds.

These were the days, it must be remembered, when a solid-body electric guitar was regarded as a symbol of teenage discontent. Rock 'n' roll, whether original and from Memphis or derivative and from London, was nothing more than a 'noise' which the older generation associated with juvenile delinquency.

My parents certainly didn't see Cliff as a good thing. I'm sure they had never checked out his worthy opinions but he just looked like a rock 'n' roll person. I can remember wanting to buy a book about him (it must have been a paperback version of *It's Great To Be Young*, his 1960 autobiography) and my dad said, 'You don't want that. It'll be full of sex.' If only he had known.

I didn't meet Cliff until 1970, at a party in London. By this time I was starting to write about rock music. We passed on the stairs and I stuck my hand out and said, 'Hi, I'm Steve Turner,' and Cliff stuck his hand out and just said, 'Hi'. It was then I realized that when you're as famous as Cliff you no longer have to bother giving your name. I saw him at various times after that through the early seventies, but didn't interview him until 1977 while he was recording his album *Small Corners*.

The genesis of this book, though, lies in a four-part documentary series for BBC TV called 'Cliff!' (1981) for which I was researcher and interviewer. I interviewed many of his friends and colleagues for these films, travelled with Cliff on the road, visited him at home and joined him on a tour of America.

At the end of it all I realized I would be well-positioned to write a much more comprehensive book about Cliff than had ever been written before. I had the access, I had the contacts and I had a pile of research material.

That Christmas I was given a copy of Albert Goldman's *Elvis*, a book which set new rigorous standards for rock biography. The previous 'definitive' biography of Elvis, written by Jerry Hopkins, had listed 112 interview sources and began the story at Elvis' birth. Goldman listed 160 interviews and started the story with David Pressley (the original spelling of the family name) who had come to

America some time during the 1740s.

Early in 1982 I made my first approach to Cliff's office suggesting there was room for a more expansive biography of Cliff than had been written before. They eventually agreed but there were long delays because they felt the market was overloaded with Cliff products, and they didn't want fans to be overwhelmed.

Final approval wasn't given until March 1991. By this time I had amassed even more material, and had the additional perspective of having co-written a song for Cliff which became the title track of his album *Now You See Me, Now You Don't*.

I didn't come to the project with a prepared thesis. I wanted simply to provide as full a portrait of the man as I could, because I considered that anyone who had been that successful for that long was deserving of detailed investigation.

There were areas I was particularly interested in though, because I thought they offered clues both to his success and to his character.

There was the question of his enigmatic sexuality. If he were a bank manager or a captain of industry I wouldn't consider this relevant, but it is when you are dealing with a man who trades in romantic fantasy. Understandably people want to know why he has never married, or whether he's interested in women at all.

The fact that Cliff has survived so many changes in musical fashion is remarkable. He has been at the top of the music business for over thirty years, and yet his success in Europe and Australasia has not been repeated in America. I wanted to find out why.

Then there is Cliff's Christian faith—not very fashionable for a popular entertainer—and his image of being a 'nice guy'. Just how much of that is due to his upbringing and how much is a result of his conversion to Christianity? I was intrigued to know whether his faith had changed or matured over the years. And whether he's a nice guy when he's not on show.

Finally there is his youthfulness. His apparent failure to grow old has become an important part of his image. I wanted to discover how much his youthful looks have to be worked on now, and how bothered he is by changes in his appearance.

Since starting work on the book the two questions I've been asked most often are, 'Hasn't there already been a book about Cliff?' and 'Is it an authorized biography?' The answer in both cases is, ... er, well, sort of.

There have been at least thirty books about Cliff published in Britain over the years. But surprisingly enough, only three of these are adult biographies, and none have been in-depth studies. In addition Cliff has written two autobiographies—*It's Great To Be Young* (1960) and *Which One's Cliff?* (1977). Both attempted a very different job from the book you now hold in your hand.

I felt that there was room for a more detailed account of Cliff's life because the expectations of a rock biography have been significantly raised by books like Goldman's *Elvis* and *The Lives of John Lennon*, Philip Norman's *Shout* (the Beatles) and David Ritz's *Divided Soul* (Marvin Gaye). No longer is it sufficient to speak to half a dozen colleagues and stitch their comments together with material from newspaper cuttings.

For this book I carried out over 200 interviews and discovered, very early on, that despite the volume of words written about Cliff over the years, I was not tramping a well-worn path. Almost all my interviewees had never been questioned about Cliff before. No one had spoken to his aunts, uncles, schoolfriends, childhood neighbours, former girlfriends and early business associates. No one had ever bothered tracing his family tree or tracking down the members of his early groups.

The book is authorized in as much I have had the full support and co-operation of Cliff and his management team during the writing, but they have not had authorial control and have no financial stake in the project.

I consider this to be the perfect arrangement. Without Cliff's blessing I would have had limited access to his friends, colleagues and office diaries. People are very suspicious about co-operating with unapproved biographers.

Yet if my involvement with Cliff had extended to include editorial approval the book would have lost any hope of objectivity. It's impossible to write an honest biography with the subject looking over your shoulder.

As it was, Cliff has given me as much of his time as I asked for. I was given an introductory letter to smooth the way in setting up interviews, and there has been no evidence of anyone having been warned against talking to me. In fact some interviews, like the one with Cliff's mother, Mrs Dorothy Bodkin, were organized on my behalf by the office.

It was very brave of Cliff to allow me to nose around in his past, digging up long forgotten associations and asking impertinent questions. I hope that he discovers his trust has been rewarded with a book which accurately and fairly sums up his life so far.

Steve Turner
London, January 1993

Acknowledgments

T his book couldn't have been written without the support of Bill Latham who, in giving me the green light to go ahead with the book, had to give the red light to a number of other well-qualified potential biographers.

It was Bill who ultimately had to reassure worried interviewees that I was alright when they called up to check with the office. Throughout the project he encouraged me to fight for objectivity knowing that this would be a difficult task in view of the closeness I had enjoyed with Cliff in the past.

Another vital support has been Gill Snow, secretary (and much, much more) to Cliff Richard. She has supplied me with phone numbers, answered all my little queries and opened the office diaries.

At Lion Publishing I'm grateful to Becky Winter not only for seeing the potential of a full-length biography of this kind but also for helping me focus my vision. Melanie Watson has ensured that the manuscript is politically correct and helped me to spell words such as occasional and commitment.

All my interviewees deserve thanks for giving up time and information, but I must mention some who have given special help.

Cliff's mother, Mrs Dorothy Bodkin, has not been interviewed for twenty-five years but graciously consented to speak to me for this book.

Peter Gormley, famed for his reticence, not only gave me an interview but was ready at the end of a phone any time I had a query.

From Cliff's family I must thank Vincent Bridgwater for his time and the use of his photographs. Joyce Dobra not only lent me photographs from the Webb side of the family but gave me access to some documents and copies of birth certificates which greatly speeded up my completion of the family tree. Olive Dazely spent long hours on the phone telling me about life in India.

Delia Wicks, Janice Berry and Betty Clarke had never spoken of their romances with Cliff to anyone in the media before and I am grateful to them for their time and openess.

Ian 'Sammy' Samwell not only spoke to me frequently on the phone but met up with me in London and gave me a small suitcase full of photographs, cuttings, sheet music, and scrapbooks. A real gold mine!

Dick Teague—who thought I was a practical joker when I first called him to ask about the days when Cliff sang in his group—sent me invaluable information about the brief career of the Dick Teague Skiffle Group. This included pages from a diary kept by his father who managed their affairs, engagement sheets, letters and cuttings.

Royston Ellis was another great discovery. Back in Britain for a short break, he went through his cupboards and discovered all sorts of helpful photographs and cuttings. He lent me copies of his books *The Shadows By Themselves* and *The Big Beat Scene*, as well as an autographed proof copy of Cliff's *It's Great To Be Young*.

Ray Mackender, who has a great memory for the 'Oh Boy!' days, sent me lots of details about incidents he remembered and was always readily available to check facts.

There were some discontinued albums and videos which I needed and Christine Whitehead, co-ordinator of Britain's Cliff Richard Fan Club, tracked them down and sent them to me.

Rachel Melville-Thomas cast a psychologist's eye over some of my research and Mick Brown, Richard Branson's biographer, was one of the first to encourage me to take on this book.

Of Cliff's current circle of close friends, Graham Disbrey was very generous with his time and Peter Graves was a reliable source of information when it came to dates of holidays and meetings. John Davey very kindly photocopied material which helped me with the chronology of events around Cliff's Christian conversion.

Finally, much of the burden of this book has fallen on my family—daughter Lianne, son Nathan and wife Mo—and I thank them for their love and patience.

1

'Only a boy from Cheshunt'

C liff Richard can't sleep. He's been lying in his bed for three hours but his mind won't switch off. He snaps on his bedside light and reaches out for a book. After two chapters the book is abandoned, the light is turned off and he again tries to drift into semi-consciousness. But something won't let him.

An hour later he's up and walking about the master bedroom. He puts on the television and watches Britain's only all-night channel with its mix of sport, chat shows and old movies. Still it doesn't tire him.

He has every reason to want this to be a good night's sleep for in just over twelve hours' time, on 16 June 1989, he will face his largest audience ever. That's what keeps him awake. It's not just the 72,000 fans who've been promised an event rather than a show, but the complexity of what he's planning to do on stage: working with 90 artists, singing 45 songs, making five costume changes and moving in style from fifties high school hop to late eighties high-tech pop while everything is recorded and filmed.

It's already taken six weeks of rehearsals at Shepperton Studios but one technical hitch, spate of bad weather or dicky throat and The Event could go down in pop history as Almost The Event. The next forty-eight hours, he knows, could raise his career to even greater heights or have him written off as the man who flew too close to the sun.

By the time he leaves his bedroom at eight o'clock in the morning and goes down for breakfast he has had no sleep. The best he has been able to do has been to lie still on the bed for two hours conserving energy.

Already in the kitchen is Bill Latham, Cliff's longest-standing and most trusted friend. Although Latham is only two years older than Cliff, with his balding head and greying hair he looks like any middle-aged man could decently expect to.

Cliff appears to have defied the years. He doesn't have an extra ounce of fat on his frame, still walks with a youthful spring and hasn't yet been dealt the curse of a receding hairline, wrinkled flesh and double chin. He has grey flecks in his hair but most are hidden by lowlights.

After a light breakfast (two slices of toast and a coffee) Cliff showers, shaves and dresses in casual clothes (a T-shirt and shorts because the weather is bright). At 9.30 a stretch limo passes through the gates and draws up on the gravel outside the front door. In the driving seat is a chauffeur dressed in a grey peak cap. In the back is David Bryce, Cliff's professional manager.

Cliff leaves the house and climbs into the back of the limo next to Bryce. He doesn't have to worry about his costumes and personal effects as they've been taken ahead to Wembley Stadium by his personal assistant Roger Bruce.

At 10.30 Bruce calls through on the car phone to check on Cliff's progress. His first shock of the day has been to discover that a member of the pyrotechnic team has been badly burned while working on the firework display. A rope he was climbing snapped and he fell to the ground clutching an armful of explosives which went off on impact. The burns are so bad it's decided to cancel the display which was to close the show.

The limo arrives at Wembley and Bruce is at the back entrance to ensure that Cliff gets free access to the fenced-off backstage area. Promoter Mel Bush has had it designed to look like a small Mediterranean village with palm trees, fountains, open-air cafés, flowers, bushes, shrubs and a marquee.

Now on site, Cliff has a coffee in his dressing cabin which has been stocked by Bruce with everything he needs. There is shampoo and conditioner, perfumed soap, a dressing gown, monogrammed towels produced especially for the day, a hairdryer and his favourite brush and comb. In the fridge there are bottles of mineral water, cans of Dexters hypotonic drink and his preferred post-concert tipple of pineapple juice and champagne.

At midday he meets masseuse Linda Kay who has been hired to ease neck and shoulder tension. She uses manual lymphatic drainage, a massage that rids the body of toxins through the lymph system, and an electro muscle stimulator to lift the contours of the face. A 'facelift without surgery' Cliff calls it. It tones his features up so well that some people think he's already been through make-up.

Wherever he goes on site he's surrounded by people making last-minute adjustments. He can't get it out of his head that he's the reason that they are all here today: 90 performing artists and 3,000 people checking tickets, selling goods, controlling the crowds, filming, recording and generally mounting the show.

After a light snack Cliff starts his soundcheck. The sun blazes down out of a clear blue sky. Everything seems perfect but he's so on edge he even forgets lines from his best-known songs. Few people who have worked with him have ever seen him so nervous.

The stadium has been made to look less cavernous by draping one end to create a huge arch beneath which Cliff will put on his most lavish and comprehensive performance yet. He knows he's one of only a few acts able to take on this venue with its daunting capacity of over 70,000.

But tickets for tonight's show sold out over a single weekend. Mel Bush then took a further gamble—a second concert on the next night—which also sold out. Cliff's nervousness is understandable: 144,000 people will see The Event.

Cliff is reluctant to give what he calls 'history lessons' in concert, which is why this isn't just another Cliff and the Shadows reunion.

But for these two nights he will celebrate the start of his career with a short set based around the idea of the 'Oh Boy!' TV show which gave him his first national exposure in 1958.

The show's two resident vocal groups, the Dallas Boys and the Vernons Girls, have re-formed. Its MC Jimmy Henney will make the opening announcement, and there will be a special guest spot.

When Henney, dressed in a pale blue and white pullover, walks out on stage it is five o'clock. 'This is how it all began thirty years ago,' he announces and the band plays the opening chords of Buddy Holly's 'Oh Boy' as five Dallas Boys, in red satin bomber jackets and white trousers, strut out.

When they move back, two central doors burst open and Cliff dances out in a pink jacket, black shirt, pink belt, black trousers and pink socks: a tribute to the fashion he wore when he first sang 'Move It' on stage. A wave of applause rises from the crowd and Cliff beams with pleasure. As he steps back, a dozen Vernons Girls in party dresses, petticoats or shorts, sashay across the stage, all of them looking surprisingly trim and elegant.

For the last verse the wispy-bearded Kalin Twins from America add their voices, walking on stage in black dinner jackets as if they've arrived late at the wrong party. They couldn't fail to remember that for the last show they did with Cliff, in October 1958, they were the chart toppers and he was the new boy.

A rumble of honky tonk piano chords announce 'Whole Lotta Shakin' Goin' On', the Jerry Lee Lewis hit which Cliff has performed ever since it was first released. In Jerry Lee's hands it was a crude song designated by rock critic Dave Marsh 'one of the strongest arguments for the idea that prudes really did have something to fear from rock 'n' roll'. In the hands of Cliff and the 'Oh Boy!' chorus it sounds about as threatening as Val Doonican singing the Sex Pistols' 'Anarchy In The UK'.

With the Kalins he sings the Everly Brothers' 'Bird Dog' and then takes off into a version of Elvis Presley's 1957 hit 'Let's Have A

Party', with all the requisite bowing of legs and knocking of knees. During this song his fears evaporate. As he rolls and jerks across the stage he is the boy who never grew up, the boy who, in middle age, is still playing rock stars in the mirror.

After eight songs with the Shadows there is a short break and Cliff returns at 8.45 as dusk begins to fall. Lights play across the crowd, and a slow drum beat starts up as Cliff, dressed from neck to foot in white, strides purposefully across the stage, wreathed in dry ice. The jacket of his made-to-measure suit is studded with 2,000 diamantés, which now sparkle beneath the pyramid of lights.

Contrasted against his well-tanned face the shimmering white costume suggests he is a figure of purity, an unbesmirched survivor from another age. He looks magisterial and immaculate.

Two or three songs into the set he starts to loosen up, picking up on the energy of the crowd. He starts to work them a little, spinning around like a half-speed dervish and urging them to clap along.

Because the Shadows had declined to appear in the 'Oh Boy!' section (they argued it would spoil the effect of their later spot), Cliff invited two original Shadows, who hadn't played together with him since October 1961, to join in his set. Tony Meehan and Jet Harris are welcomed onto the stage.

Jet, gaunt and balding, saunters on in a Mississippi gambler's jacket and leather boots, his red guitar hanging over his right shoulder. Meehan settles behind his drum kit. 'This is the song that started it all off,' says Cliff, strapping on a white guitar and playing the rhythm line of 'Move It'. He's now played it so many times that it rarely sounds like the raw, earthy original.

The night sky is now pitch black, the show is reaching its climax. 'For thirty years you have given me a really glorious career,' Cliff says after singing 'I Just Don't Have The Heart' with the production team of Stock, Aitken and Waterman on backing vocals.

'What can I say? All I've been able to do in return is the best I can do. But the best I can do is not going to change your lifestyle in any way, it's not going to mean anything in any great eternal terms.

'I always feel that if I have one thing to offer that's of any value it's the message that God exists, that Jesus is alive and that he's yours if you want him. I've been criticized for saying that many times in situations like this but I thumb my nose at the criticism. Here are two songs I hope you like.'

He then sings the gospel songs 'God Put A Fighter In Me' by Graham Kendrick, Britain's best-known contemporary hymn writer, and 'Thief In The Night' by Paul Field.

That he bothers, at this climactic point in his biggest concert ever, to turn the attention away from himself, is evidence of the depth of his religious feelings. He would feel he had short-changed his fans if they left Wembley Stadium only thinking about how wonderful Cliff Richard is.

The finale comes with 'From A Distance'. Cliff stands on a plinth swathed in light while the rest of the night's performers congregate around him. During the instrumental passage, as the lights sweep the stage and flags flutter in the breeze, he grasps the radio mike close to his lips with both hands and then when he lets it drop it's clear that he's close to tears. He wants to smile but his mouth is going in the wrong direction.

He regains his composure long enough to get through the last verse and then when it's all over he says, 'Thank you. Good night and God bless,' and walks away wiping his eyes.

As soon as he is off stage Roger Bruce puts a coat over his shoulders and guides him towards his dressing cabin. Those who've been working on the site—cleaners, ticket collectors, police, first aiders—spontaneously line up and leave a path for him, applauding him as he moves between them.

When he gets to the cabin he flops onto a leather sofa and bursts into tears. Bruce puts his arms around Cliff's shoulders to comfort him and then he too begins to sob.

It's as if all the love and affection that Cliff has worked to generate over the past thirty years has just rolled over him in one single wave. It's at times like this that he says to himself: 'I can't believe all this is happening. I'm only a boy from Cheshunt.'

2

Roots in the Raj

T he fact that the boy who became Cliff Richard was born in India and baptized Harry Rodger Webb has been presented a million times. But nothing has ever been said about how his parents, Rodger and Dorothy Marie, came to be on the subcontinent and there have been only the sketchiest descriptions of his grandparents.

Perhaps because of this it has often been rumoured that Cliff's dark good looks are due to mixed race. When he was a teenager in Cheshunt the question for his friends was not whether he had Indian blood, but from which parent it came. Most of them plumped for Mrs Webb because she was most like Cliff in appearance and had the same darker skin tone.

Cliff has never been a good source of information on family history because he has never been interested. The most he has ever said is that his grandparents were 'as English as roast beef', and that it had been they who had made the move to India. He once told a journalist that he thought one of his grandfathers was born in Threadneedle Street, in the City of London, but that 'every time I pass through there all I can see are banks and insurance offices'.

The truth is that only one of his grandparents was born in England—but not in Threadneedle Street—and it's possible that some of his great-great-grandparents never knew any country other than India.

The mystery of the skin pigmentation is partly solved by the records of baptism, marriage and burial held by the India Office Library in London. They show that a great-grandmother on his mother's side was half Welsh and half Spanish, born to George David Smith and Emiline Josephine Rebeiro who had married in Calcutta in 1869. Photographs of her in middle age show that she had distinctively dusky Mediterranean looks which passed to her children.

The Portuguese had planted themselves in India in 1510 when they captured Goa on the west coast and turned it into a colony. A steady flow of Portuguese and Spanish workers came to that first settlement and soon moved northwards to Bombay.

The British didn't come into India for another hundred years, when the East India Company began building trading posts and forts. Although the company hadn't intended to govern, merely to make money out of commodities such as spices, cotton, sugar, jute and silk, effectively it became an imperial power dividing the country into the presidencies of Bombay, Bengal and Madras and organizing its own massive private army.

By the time Victoria came to the throne in 1837, Westminster was firmly in control of India and the Crown had appointed a governor-general. Whereas the original merchants of the East India Company had set up in the ports and worked alongside the indigenous population, the Victorian imperialists had no such respect for the natives and their ways. They saw the Indians as people to be tamed.

Cliff's ancestors came to India as part of this exercise. His father's family came as part of the task force needed to build the railway system that would transform India from a collection of outposts to a modern nation. On his mother's side they came as soldiers, equipped to defend the British Empire against restless natives.

The earliest ancestor on record is Thomas Webb, Cliff's great-great-grandfather, who was born in London's East End in 1805. He became a book-keeper, married a girl called Mary Taynton, who was two years his junior, and lived at 2 Wilson's Place, a small cul-de-sac near Commercial Road in Limehouse. Here, in 1841, Mary gave birth to Cliff's great-grandfather, Thomas Benjamin Webb, the man who was to lead the Webb family to India.

Wilson's Place today is an area of lock-up garages with the outline of Canary Wharf visible in the distance. The houses that Thomas Benjamin Webb would have known were torn down long ago.

Nothing is recorded of his life until 1865 when he married Amelia Sophia Smart, a West Ham girl, and moved over the river to Woolwich where they settled at 135 Plumstead Road.

The 1871 census shows that Amelia was then a dressmaker and Thomas Benjamin was working as an engineer at the Woolwich Arsenal. This meant that they were affluent enough to employ a live-in nursemaid, Jane Brown, to look after their first child, probably their eldest son Thomas.

It was in this house in 1872 that Cliff's grandfather, Frederick William Webb, was born. Again we don't know much about his early life, but the stark facts show that he was frequently hit by tragedy. Two more children were born to his mother in quick succession. Then shortly after his second birthday she died, age 33, from typhoid fever, leaving her husband with four children to care for.

In view of this new responsibility it's hard to account for what happened next. In 1877, the year Queen Victoria became empress of India, Thomas Benjamin packed his bags, left his children and went to work as a mechanical engineer on the South India Railway.

There may have been sound economic reasons for the move. The railway system in India was in its infancy and British labourers were being recruited to lay new track. Maybe the wages of an engineer at the Woolwich Arsenal weren't sufficient to cover the care and education of his children, whereas those of a covenanted engineer in India were. No one knows who looked after his children or whether he ever intended to return.

All that is known is that the young Frederick William received a grammar school education in Holborn and then, at the age of twelve, left England to join his father. On 10 April 1885 we find him in Perambur in South India where, according to the ecclesiastical returns, he was baptized by a chaplain of the Madras Railway. His brother later joined him, but the fate of his two siblings remains a mystery. Neither of them went to India or saw their father again.

Two years after Frederick William arrived in Perambur, further tragedy struck. On 27 August 1887 Thomas Benjamin was tending a damaged valve on an engine when it burst open. The escaping steam could have caused an explosion so he laid himself across it to prevent a disaster, and died of terrible injuries.

Thomas was buried the same day, which happened to be Frederick William's birthday. Conducting the funeral service was the same railway chaplain who had baptized the boy two years before. At fifteen Frederick was an orphan, alone in a still strange land, and with no means of returning to the familiar streets of South London.

No one alive today can remember him mentioning this calamitous time. 'We didn't ask our parents about their backgrounds in those days,' says his daughter Joyce Clarkson. 'It just wasn't done.'

The next entry in the ecclesiastical returns is Frederick's marriage in 1896 to Donella Eugenie Woodfall, Cliff's paternal grandmother. Donella Eugenie, known because of her initials as Dewy (a nickname that passed briefly to Cliff's oldest sister who was baptized Donella Eugenie Webb), had slightly oriental looks. Rumour had it they were due to a Burmese princess who married into Donella Woodfall's mother's family. Her direct ancestry was Dutch and English but, if the Burmese connection is true, it would further explain Cliff's dark colouring.

Donella and Frederick started their married life in Negapatam but by 1899, when their first daughter Dorothy May was born, they had moved to Burma where Frederick William was involved in bridge construction in the capital city of Rangoon.

He was a handsome man with a commanding manner, but had a

foul temper which sometimes lost him work. 'But there was another side to his character,' his granddaughter Joyce Dobra points out. 'He would spend a lot of time in the juvenile courts where he would bail out young men, take them home, get them good apprenticeships and see them on the right path.'

Donella Eugenie gave birth to a total of eleven children. Rodger Oscar Webb, Cliff's father, was born on 23 December 1904 at Tramway Quarters, Rangoon. Although it was company accommodation, the Webbs were well off by the standards of their contemporaries back in England. They enjoyed the services of a cook, a bearer, a sweeper, a washer, and an *ayah*, the servant who looked after the small children.

They stayed in Burma until 1914 when the family began to move around Indian railway towns such as Howrah, Allahabad and Lucknow. By the time Rodger started at Allahabad High School his oldest brother, Harry, was seventeen and his youngest sister, Joyce, was a baby.

Frederick William was a tough disciplinarian who caned the boys and took the attitude that if girls misbehaved while boys were present it was the boys' fault for letting it happen. He kept his servants in order and told them that a spare glass eye which he kept in a drawer was able to see everything that they did in the house. (He had lost his left eye in an accident.)

He was also deeply religious, reading the Bible regularly and making notes of his studies in the margins. 'We were always taught from the Bible,' says his youngest daughter Joyce Clarkson. 'I remember having to go to Sunday school when I was young. The local priest, Reverend Vetichan, was a wonderful man and it was through him that we became regular churchgoers.'

The Webbs were a happy family and the children enjoyed the sheer fun of being let loose in a country of exotic smells, wild animals and brilliant sunshine. Rodger was often dragged around with his older brothers and sisters and unwittingly got involved in their mischief.

'Once they went to a Hindu cremation,' Joyce Dobra remembers being told. 'They hid in the bushes to watch and as the heat affected the muscles of the body being burned it began to sit up and the children fled in terror. Rodger was only a toddler and he had terrible nightmares for a long time afterwards.'

During the First World War life changed dramatically for the Webbs. Harry was sent to fight in Tanganyika, German East Africa. He was killed there in Dar es Salaam at the age of twenty. Around the same time Rodger's older brother Frederick died of typhoid at fifteen. The one bit of bright news was that Donella Eugenie was expecting yet another child, but even this turned into tragedy. She died of 'malarial cachexia and childbirth' in Lucknow. Eight months later the child, a little boy baptized Valentine, died of a heart defect.

Frederick William was badly affected by these tragedies. He locked himself away in a room alone for several weeks and drank heavily to numb the pain. 'When he finally came out his hair was absolutely white,' says Joyce Dobra.

Rodger must have left school around this time. No one is sure what he did immediately afterwards. His sister, Joyce Clarkson, thinks that he returned to Burma to work in a factory that made chocolate. What is certain is that he eventually took an office job with G.F. Kellner and Co., a Calcutta-based company described at the time as being 'wines, spirits and provision importers, wholesale and retail distributors'.

Established in India during the middle of the nineteenth century, Kellner's was well known to the European community for its railway catering. Rodger became a steward on trains travelling between Calcutta and Dehra Dun and then a regional manager, which is what he was doing when he met his future wife.

Cliff's maternal lineage is a military one. His grandmother, Dorothy Edith, was the daughter of William Brock Bridgwater and his wife Marie Beatrice. William Brock had been born in the Vale of Health, a beautiful hamlet tucked into a fold of Hampstead Heath.

He joined the army as a boy, trained in Ireland and went to India with the Essex Regiment. It was here he met Marie Beatrice Smith, a dark-eyed half-Spanish beauty who was living in the hill station of Naini Tal looking after the children of a high-ranking military officer. They fell in love and married in 1898 in Allahabad.

Their daughter Dorothy Edith was born with a club foot and grew up to be a short, plump girl. The children at school made fun of her and called her 'lungi' ('lame one'). She visited England for operations to correct the foot but it only made matters worse. William Brock instead taught her to defend herself by giving her boxing lessons.

When the First World War broke out William was far too old to serve and had already done seven years' service in the army but he insisted on re-enlisting.

'They were taking people up to the age of forty,' remembers his son Vincent Bridgwater. 'He was forty-five and put his age down as forty and five months, and he was accepted.

'He returned to England where he was reunited with his family and then he was sent to France. He fought in the second battle of Ypres in April 1915 where the Germans used poison gas for the first time. He was gassed and the trench he was in was blown up. Fortunately he was discovered. They took him to hospital and found that he had broken his spinal cord. He came back to us in India in 1916 as a cripple.'

He spent the rest of his life in a wheelchair and Dorothy Edith had to look after him. Perhaps to escape the pressures of home life, at sixteen she married William Edward Dazely, a young soldier stationed in Bangalore with the Supply and Transport Corps. Nine months and three days later, in Lahore, she gave birth to a baby she had baptized Dorothy Marie.

Although she never discussed the marriage with her children, it can't have been happy. Two years after Dorothy Marie's birth there was a second daughter, Olive Queenie, born in Jubbulpore. Then in the spring of 1924 William Edward 'disappeared'.

Vincent Bridgwater, who was ten years old at the time, remembers being told that his brother-in-law had been sent up to the north-west frontier where British troops were defending themselves against Afghan tribesmen, and had never returned. There was no death certificate, he was told, because the body had never been found, but that in itself was not unusual in a conflict where soldiers were often captured and slashed to pieces with swords.

'He was attached to the army in some respect and he vanished,' he says. 'We never heard from him again. My sister and mother tried to find out where he was but they couldn't come up with anything. The army gave no details at all.'

Dorothy Marie and Olive Queenie grew up believing that their father was dead. They knew nothing about him because everything connected with him, including photographs, had been destroyed after he failed to return.

'She seemed to blame him for dying,' says Olive Queenie. 'She wouldn't talk about him and yet sometimes, when I had done something wrong, she would say, "You're just like your father". But how I was like my father I didn't know because I didn't know anything about him. I didn't even know what he looked like.'

It was only during research for this book that, after seventy years, the true story finally emerged. There are no records of a William Edward Dazely having died in India between 1924 and 1948 but there is a record of a William Edward Dazely arriving in Karachi in 1929 and marrying a 23-year-old spinster named Maizie Sherard. Thirteen weeks later Maizie gave birth to a child. Mr Dazely's given age, thirty-three, was exactly that of Dorothy Edith's husband who had been born in Kirkee in February 1896. Significantly he described himself in the church register as a 'widower'.

Clearly he wasn't telling the truth, but whether he abandoned Dorothy Edith and his daughters or whether there had been an agreement to split up and start their lives anew will never be known. The fact that she harboured such long-lasting resentment towards him suggests that his disappearance was half expected.

Olive Queenie remembers overhearing her mother discussing

the matter with an aunt. 'They were saying that he couldn't be dead and that he had only been reported missing,' she says. 'They were suggesting that he might still be alive and other bits of gossip.

'I used to ignore it and then one day a friend of the family showed my sister a photograph of him and she was more or less saying the same thing. I never believed it though. As far as I was concerned no one in the British Army could possibly get away from his family and live because he couldn't get out of the country.'

Yet he did manage to get away from his family. In Karachi he worked first as a policeman and later as a motor mechanic. He fathered five sons in fourteen years, though he was always known to have wanted a daughter.

In 1944 he moved his family to Poona and then four years later left for England where he settled in Balsall Heath, Birmingham, and worked as a storekeeper at the Rover factory in Solihull.

William Edward Dazely died of coronary thrombosis in 1969 never knowing that Cliff Richard was his grandson, and never having told his family about the wife and two daughters that he had left behind in Ambala in 1924. When, during the writing of this book, his family found out, the news came as a great shock to them.

Within two years of William Edward's 'disappearance' Dorothy Edith had found a new love in Richard Dickson, an Anglo-Indian who claimed Indian royal blood. In 1927 their first daughter, Edna, was born.

As a chief inspector on the railway Richard commanded respect, perks and a good salary. When the family travelled by rail they had their own special carriage and at home there were up to fifteen servants doing everything from cooking and washing to nursing the children and gardening.

Dorothy Marie and Olive Queenie loved him as if they had never had any other father.

'I had no feelings for my real father,' says Olive Queenie. 'The only father I knew was my step-father and I thought the world of him because he was a very clever person and he was very good to me.'

Dorothy Edith ruled her family with a rod of iron and had a fierce temper. 'When she went wild she would nearly kill you,' says Olive Queenie. 'People would have to grab hold of her to stop her. I remember once we were at a Railway Institute dance and a soldier turned and said something to my sister which involved referring to her as a "fair wench".

'My mother came up to this fellow and caught him right across his head with her hand. It sent him flying. He was enormous, she was only five-foot tall, but it sent him reeling backwards.

'She became known as "the battle-axe" but everyone respected her. She was good and kind but you couldn't act the fool and you couldn't use bad language when she was around. If she heard soldiers using bad language she would order them out of the room. She wasn't afraid of anyone.

'There was nothing religious about her morals though. She was just plain Victorian. My grandmother, on the other hand, was slightly of the religious kind. Behind her way of talking and teaching was always the Bible. Her point of view was that God wouldn't like that.

'She wasn't a Bible thumper but a lot of her goodness came from the fact that she always read the Bible and we all had to say our prayers at night before we went to sleep. If she wanted something done her way she would bring the Bible out to prove it.'

Dorothy Marie and Olive Queenie had spent most of their early life as boarders at the Lawrence Royal Military School in Sanawar, which offered a limited number of free places each year to children who had lost fathers in military service.

When William Edward Dazely went missing in 1924 Dorothy Edith was living in an army cantonment in Ambala, close to Simla, and of the five Lawrence schools in India the one at Sanawar was the closest. Shortly after the two little girls entered the kindergarten their mother moved down to Asansol to be with Richard Dickson and so the girls spent their early years hardly ever seeing her.

'For the first few years we never went home at all,' remembers

Olive Queenie. 'We were just kept at school because it was a good ten-day train journey to Asansol. We used to go for treks into Simla and further on up into the Himalayas. Then we went home when it was Christmas time but not for the summer holidays.'

Sanawar was a beautiful location high in the foothills of the Himalayas, close to the glamorous hill station of Simla where the Viceroy and his government spent their summers. The Lawrence school was mixed, and designed to produce soldiers, nurses and the wives of soldiers.

The two girls were very different—Dorothy Marie was outgoing, sporty and good at knitting and sewing, Olive Queenie was desperately shy and bookish. Dorothy Marie shone at tennis, badminton and hockey and was renowned as an aggressive team player, a quality that her son was to inherit along with her love of sport.

It was while at Sanawar that she started wearing glasses. 'Some children started calling her "four eyes" and "goggle eyes" but she was such a good fighter that very few of them would call her names except behind her back,' says Olive Queenie. 'She would fight anybody tooth and nail. I wouldn't fight anybody and I used to rely on her to defend me.'

Her second family now well established, Dorothy Edith decided in 1934 that it was time that the girls came to live at home, and they were enrolled in a local Roman Catholic school in Asansol, the Loretta Convent. It was at Asansol that Dorothy Marie was to meet her future husband.

3

'He was a terror for music'

lthough she was an attractive girl with many admirers, especially from the nearby Catholic boys' school, Dorothy Marie had never loved a man before Rodger Webb. Up until then there had only been coy looks and flirtatious chatter. Actions more serious couldn't be contemplated in the climate of the times, especially with Dorothy Edith keeping a keen eye open for anything that might suggest misbehaviour.

It often fell to Vincent Bridgwater, her mother's younger brother, to discourage potential suitors. 'I had to warn some of them off because they weren't the type that I thought should be mixing with my niece,' he says.

Olive Queenie remembers the time: 'You could say she had boyfriends before Rodger but they were kept secret and they weren't boyfriends like young girls have nowadays. You didn't go out with them. You met them after school and cycled home with them or you'd go into the park and chat to them. To our way of thinking at the time they were boyfriends though.'

The British India of the 1930s was still in a Victorian time warp. Children whose parents had grown up in Britain were considered terribly modern, and slightly dangerous. A girl was treated as a child until she was at least sixteen and then, on leaving school, she would be expected to clean, wash and darn at her parents' home until a man with an appropriate income came to ask for her hand in marriage. Except for those bold few who learned to type and thought in terms of a career, the late teens were spent learning how to be a housewife.

'We were terribly old-fashioned,' says Olive Queenie, looking back. 'The atmosphere we were raised in was the same one I was reading about in books written in nineteenth-century England.

'You weren't supposed to speak to a boy unless you were actually introduced to him and you certainly wouldn't be able to go out with a boy unless a *duenna* [governess and chaperone for young women] or your parents were with you. You weren't allowed to go out alone with a boy not even when you were engaged. I used to smile when Dorothy was engaged. She used to have to kiss Rodger in the sitting room. She couldn't go outside and kiss him.'

Dorothy met Rodger Webb in Asansol in 1936 when he came to visit his sister, Dorothy Cooke, who lived in the apartment above. The Cookes and the Dicksons had become close friends and were always in each other's homes. Now sixteen years old with dark bobbed hair and large flashing eyes, Dorothy Marie fell for this smartly-dressed man with his impeccable manners. She thought he looked like a matinée idol. 'He was a thorough gentleman,' she says. 'And handsome too.'

Remembers Olive Queenie, 'In those days he had smoothed-down hair and he was very good looking. He used to remind me of the actor Leslie Howard. He had the same bone structure.'

There were drawbacks though, the biggest being the difference in their ages. Rodger was thirty-one, almost twice Dorothy Marie's age and only two years younger than her mother. Then there was the question of distance. Rodger was based in Howrah, a district of Calcutta, and wouldn't be visiting Asansol more than twice a year. Dorothy Edith made it clear that much as she admired Rodger, she didn't think him a suitable boyfriend for her daughter.

Nevertheless Rodger and Dorothy Marie courted for three years, mostly by letter. When they were able to see each other in Asansol there wasn't much opportunity for intimacy because the visits were turned into huge family affairs with the Cookes, the Dicksons and the Webbs gathering to eat, sing and play parlour games.

Rodger had a sister, Marjorie, and a brother Tom, who also lived in Howrah and they would travel up for these parties. They were quite unlike the debonair Rodger and were both, in their own way, eccentrics.

Tom appears to have been the black sheep of the family whose life consisted of a cycle of making money and giving up his job for a life of pleasure, before he eventually returned home broke. Marjorie, who worked as a ticket collector on Howrah station, frightened the younger children with her loud voice and her strong language. She dressed in men's clothes and smoked a cigar. 'You didn't think a woman could be like me, did you?' she once asked a rather timid Olive Queenie. Neither Tom nor Marjorie ever married.

The two brothers were very close and teamed up to make music, Rodger with his guitar and mandolin, Tom singing while playing ukulele or banjo. Later, Tom would provide Cliff with one of his earliest musical memories by sitting at the foot of his bed and singing him to sleep.

To the impressionable Dorothy Marie, Tom was as smooth and accomplished as Bing Crosby and she would sit out on the steps of the quarters as he sang songs like 'Ramona', 'The Bells Of Sorrento' and 'Red Sails In The Sunset', while Rodger accompanied him and Marjorie huffed away on tissue paper and comb.

On 26 April 1939 Rodger and Dorothy Marie were married at St Paul's Church, Asansol, and moved north west to a large company bungalow in Dehra Dun. Life was wonderful for Dorothy Marie. Rodger was doing well in his job, managing the local Kellner's restaurant, and she was happy in her home where most of the housework was carried out by servants.

Although she had lived in India all her life she would never have known a native Indian as a close friend. The Indians had their homes on the outskirts of the big towns and lived entirely separate lives. Although she would have respected them there was no question of them being regarded as equals.

'The Indians didn't like the idea of a mixture of races,' says Olive Queenie. 'They thought that any white person who mixed with an Indian was trash, any white girl who went with an Indian man was trash to them. They wouldn't respect her. Similarly any of their girls who went with a white man was automatically considered trash.'

The largest employers in British India were the post and telegraph, the railways, the civil service and the army, and each occupation bred its own community.

'There was a very great class distinction,' Joyce Dobra remembers. 'I had the education of a civil servant and could get into almost any club. But because my father had been born in India he was looked down on by those who had been born in Europe. We in turn looked down on the railway people who, like the post and telegraph, lived in rented accommodation.

'There were very strict social codes laid down by the wives of army officers and diplomats. The rich Indians were allowed to socialize with the whites but even they weren't admitted to any of the clubs.'

Rodger and Dorothy Marie's club was the local Railway Institute where they regularly went to play cards or tennis and badminton. 'There were dances almost every day,' remembers Dorothy Marie. 'It was a lovely life.'

In 1940 she discovered she was pregnant. There were no large British hospitals in Dehra Dun, which then had a population of fewer than 250,000, so she planned to travel three hundred miles south east to Lucknow where Rodger's father was now living in retirement, to have the baby at the King's English Hospital in Victoria Street.

Britain was by now feeling the effects of the war with Germany. There had been skirmishes with fighter planes over South-East England and bombs had been dropped on London. There was little danger of India being attacked but there was a feeling that the days of the British Empire might now be numbered.

When Dorothy arrived in Lucknow the local papers were running stories on the ambitions of the Axis (the alliance of Germany, Italy and Japan) to capture the oil fields of Iraq, and Mahatma Gandhi's plan to fast for the cause of Indian independence. The big films in town were Laurel and Hardy's *Ships At Sea* and *Broadway Melody Of 1940*, starring Fred Astaire.

On Monday 14 October 1940 Dorothy gave birth to the dark-haired boy who would one day be known as Cliff Richard. He weighed nine pounds. That day the *Lucknow Pioneer* printed the text of the first BBC radio broadcast by Britain's Princess Elizabeth which read, in part: 'When peace comes remember it will be for us, the children of today, to make the world a better and happier place.'

Rodger didn't see the new baby until his wife returned to Dehra Dun, where they agreed to name him Rodger Harry Webb—'Harry' in memory of Rodger's eldest brother. This was the name they had prepared as they set off on Saturday 2 November to take the child to his baptism at St Thomas' Church.

'When I got to the church I saw his godmother and mentioned that I was naming him Rodger Harry,' remembers Dorothy Marie. 'She immediately said, "Oh no. I think it should be Harry Rodger." I just stood there unable to do anything and of course the vicar was holding the baby at the font as they do and I heard him saying, "I baptize thee Harry Rodger Webb."'

Harry was placid but tough. Many white children were susceptible to tropical disease but he remained strong and healthy, playing around the house under the eye of his *ayah* while his mother embroidered, sewed and knitted. She made all his clothes until he was six years old.

A year after Harry's birth she became pregnant again, this time returning to her mother in Asansol where, on 10 June 1942, she gave birth to a boy whom they named Frederick William, after Rodger's father.

The baby Frederick William hardly features in Cliff's biographies and autobiographies, the only mention coming in *It's Great to Be Young* where he says, 'Back in India Mum's second child had been a boy but the poor chap died very shortly after birth. Things like that don't mean much to children, and much as I wanted a brother then, I can't think what life would be like without my perky younger sister, Joan.'

There's disagreement over how long the child lived. Olive Queenie thinks he was over twelve months old. Dorothy Marie thinks it was less than three weeks. The ecclesiastical returns don't record his burial. He must have been alive at the age of eighteen days when he was baptized at St Paul's Church in Asansol.

He was born a 'blue baby' and never enjoyed full health. Often he cried all day. Dorothy Marie and Rodger went out dancing one night and returned to find him so ill that a doctor had to be called. The next morning young Frederick William was dead.

'Dorothy always felt she was to blame,' says Olive Queenie. 'But it would have made no difference if they had stayed at home that night. He would have died anyway.'

Dorothy Marie now thinks the death had a far deeper effect on Harry than she had at first thought.

'He was too young to explain what he was feeling but Rodger and I felt that he had lost something in that moment,' she remembers. 'I think he is always conscious that the brother he had was lost. When he was young he didn't show anything but when he grew older he would sometimes say, "I had a brother." Funnily enough when I was in Bermuda a few years ago I heard him say, "If my brother had lived he would now be forty." It's obviously never left him.'

After three years living in Dehra Dun Rodger was promoted, and the family moved to Calcutta where Kellner's had its headquarters in the prominent thoroughfare of Chowringhee Road. They were given a small first-floor apartment over a chocolate factory close by Howrah Station, Calcutta's teeming gateway to the rest of India, where a rickety wooden staircase on the outside of the building took them to their front door. Soon after moving in their first daughter, Donella Eugenie, was born.

Harry was remarkably even-tempered as a child. Interviewed in

1964 by Bob Ferrier for his book *The Wonderful World of Cliff Richard* his mother said, 'I never found any fault in that child. He never lied to us, he never hurt anybody, he still doesn't.' Today her opinion is much the same. 'He was very good,' she says. 'He has all his life been that way. He has always been very kind and I can honestly say that he has never driven me to despair like some children can.'

Yet he wasn't spineless. 'Cliff was undoubtably a toughie,' says Olive Queenie. 'He was always very fit and was able to weather all the sicknesses. His sister Donna had a habit of deliberately getting him into trouble with his mother and he would get soundly walloped but because he was such a tough little guy he never used to let on that he was innocent.'

In the summer months they would leave Calcutta and holiday in Lucknow with grandfather Webb and then go on to Buxar where grandmother Dickson was now living. These times away from home provided Harry with some of his few lingering memories of India— chasing bees, watching monkeys jumping in the branches of trees, fishing, flying kites and hearing tales of his father's exploits as a tiger hunter.

Rodger was a typical chauvinist of the period who expected everything to be done his way. He would come home from work and sit in his favourite chair while Dorothy Marie and the servants arranged things according to his wishes.

'If things weren't going exactly the way he wanted them to go he would become very Puritanical,' Olive Queenie recalls. 'He could be very strict with Dorothy. She would be quite tired by the time he came back home from work and yet he would want to go out to one of the company dances.'

It was in Howrah that Harry discovered that he could operate the family gramophone and sing along to records.

'He was pretty smart with that machine and would always choose the exact records that he wanted to hear,' says Dorothy Marie. 'He would wind it up himself. We asked him how he knew which records he liked and it was because he recognized different marks on the labels. After discovering the gramophone, music was his number one thing.'

His three favourite records were 'Ragtime Cowboy Joe' by Geraldo and his Orchestra featuring Dorothy Carless, 'Chewing A Piece Of Straw' by Jack Payne and his Orchestra and 'Jersey Bounce' by the Glenn Miller Orchestra.

'He was a terror for music,' remembers Olive Queenie. She was in the army, and used to take the children out for walks in Calcutta's Botanical Gardens when home on leave. 'He used to stand by the gramophone with his finger in the air beating time to the music as if he was a great conductor.'

On September 1945 Harry started at St Thomas' Church School in Church Road, Howrah, a building set among banana trees. He remembers one of the family servants, Habib, bringing his lunch up to him each day wrapped in a napkin.

He was already learning to speak Hindi, which his father spoke fluently, and at school he learned Bengali. His best friend Lal spoke no English and so all their conversations were in Hindi.

The war had only just ended, Japan had been crushed by two atomic bombs and the British, who had promised Home Rule to the Indians in return for their wartime co-operation, were now nervously working out the details of a transference of power.

For those like Rodger and Dorothy Marie who although British by family origin had never known any other home but India, it was a worrying time. Their days living in the sun with servants at their beck and call were numbered because there would be no place for the old ruling class in an India run by Indians.

Harry began to notice that gradually schoolfriends were leaving, saying that they were going to a place called 'home' which was small, cold and thousands of miles away and which most of them had only read about in books.

The prospect of independence re-awakened old religious feuds. Under British rule the Moslem and Hindu factions had no power and so they set aside their differences. Now the Moslems were wanting to ensure that they would get their own state within the boundaries of the old British India.

In June 1946 the Moslem League voted to accept a British plan that granted them the territory of Pakistan but within seven weeks they withdrew their acceptance and accused Britain and the Congress Party of going back on their pledges. The All-India Moslem League in Bombay called for 'direct action' and set up a committee to launch a struggle 'as and when necessary'.

At this point violence spilled into the streets. Dorothy Marie was jostled while out shopping and Indians shouted at her, 'Go back to your own country white woman.' The young Harry was frightened. 'Leave her alone,' he screamed. 'She's my Mummy.' The old India his parents knew, where the natives 'knew their place', was fast vanishing.

On 16 August 1946 riots came to the streets of Calcutta. The Moslem League mounted a Direct Action Day as a protest against the British Independence plan, and were attacked by Hindus. British troops and police had to fire on crowds as shops were burned and looted. In three days there was damage estimated at one million pounds, a death toll of 3,000 and 10,000 casualties. The Calcutta Fire Brigade dealt with 900 fires and the streets were littered with bodies.

The Webbs, who lived in a predominantly Sikh area, were terrified. A family of Moslems nearby had been attacked and killed by Hindus leaving only one boy who they could see was hiding in his garden. They kept him alive by dropping food parcels on a rope from their window at night and eventually got in touch with Dorothy Marie's uncle who was serving in the Calcutta Police and he came over in an armoured car to take the boy to safety.

'When he drove up we looked out of the window and we could see that there was human flesh hanging off the tracks of his vehicle,' remembers Dorothy Marie. 'It was a terrible sight. We could see a bit of the Hooglie River from our apartment but that day you couldn't see the water for dead bodies. It was dreadful.

'That was when we knew we had to leave eventually. We knew that if this was what it was going to be like then it wasn't going to be worth living in India.

'My uncle Harry made sure that we got safely out of our apartment and we went and stayed with Rodger's sister, Marjorie. But we hadn't been there for two days when threats were made to burn the place down. Some Moslems guided us out and they didn't hurt us but the whole street was strewn with dead bodies and glass and bricks. They took us to a cinema for safety.'

Thus began the speedy wind-down of British rule. In February 1947 Lord Louis Mountbatten was despatched from London to replace Field Marshal Lord Wavell as viceroy of India and to begin negotiations with Hindu and Moslem leaders over the future of their land.

Although the Hindus were fiercely resistant to the idea of partition it was obvious, with such hatred abroad, that this was the only workable solution. By June both the Congress Party, led by Pandit Nehru, and the Moslem League accepted a plan which would set up a state of West Pakistan in the north west and the much smaller state of East Pakistan in the north east.

On the stroke of midnight, on 14 August 1947, 163 years of British rule in India ended and the transference of power was complete.

But freedom for India didn't bring immediate peace. Months of turmoil followed as millions of refugees fled over the Indo-Pakistan borders in both directions and an estimated 400,000 Moslems and Hindus were slaughtered.

Into this India, on 21 November 1947, came Jacqueline Ann, the Webbs' second daughter. Two months later, in New Delhi, a Hindu fanatic assassinated Mahatma Gandhi, one of the inspirations behind the independence movement, as he made his way to a prayer meeting, thus precipitating a further series of riots. By now the British were streaming out of India towards destinations that they hoped would provide them with as good a life as they had left behind.

It was Rodger's inclination to go to Australia where Charlie Holder, one of the men who worked for him, had emigrated, but Dorothy Marie wanted to follow her mother to England where she gone with her new family of seven, the youngest of whom was the same age as Harry.

A scheme had been set up where those who could prove British ancestry had half of their fare paid by the British government and so the Webbs put all their savings towards getting Bombay to London tickets and packed their few belongings into suitcases. They had always lived in company accommodation so there was no house to sell, no furniture to put into storage and most of the clothes they owned they knew would be hopelessly impractical in the English climate. Their pet dog was left with Dorothy Marie's uncle Vincent, who was staying on in India along with Tom and Marjorie Webb and Frederick William.

They left their home in Howrah for the last time on Saturday 21 August 1948 and took a train from Calcutta to Bombay where, three days later, they boarded their boat for England.

The *Ranchi* was a 23-year-old P&O passenger liner which had spent the war as an armed merchant cruiser and then as a troopship in the Middle East. This was its first round trip since being refitted as a passenger ship. (All other books have mistakenly identified this as the *Ranghi*.)

Built as a liner for 587 passengers, including a first-class section, it had been re-designed for 950 'tourist class' passengers, which meant that it was functional rather than luxurious. Rodger was told that this was to be the ship's last voyage before being scrapped— which wasn't true—and so they were pleasantly suprised to have a comfortable cabin to themselves. (The *Ranchi* stayed in service until the end of 1952 and was then sold to the British Iron and Steel Corporation.)

'The dining rooms were alright,' remembers Dorothy Marie. 'They had a cinema on board and I remember Cliff crawling under the tent without paying to see the films.

'He and I were quite ill when we started on the journey and couldn't even leave the cabin. We felt a little better during the middle of the journey and then when we reached the Bay of Biscay we both fell ill again.'

Having left Bombay on the evening of 24 August the *Ranchi* sailed through the Arabian Sea, arriving in Aden on the morning of the 29th where it docked for four hours, before setting off through the Red Sea towards the Suez Canal.

While sailing up the canal Harry learned how to whistle by imitating other passengers who cat-called the Egyptians watching from the banks. His father's response was to give him a memorable belt around the head. After a six-hour stop-over in Port Said on 2 September the liner made its way across the Mediterranean, arriving at Tilbury Docks at 6 a.m. on Monday 13 September.

The story that Cliff has always told is that after disembarking his father hired a taxi to Carshalton with his last five pounds (or seven pounds as it was being reported in 1960) but Dorothy Marie remembers it differently.

She believes they were picked up by a private car from Tilbury and that their first few days in England were spent with an aunt of her mother's who lived somewhere in south-east London. It was only then that they made it down to Carshalton where the Dicksons, Dorothy Marie's mother and her family, had set up home.

Harry's first impression of his new country was the typical one of those who had never seen the motherland—the striking appearance of vegetation after a lifetime surrounded by brown dust.

'I can remember nothing of the white cliffs of Dover or even of Tilbury,' he once said, 'but I shall never forget the green fields, the trees and the flowers; particularly the flowers on Carshalton station.'

More striking to Rodger and Dorothy Marie must have been the effects of the wartime rationing of clothes, food, petrol and confectionery, which was still in force, and the bomb sites which blighted London. This was not the colourful, confident Britain of the picture books but a nation suffering austerity.

The latest news in the *Wallington and Carshalton Times* was of a serious bread shortage and a worrying lack of telephones. Apparently there were only 8,000 phones in the whole area and even the chief engineer at the local exchange could not get one installed.

For Rodger, whose whole life had been spent promoting fine wines and good food, the prospects of work in the home country didn't look at all promising.

4

'Like a dream come true'

Richard and Dorothy Dickson had bought their three-bedroomed house at 47 Windborough Road, Carshalton, for £2,500 but it was barely big enough for them and their children—Edna, Jean, Nora, Vincent, Peggy, Geraldine and Christopher.

Then had come the news that Rodger and Dorothy Marie—their daughter and her family—were on their way with Harry, Donella and Jacqueline. It didn't seem possible that they could all fit into a suburban semi-detached so the neighbours at number 45, Norman and Elizabeth Luscombe, agreed to let the Webb family sleep in their small front bedroom until they found a home.

'The room was the size of a box,' remembers Dorothy Marie, 'and everything had to be done in that small space. Because the children were young I had to have a little cooker there to boil their milk and make them porridge.'

The arrangement didn't last long and the Webbs returned to number 47 where they were put in an equally small room. This meant that the Dicksons' house now had to sleep fourteen people, including two married couples and two children over twenty.

'We were sleeping all over the place,' remembers Vincent Dickson, the eldest son. 'We hadn't been in the house very long ourselves so it was a big upheaval.'

Soon after their arrival Harry started at Stanley Park Road Junior

School which was only a five-minute walk away. Here he learned for the first time that he didn't have the milky-white skin that most English-born children had during the winter.

His deep tan hadn't stood out in India. In fact, there he had been the 'white boy'. But here in south-west London, where very few children had ever seen a person who wasn't white, he was thought exotic. The difference was accentuated by his Anglo-Indian accent.

Discovering that he was newly arrived from India his classmates concluded that he must be an Indian and, in 1948, the only Indians that British school children knew much about were the ones who threw tomahawks and attacked cowboys.

Harry was teased and asked where his head-dress was. It didn't make it any easier that most of his household were part-Indian and stood out in the street with their dark hair and brown skin.

To this day there are those in Carshalton who are convinced that Cliff is part Indian. 'I think there was Indian blood in him because the Dicksons were Indian weren't they?' says Dorothy Willis, who as Miss Olstead taught him in Sunday school.

The most effective way of gaining respect, Harry soon learned, was to hit back rather than to trade insults. Rodger wanted to lodge a formal complaint, especially after a teacher had said to his son, 'Come on Webb, you can't run off to your wigwam any more.' But Harry wanted to stand up for himself.

It was while in Carshalton that he had his first experience of evangelical Christianity. He had sung in the choir of St Thomas' in Howrah, a traditional Anglican church, but at Stanley Park Evangelical Mission, a crude corrugated hut in Stanley Road where he started to go to Sunday school, they talked about 'asking Jesus into your heart' and sang lively choruses.

'His interest in religion in those days was no more than any of the other kids in the class,' remembers Dorothy Willis, who taught him for half an hour each week. 'And he certainly had no thoughts of singing.'

In photographs taken at the time his Sunday school friends beam cheekily and confidently at the camera where he appears subdued and worried. His front teeth were beginning to protrude and he had a noticeably fang-like upper left tooth. His father had told him to straighten his teeth by sucking them in.

His insecurity was a natural part of finding a new place in the world. Back in India he had been treated like a prince by adult servants. Here he was being made to feel racially inferior by white children. Also his father was penniless and out of work and they had no home to call their own.

'The British in India were top dogs,' says his cousin Joyce Dobra. 'We were white and were always brought up with the idea that one day we would be going "back home to England". We were used to telling other people what to do. Our servants were all adults and yet we treated them as if they were children.'

Rodger finally found work as a wage clerk in a local hospital. It gave him money but it was a blow to the pride of a man who had been used to running the show. Dorothy Marie was so unhappy that she wondered whether it might not be best to find another country to live in.

'I was making all sorts of plans to leave England,' she admits. 'I had a brother-in-law who had gone somewhere in the East and he had written and said he could get Rodger a job. I wanted him to go.

'I told him that he could have a job and we'd have free accommodation but he felt that Britain was losing colony after colony and that soon that place would go. And it did.

'A year later my brother-in-law was in England himself and living not far from us but I still hated it here. Rodger hadn't wanted to come in the first place but he never once reproached me.'

Rodger's sister Dorothy Cooke and her husband had by now left Asansol and were living at the opposite end of London in Waltham Cross, Hertfordshire, in a semi-detached house. They suggested easing the situation in Carshalton by having the Webbs stay with them.

Their local council was building a lot of rented accommodation as part of the post-war resettlement and they believed the Webbs could then be put on the waiting list. So, on Harry's ninth birthday, after one year and a month in Carshalton, they went to live with Dorothy and Ernest Cooke and their two boys, Rodger and Ernie.

It may have been slightly less cramped than the Dicksons' house but the Webbs still found themselves squatting in a small room with mattresses on the floor. The only difference was the glimmer of hope that within months they might get their own council house.

Harry was taken to the nearby King's Road school where his teacher was the second-year junior mistress Mrs Tonks.

'I'll always remember the day he came into my class,' she says. 'The headmaster, Harold Cooper, brought in this lad who was very dark with big brown eyes. He was holding his hand because he was quite young and he said to me, "Well, there you are Mrs Tonks. Here's another one for you," because the term had already started and I already had between thirty and forty children in the class. Harry stood there and he bowed. I'll never forget that. He bowed!'

One of Harry's new classmates was a tall blond-haired boy named Norman Mitham whose family lived near the Cookes. The two boys took to each other straight away. They shared a love of football and other sports and would stay close friends right through school, then becoming musical partners in Harry's first major venture.

Norman remembers the racial taunting starting up again at Waltham Cross, this time with Harry being nicknamed 'Sabu' after the subject of Alexander Korda's 1937 documentary film *The Elephant Boy*.

'In those days anyone who didn't come from Waltham Cross was an alien,' he says. 'He was very unafraid of it all though. He didn't try to hide from the fact or kowtow to them. He stood up for himself. He could certainly lose his temper and he knew how to handle himself.'

On 6 January 1950, Rodger, who was now working as a clerk in the City for Eastwood's Ltd. at 158–160 City Road, filled out his first application form for a council house. He explained to Broxbourne Borough Council that his family of five had lived for a year with nine other people in a three-bedroomed house and now, with his wife expecting a fourth child, they were still having to live and sleep in one small bedroom.

They were added to the waiting list but by the summer he still hadn't heard anything so on 7 August he filed a second application. Christmas 1951 came and went without any news.

After fourteen months with the Cookes, tensions were rising, especially between the two women who found themselves trapped together in the house for long hours each day.

'We had to sleep on two mattresses which just fitted into the room and we had to stand on them when we got dressed,' says Dorothy Marie. 'She wouldn't let us use any other part of the house except to eat.'

Dorothy Marie began to get friendly with the woman next door, Marcelle Henrit, who was outraged that a young family was expected to live in such appalling conditions. Her son Bob Henrit (now drummer for the Kinks) remembers the time well.

'We had a family friend who was on the Waltham Abbey Council,' he says, 'and she started to pull some strings. She wasn't able to get anything going in Waltham Abbey itself but she had a friend in Cheshunt who she got in touch with and asked for things to be speeded up.'

In March 1951 things finally started to move. 'It all happened so quickly,' says Dorothy Marie. 'Within a week this fellow came and I told him that I couldn't take him over the house because that was out of bounds but he could come to the room where we all lived, slept, ate and drank.

'He got such a shock when he saw it. By that time Joan had been born and there was a line running across the room with nappies hanging out to dry, a burner to boil her milk and absolutely no room to move about.

'In two weeks' time we had the key to a brand-new council house. We went there to three bedrooms, a kitchen, bathroom and a huge living room downstairs. It was like a dream come true!'

Cheshunt, at that time a small town, is in the Lea Valley just north of London. It is only five miles from Enfield and a short train journey from Liverpool Street Station. After the war it had attracted some industry from the City and was a centre for garden nurseries.

The Bury Green estate, where the Webbs had been housed, represented the post-war ideal of reasonable rented accommodation surrounded by wide streets and playing areas for children. Hargreaves Close had eighteen houses, with number 12 part of a terrace at the far end looking down the close. The Webbs moved there on 11 April 1951—two years after arriving in England.

Rodger and Dorothy Marie soon found work at Thorn Electrical Industries on the Great Cambridge Road in Enfield which incorporated the Ferguson Radio Corporation and Atlas Lighting. Rodger became a blue-collar worker in the credit control office while Dorothy Marie sorted components on the assembly line.

Their total wages barely added up to twenty pounds a week and it became a struggle to feed and clothe four children while furnishing a new home. Shoes had to be shared around, a lot of rice was eaten and Rodger improvised by making dining-room chairs and tables out of old packing cases he picked up at work for a pound. There was no television set, telephone nor gramophone.

'There was no furniture as such,' remembers Norman Mitham. 'When they first moved in you'd have to sit on boxes and quite often on the floor. None of us was rich but they probably had less than any of us.'

The values that the Webbs brought with them from India seemed strangely out of place in a world that was frantically trying to rid itself of Victorianism. Rodger didn't like the new air of informality. He was determined that in his family, at least, the old values of honesty, courtesy and diligence would be upheld.

Although not a church member, Rodger Webb had a firm belief, possibly inherited from his father, that the Bible was the supreme guide for living, and he would regularly read chapters of it to the children by the fireside in the evenings. When he admonished them it was always with an appeal to what the Bible said.

'He would always tell us that this was what God said,' recalls his daughter Jacqui. 'I remember him saying that we shouldn't do this or that because God wouldn't approve of it.

'I think he felt there was a lot wrong with the church system and that you didn't need to go to church in order to be a Christian. I suppose he sent us all to Sunday school because he felt that at least it was better for us to be doing something.'

This moral code was rigid and enforced quite severely at times. He demanded unquestioning obedience and was a stickler for the letter of the law. The children would be punished for being five minutes late. Harry would get a slap.

To his daughters, whom he never hit, he was a warm and friendly figure. 'I saw my dad as the most wonderful person in the world,' says Jacqui. 'What I most remember is sitting on his lap. He would always sit on the armchair and leave a little corner for me to sit on.'

But to Harry he was a prickly character who never openly displayed affection and in whose presence he was very wary. In some children this would have created wilful disobedience but in Harry it created respectful conformism. 'I knew I couldn't get away with anything,' he explains, 'and I never tried.'

He went to his mother for consolation. Whereas his father seemed old and crusty she was young, vivacious and attractive, and a big hit with the schoolfriends he would bring home for tea.

'She became a great guiding light for Cliff,' says Olive Queenie. 'In all the old-style families the father was respected. He was the master. He dished out the punishment. There wasn't the same close-knit attachment that there was with the mother.

'After coming to England things did drift between Cliff and his father because he saw a lot less of him than when he was in India. Rodger didn't have the time to take him out anywhere because he was either working or too tired.

'She adored Cliff and a bit of spoiling would go on. Sometimes Rodger would arrive home and find that Dorothy had allowed her son to do something which he had said he couldn't do.

'Cliff never argued back though. He would get chastised but wouldn't then turn round and say that his mother said he could do it. He knew that would have got her into trouble and Rodger could be very strict with her too.'

'His father could be unyielding,' remembers Mitham. 'If he wanted Cliff in by 9.30 and yet the film we wanted to see didn't end until 9.45 he'd say, "I don't care. It's 9.30 and that's that." Cliff would never argue with him. He set the law and that was it.'

'His family wasn't as flexible as most of ours were,' says Pete Bush, one of Harry's closest schoolfriends. 'We were the first generation to be a lot more free and easy with our parents but it didn't seem to apply to him. He respected his father but I think that it was respect out of fear rather than respect out of love.'

The Webbs stood out among their neighbours for their strictness. Harry didn't seem to enjoy the rough and tumble of life out on the streets and was only allowed out of the house at certain times to play. 'He was a mummy's boy,' says Ivy Clare, the Webbs' next-door neighbour. 'Mrs Webb had a real hold over him. I never saw him out at all.'

Another neighbour, Richard Holmes, had twin daughters who sometimes played with Joan and Jacqui.

'He may have had his own friends at school but I didn't see much of him playing outside,' he says. 'The only time I can remember seeing him is when he was flying his kite out in the close with his dad.' His daughter Linda confirms this. 'He just didn't mix with the other boys,' she says. 'He didn't play with other people outside.'

The only person who saw another side of Harry and his father was Norman Mitham. He remembers Rodger hiding coins around the house and getting the boys to find them. He also remembers being entranced by Rodger's stories of hunting tigers in India. 'To a boy in Cheshunt, hearing someone describe life in the jungle was quite amazing,' he says.

Norman and Harry would sometimes go 'scrumping'—stealing

apples—or knocking on doors and running away. 'During the conker season we would fill our pockets with conkers and we would run down the road throwing conkers at people's front doors,' says Norman. 'I can remember he was absolutely over the moon one night because he had thrown a conker and it had hit a doorbell and made it ring.'

The biggest blow of Harry's early life came in the summer of 1952 when he failed the eleven-plus. The blow was all that much harder to take because it had been assumed that he would pass without any problem.

'I was top boy at my junior school,' he says. 'I have a book somewhere which I was given as a prize and then, within weeks, I had failed the eleven-plus and people below me had passed. I was shattered.'

In September 1952 he went to the newly-built Cheshunt County Secondary School which was taking in 800 pupils, and he soon fell in with a crowd of high achievers.

It was for his accomplishments on the sports field rather than in the classroom that Harry would be remembered. He played soccer for Hertfordshire, rugby football for the school, broke the over-13s javelin record with a throw of 106 feet 3 inches, was a top sprinter and had a reputation for fierce tackling that equalled his mother's tough tactics on the hockey pitches of Sanawar.

'He was good at football and played rugby like a lunatic,' says Brian Cooke. 'Also he was undoubtably the best scrapper in the school. You didn't play around with Harry Webb. I think he had to look after himself when he arrived in this country and that toughened him up.'

By the time he arrived in the second year, in September 1953, he was well established and popular. 'He was different from the other boys,' says his classmate Frances Slade. 'He seemed quieter and more gentle. He wasn't sloppy. I think a lot of it was due to his background in India. He was definitely the most polite and charming boy I knew.'

One woman Harry was able to charm was Jay Norris, a young English and drama teacher who, like Harry, had come to the Cheshunt school when it opened in 1952. They established a relationship which has never been broken and she was to become the first person to persuade him to get up on a stage and sing.

'I remember him coming to me one day because he hadn't done his homework,' she remembers. 'He had this really charming smile and he said something about having had to go out the night before and I said, "I'll tell you something, Webb. When you leave school you'll go into a job where the measure of success is smiling at women because you do it very well."'

Jay Norris had a unique ability in getting teenagers excited about poetry and drama. She read them Shakespeare and brought in a reel-to-reel tape recorder so that they could hear themselves recite. After school she ran a drama society which entered productions into local competitions.

'We were just an ordinary bunch of secondary modern kids,' says his schoolfriend John Vince, 'and she had us acting and singing and recording. We got to learn what a stage was and how to put theatrical make-up on. I'm sure a lot of kids today from backgrounds like ours wouldn't even know who Shakespeare was.'

Harry was only average at his schoolwork but he responded to Jay Norris. He joined the drama society and discovered that despite his shyness he had a real feel for acting.

His acting debut was in *The Price Of Perfection* by Sheila Buckley in February 1954. This was followed up in October by A.A. Milne's *The Ugly Duckling* in which he played the chancellor and then, in February 1955, he had a part in *Willow Pattern* which won first prize in the Youth Drama Festival.

'He had the right kind of voice,' says Jay. 'He had a feeling for words and a feeling for putting something over. It's very rare to find a boy with a really good, interesting voice.'

'I think Jay was very instrumental in getting him motivated,' says

Frances Slade. 'He was very shy when he first came to the school but she spotted something in him. He could read aloud so well.

'To get a class of idiots like us to sit down and listen to someone reading was quite something and she managed to get us all doing it with Shakespeare and the sorts of things you normally have to bludgeon kids with.'

Life at 12 Hargreaves Close had been complicated by the arrival of Harry's grandfather, Frederick William Webb, who was now in declining health. 'When everyone else left India in 1948 he didn't want to come to "Freezeland", as he called it. It was too cold,' says granddaughter Joyce Dobra. 'Then suddenly when he was about eighty he decided he wanted to come.'

He looked out of place in England. He insisted on wearing the lightweight linen suits he had always worn in India and with his long white beard and walking stick the local children believed he was Father Christmas. The fact that he frequently handed out sweets and apples to them reinforced the suspicion.

He took over the small front bedroom and Harry had to move in with his three sisters. It wasn't to be for long though. In 1954 Frederick went to stay with the Cookes where he died one morning of a sudden heart attack.

Dorothy Marie was now cycling every day to a wiring factory in Broxbourne where she would work until five o'clock. This meant that Harry had to look after Donna, Jacqui and Joan from the time they left school until she arrived home.

In September 1955 Jay Norris became Harry's form teacher and the school's Christmas production was to be A.A. Milne's *Toad of Toad Hall* based on Kenneth Grahame's *The Wind In The Willows*. Harry was her choice to play Ratty. 'That should tell you what sort of boy he was,' she says. 'Ratty was the sympathetic one, the nice one, the sensible one.'

The only problem was that if he took the part he would have to sing and although he had enjoyed singing since childhood he was not a confident performer. 'As far back as I can remember he had enjoyed music and he was always singing,' says Jacqui. 'But if anyone was around he would hide behind the settee. He wouldn't stand up and sing in front of our aunts and uncles if they could see his face.'

He told Jay that he wanted the part of Ratty but, unfortunately, he couldn't sing. 'I told him that was rubbish,' says Jay. 'I said it's actually quite simple. If you can't sing you can't play Ratty. Of course he did sing it and he sang it beautifully. I can see him now in his Ratty suit, twirling his tail.'

At the same time that Harry was fronting his first audience as a singer, a new form of American music had come over to Britain. It was called rock 'n' roll and 'Rock Around The Clock', a record by Bill Haley and the Comets, had come into the *Record Mirror* charts at number twelve on 15 October 1955 and had risen to the number one spot on 12 November, staying there through to the second week in January 1956.

Haley was a most unlikely looking hero for teenagers. Thirty years old, with an egg-shaped face, he appeared on stage in a tartan dinner jacket with a silk collar and had a precious kiss curl sprung on his forehead. With their receding hairlines, moustaches and spectacles, the Comets didn't look any more youthful.

Born in Michigan in 1925, Haley's musical background was in country and western but in 1951 he became the first white singer to cover a rhythm and blues song when he recorded Jackie Brenston's up-tempo song 'Rocket 88' with his group the Saddlemen.

At the time music like this made by blacks was categorized as 'race' music. It was produced mainly for what was then termed the 'negro' market, which didn't have the purchasing power to make an impact on the national charts.

'Rock Around The Clock' was recorded in New York on 12 April 1954, produced by Milt Gabler of Decca Records, and was an immediate hit in America. Its international success though happened only when the producers of *The Blackboard Jungle*, a film about rebellious New York schoolchildren, seized the opportunity of using what was then considered a novelty song over the credits.

The effect of Haley's record on British teenagers was profound. The pop music of the day was dominated by Rosemary Clooney, Dickie Valentine, Alma Cogan, Ruby Murray, Teresa Brewer and Frankie Laine who soothed rather than excited. It was music that appealed to those who had come through the war and were now looking forward to a future of peace, prosperity and family life.

But their children wanted something more vigorous and stirring. Rock 'n' roll, with its brash American sheen, pointed to the sort of future they wanted.

'I think we were all desperate for something new,' says Frances Slade. 'We all had been born either just before or during the war, many of us had experienced separation from our fathers, we had gone through rationing and everywhere looked grey. There was no colour anywhere. It was just dull, grey and boring.

'The word teenager had hardly been conceived. Entertainment for people in this age group was non-existent. We couldn't buy the clothes we wanted. The thing is, we didn't really know what we wanted. All we knew was that we wanted something different.

'Then along came Bill Haley and rock 'n' roll and suddenly there was something we could relate to and, what's more, it was something we could do.

'I think we were all being cloned into becoming very good safe little factory workers and office girls or, if possible, into doing some further education in order to become a teacher. But we weren't supposed to rock the boat because we were putting the country back together again. I think we just thought that there was more to it than that.'

Bill Haley inspired Harry. He never wanted to look like Bill Haley or to emulate his stage act but at least he knew there was more to pop music than Jimmy Young singing 'The Man From Laramie'. For the real epiphany, the one that was to change his life, he had to wait. But only for another five months.

5

'I heard Elvis and the next step was to do it'

One Saturday, in May 1956, Harry was walking with friends in the Four Swannes area of Waltham Cross when he passed a Citroën, parked outside Asplan's the newsagents, with its engine ticking over and its radio playing. What he heard from that car radio transfixed him.

It was a pop song but it was unlike anything he had ever heard. It seemed like a surge of energy, an attitude transformed into noise. He had no idea what it was and had to tune in regularly to AFN (American Forces Network) to find out that it was 'Heartbreak Hotel', by an American singer named Elvis Presley. There were no BBC radio or television programmes at the time which were likely to play such music.

The effect of that moment has never left him. It marked a change in his aspirations. 'The day I first heard Elvis's voice I thought of it as a sound or an instrument,' he says. 'I had never heard anyone sing like that before. I had liked songs by Perry Como and Frank Sinatra but I had never wanted to be like them. When I heard Elvis the next step for me was to try to do it.'

Bill Haley had introduced the rhythm to the young white audience but Elvis brought the style. He was twenty-one when he cut 'Heartbreak Hotel' and had been recording for only eighteen months after having been discovered by Sam Philips whose Sun Record label in Memphis had released Jackie Brenston's 'Rocket 88' in 1951.

Philips' great idea—which must have been encouraged by Bill Haley's cover version of 'Rocket 88'—was to find a white boy with a black-sounding voice who could make rhythm and blues widely acceptable to the racially-prejudiced white community.

Hip white American teenagers were already tuning into black radio stations but as yet there were no artists they could identify with. There were no James Deans or Marlon Brandos singing rock 'n' roll.

Elvis was white with a voice that sounded black, and he looked great. He had the lips and nose of a young Greek god, held his long dark hair back with grease and wore flash pimp's jackets that would have branded a white man a homosexual in many parts of America.

'He had a strange kind of appeal to both sexes,' commented Jerry Leiber, who co-wrote many of his hits. 'He didn't intimidate or look too much like a grown man. He was innocent but still provocative. There was a feminine undertone to his features. He wasn't handsome, he was beautiful.'

Not that fifteen-year-old Harry even knew what Elvis Presley looked like in May 1956. All he knew was that he needed to buy a copy of 'Heartbreak Hotel' and he needed to try to sing like Elvis. The first that his friends knew about his Four Swannes experience was when he arrived at school one morning with the record begging them to listen to it.

'We had managed to commandeer the school record player,' says Frances Slade. 'We had it hidden in our stock room for months and we were allowed in school before everyone else because we were prefects. In Room 9 we used to have our own private club.'

Harry put 'Heartbreak Hotel' on the turntable and raved about his discovery. 'He came in at around half past eight and he played this record over and over again,' remembers Pete Bush. 'He then tried to mime to it. That to me was the first sign of his fascination for Elvis. He used to take the microphone from the tape recorder and sing through it as the record was playing.'

He soon saw photographs of Elvis in weekly magazines and developed a passion for wanting to look like him. He pushed Brylcreem through his dark hair, combed it back into a powerful wave and then practised curling his upper lip and staring moodily beneath lowered eyelids in the mirror over the fireplace.

'He used to keep asking us if he looked like Elvis,' remembers Jacqui. 'He used to do his little movements and then he'd say, "Do I look like Elvis? Do I look like Elvis?"'

There was a weekly dance on Saturday nights at Holy Trinity Youth Club in Waltham Cross. Harry would go with a group of friends and dance to chart records played on a small Dansette. Two of the girls, Betty Clarke and Freda Johnson, liked singing to the records and when Harry, John Vince and a girl called Beryl Molineux began to join in it took on the shape of an informal group.

They harmonized on songs like 'Water' by Frankie Laine and 'Only You' by the Hilltoppers but had a special affection for the doo-wop sounds of the Crew Cuts ('Sh-Boom') and the Teen Queens ('Eddie My Love').

Doo-wop was a convenient label to describe the new vocal harmony music coming out of New York from groups like the Clovers, the Moonglows, Frankie Lymon and the Teenagers and the Cleftones. It wasn't strictly rock 'n' roll but it was inspired by rhythm and blues and a lot of the groups were black.

There had been no serious intentions behind the sessions around the record player but when, in July 1956, Trinity Youth Club put on an Anglo-French dance as a fundraiser for Holy Trinity School the five were asked to perform a cabaret spot. They called themselves the Quintones, a suitably doo-wopish name, and began rehearsing in a friend's house.

'Harry would sing the song,' remembers John Vince, 'the girls would harmonize and I would do the boom-de-boom bass line.' One song, however, wouldn't require any help from the others. Harry was going to do 'Heartbreak Hotel' on his own.

When it came to the event on Bastille Day, 14 July 1956, at the Holy Trinity School in Waltham Cross, Betty Clarke suffered stage fright at the sight of an audience of 250 people and was substituted at the last minute by her friend Irene Fowler.

The brief performance, which included Harry's 'Heartbreak Hotel' solo spot, has gone down in history as his first concert. It also earned him his first publicity. The *Cheshunt Weekly Telegraph* carried a large photo of the Quintones with Harry clearly distinguishable in his light jacket and greased-back hair.

'The dance, which was in connection with the school's birthday and fête, also Bastille Day, raised £20 for the school funds,' ran the report above the picture.

'Posters, supplied by the French Embassy, advertising the day and the beauiful French countryside, decorated the hall, and the stage accommodating Jack de Benham and his band, represented a French café. Appropriate lighting completed a most effective scene.

'Cabaret turns were provided by members of the club; Mr Eric Frith, the leader, impersonated Liberace.

'Proceeds from the competition were given to the Duke of Edinburgh's playing fields fund.

'Refreshments were provided under the direction of Mrs Rix and Mrs Matthews.'

The Quintones rehearsed more than they played. The only other event that anyone is certain they performed at was the twenty-first birthday party of John Vince's sister Pamela, in September of that year. A photograph taken of the cake-cutting shows Harry still looking shy and out of place. While John Vince and his brothers are sniggering and wearing casual white shirts Harry is standing behind them in a dark jacket and tie with his lips gripped together.

Besides giving him his first performing experience the Quintones brought Harry closer to Betty Clarke, a petite girl with dark hair who he'd known since junior school in Waltham Cross. They had always liked each other but now they were both fifteen things became more serious.

'I think Betty Clarke was my first girlfriend,' he says. 'In those days you took bets on who you could catch and kiss. We used to say, "Well, if you're so crazy about her then grab her in the corridor during the break and kiss her."'

'So from chasing girls, catching them and kissing them suddenly you found that you were with someone and you were seen as a couple. Betty and I were boyfriend and girlfriend and went to the pictures and to parties together.'

One of their first times together had been at the 1955 school lunch. 'It was usual that a boy and a girl would choose a member of staff to take to the lunch,' remembers Betty. 'This year both Harry and I had chosen to take Jay Norris and she said, "I think really it's Harry taking Betty!" At school we were just friends but then, at the youth club, we walked out together for a little while.

'He didn't send me flowers because none of us had that sort of money in those days, but he would send me cards and once he put a box of chocolates inside my desk at Christmas. It was just those little things that meant you were a closer friend than just an ordinary schoolfriend and other people regarded you as boyfriend and girlfriend.'

Teenage relationships in the fifties were still very innocent, unaffected by commercial pressure to couple up and become 'sexually active'. Over eighty per cent cent of English children still went to Sunday school, so in many cases there was a moral foundation for chastity, but the biggest fear was putting a girl 'in the family way', which inevitably meant an early marriage. Teenagers who went 'all the way' were generally considered a bit fast and not 'nice'.

Harry and his friends were definitely a 'nice' bunch who believed in socializing as a group rather than pairing off for intimate moments. With little money and no commercial teenage culture they spent their time swimming, walking, bike riding and going for picnics. They spent more time in one another's homes than they did in cafés or cinemas.

'We didn't have the opportunity to go to many different places so we used to take our bikes and go to Epping Forest,' says Betty. 'Sometimes we went out as a group. There weren't discos in those days—only the record player down at the youth club.'

What struck Betty about Harry was his respect towards girls. He never used his good looks to flirt outrageously.

'He never pushed himself around,' she says. 'I think it was to do with the way he was brought up. He was taught that it wasn't nice to go out with one girl after another and that you should never take advantage of anyone.

'I'll always remember someone asking him whether he had a girlfriend and he said, "Yes. I've got her picture in my pocket" and he dived into his pocket and brought out a photograph of his mother.'

Most of the children in Harry's year, including Betty Clarke, left school that summer but he was included as part of an experimental group of fifteen pupils who stayed on to sit O levels. Their relationship didn't survive the summer holidays as Betty started courting another boy from the youth club.

'We parted good friends,' she says. 'We just went our separate ways. When I saw him on TV just a few years later I couldn't believe that I'd actually been out with him and he'd been in my home.'

'I'd always remember him whether or not he had become famous. Harry Webb was an important part of my schooldays.'

There were two other girlfriends from those days that he can still remember—Sheila Bevan and Heather Harman. 'Sheila was the girl that all the guys wanted to go out with,' he says. 'I also remember being besotted with Heather when we were doing *HMS Pinafore*. I went out with her for a short period.'

In the group that had stayed on in Jay Norris' fifth form there were thirteen boys—including John Vince, Pete Bush and Brian Cooke—and two girls—Janice Berry and Frances Slade.

They were an unusually close-knit form. Brian Cooke can remember the time when Pete Bush received a cuff around the head from a member of staff and the whole class walked out and protested to the headmaster. Groups of them would often go for tea at Jay's home.

'They were the first class that I knew I'd miss because they were so nice,' says Jay. 'We had been together such a long time and had developed a mutual trust and goodwill.'

Harry studied for O levels in Religious Education, English Language, English Literature and Maths, but he was never a star student. No one would have picked him out as a boy who was going to do great things.

'His problem wasn't in being lazy but in wanting to do too many other things so that he didn't want to sit down and do essays,' says Jay Norris. 'He was also extremely interested in rock 'n' roll. That didn't leave an awful lot of time for school work.'

At the age of sixteen Harry was a mixture of respectful conformism and determined individualism. In his reluctance to blaspheme, smoke, drink or argue back with his parents he seemed, even to his contemporaries, to be a little old-fashioned.

But no one mistook his politeness for compliancy, because beneath the well-mannered surface was grit. He showed this in his competitive nature on the sports field and in his reputation as a fighter.

'He was not a guy that you would upset,' says Cooke. 'He'd knock your block off. By far the biggest boy in our class was a lad called Chris Green, and I remember that one day he said something Cliff didn't like, and Cliff knocked two of his teeth out.'

For his final Christmas play at Cheshunt School Harry took the part of Bob Cratchit in *A Christmas Carol*. It was then, according to Cooke, that the future rock 'n' roll star began to emerge.

'For his part in *A Christmas Carol* he had to dress up in tight black trousers and you suddenly noticed that the girls were looking at him as a bit of all right. Up until that time there had been nothing. During rehearsals he used to sing "Heartbreak Hotel" and "Hound Dog" just as a joke.'

A Christmas Carol earned him his first review. 'Harry Webb acted well as Bob Cratchit,' said the *Cheshunt Weekly Telegraph*, 'but he was rather let down by the make-up team and, hard as he worked, he could not dispel the impression that he was a teenager and not a harassed father.'

That Christmas he visited his grandmother in Carshalton and his aunt Ruth (married to Vincent Dickson) can remember him singing Tommy Steele's two hits 'Rock With The Caveman' and 'Singing The Blues', which were the first attempts at British rock 'n' roll, and telling her, 'I'm going to be famous one day.'

Although rock 'n' roll was being heard more frequently it was still considered a passing phase and wasn't receiving any specialized television coverage until '6.5 Special' started in February 1957 on BBC TV, the same month that Bill Haley arrived in Britain for his first tour.

Pete Bush remembers that by this time Harry was becoming very conscious of his looks. 'In our last year at school he became very meticulous about his appearance. He was always combing his hair. It wasn't a fashion show because none of us had a lot of money. It was just that he liked to keep looking good.'

There was enormous anticipation for Haley's concerts. The *Daily Mirror* had been orchestrating a publicity campaign which would culminate in the organization of a four-hundred-seater Rock 'n' Roll Special train from Waterloo to Southampton to greet Haley and the Comets when they docked on 6 February.

The film *Rock Around The Clock*, which starred Bill Haley, had gained notoriety because Teddy boys had decided that they shared an affinity with rock 'n' roll and were turning up at the cinemas to jive in the aisles and slash seats. The film was banned in some cities and Bill Haley was given space in the *Daily Mirror* to declare how sorry he was that his music had got people over-excited and to explain how virtuous it really all was.

In hyping Haley to such an extent the *Mirror* was walking a fine line between promoting a series of events and inciting teenage frenzy. When Haley finally arrived he was faced with a crowd of

5,000 at the dockside and more at Southampton station. The fans were so out of control at Southampton that he was virtually carried by the force of the bodies towards his train. All along the route to London those who'd read the *Mirror*'s timetable for the progress of the Rock 'n' Roll Special stood beside the tracks and waved.

The behaviour so alarmed Haley that he threatened to cancel the concerts if any rioting occured. Strict security was enforced, dancing in the aisles was banned and the *Mirror* soberly advised its teenager readers to 'take it easy'. The warnings proved worthwhile. When he took to the stage at London's Dominion Theatre, Tottenham Court Road, there was a full house of 3,000 but no riots.

On 23 February Haley was able to write in *Melody Maker*: 'There haven't been any disturbances at the concerts. The boys and girls clap and they sing with us. That is the general pattern that we follow in our presentation. If we entertain the crowd, then the crowd will watch and listen quietly.'

The tour, as scheduled, was a brief incursion but shortly before Haley arrived in Britain a further twelve dates were added, one of them at the Regal in Edmonton, just a few miles down the road from Cheshunt. Harry and his friends were in line for tickets the morning they went on sale, which was a school day.

The plan had been to go on to school but by the time they were served it was after midday so they killed the afternoon at Terry Smart's house. What they didn't know was that a member of staff had seen them in Edmonton and so the next day they received a dressing down from the headmaster, with the prefects among them temporarily losing their badges.

The concert was on Sunday 3 March 1957, and was an eye-opener for these sixteen year olds from Hertfordshire who had never been able to see a live rock 'n' roll performance.

'We were absolutely bowled over by the whole thing,' remembers Frances Slade. 'It was so exciting. At last there was something we could relate to instead of all this Guy Mitchell and Perry Como stuff that was being churned out at us.'

Haley was preceded by a fifty-minute set from the Vic Lewis Orchestra and then came on playing 'Razzle-dazzle' dressed in his tartan jacket. The volume, although low by today's standards, took the audience by surprise. *Melody Maker*'s Laurie Henshaw had described it as 'hitting the crowd like a battering ram' even though it only came through three small speakers.

Bass player Al Rex threw his stand-up bass around, eventually straddling it like a horse while tenor sax player Rudy Pompilli climbed on his back in what appeared to be wild abandon to youngsters more accustomed to a band seated behind its music stands.

'What struck me was that everyone was standing up,' remembers Norman Mitham. 'It was electrifying. We'd never seen anything like it before. The sound seemed so full. We came home afterwards on the bus and talked about the concert for days.'

Says Cliff: 'I can still feel the excitement I felt that night. We were in the circle and we had to stand up to see and you could feel the balcony shake when he came out singing, "On your marks, Get set, Now ready, Ready Everybody, Razzle-dazzle..."'

'It's hard for me now to think of anything that has been as good as that. There must have been, but that was my first encounter. I had never been to a concert before and suddenly everything we had heard on the radio was happening right before our eyes.'

In 1960 he wrote: 'This, I think, was the moment when I knew what I wanted to do above everything else in the world.'

The month of the Haley concert saw another musical phenomenon, skiffle, gripping Britain. Like rock 'n' roll it was an American music but its origins were further back in negro spirituals, folk songs and acoustic blues rather than the electrified Chicago blues.

Unamplified and largely unrecorded, skiffle tended to appeal to the better-educated and more middle-class teenagers who wore thick pullovers and corduroys rather than coloured shirts and drainpipes. They admired the music for its 'authenticity' and 'purity' and rather scorned rock 'n' roll because of its deliberate commercial appeal and its associations with Teddy boy hooliganism.

Nevertheless, that didn't stop the music papers from gleefully declaring the death of rock 'n' roll and predicting that skiffle would be the next big thing. The point was considered proven when the Vipers scored a hit with 'Cumberland Gap', Chas McDevitt with 'Freight Train' and Lonnie Donegan with 'Don't You Rock Me Daddy-O'.

Harry never really liked it. To him it was as far removed from rock 'n' roll as was opera. He bought Donegan's records but the releases that he really loved were those by Elvis, the Everly Brothers and the Platters. He could never have imagined himself singing skiffle.

6

'I unashamedly used skiffle'

During July and August 1957 Harry took a summer job picking tomatoes in a local garden nursery while waiting to hear how he had fared in his O level exams. He had a horrible feeling as he trudged home each night with his hands stained dark green that he could be doing a job like this for the rest of his life.

When the results came through they were a severe disappointment. His father opened the letter and broke the news that he had passed only in English Language. In real terms this left him no more qualified than his classmates who had gone out into the world after the fourth year. Career opportunities for people with one O level were limited. If he didn't take up an apprenticeship he was left with the options of being a manual labourer or an office junior.

Fearing the worst, his father had already been making enquiries at Thorn Electric and knew of a vacancy in the credit control department at Atlas Lighting. It was an unskilled position checking orders against the different trade discounts and passing the information on to regional despatch centres. It wasn't a demanding job but there were 'prospects' for the right hard-working lad and it brought in extra money for the still-struggling family. Most of his four pounds a week wage packet would be handed straight over to his mother.

Thorn Electric was a major employer in the area but didn't offer the ideal work environment for a sixteen-year-old boy. The average age of its workers at that time was forty and many of these were housewives working on the assembly lines. June Pearce, who, as June Turner, was a personnel officer when Harry joined the company, remembers him mainly because he was one of the few young people on the pay roll.

'He just seemed like most other young people of the day,' she says. 'He was very quiet, very polite and sort of orderly. He wasn't a tearaway by any means. He belonged to the Sports and Social Club and used to play a lot of badminton with his father.'

While sorting out the orders and looking up maps to find out where the closest despatch centre to Macclesfield was, he secretly dreamed of being Elvis. He had been doing his best to look like his idol, studying the photos that Donna was collecting and pinning up in the girls' bedroom, but he now wanted to be able to do what Elvis did—to sing, make records and appear in films.

He had been encouraged by singing with the Quintones but since then he had entered some local competitions as a solo act. In one talent show, held at the Capitol Theatre in Winchmore Hill, he had sung a version of Frankie Laine's 'A Woman In Love' and taken second place.

'I wasn't frustrated at the office,' he says, 'because I never thought about it that much. I was only thinking about becoming a singer. I was convinced I could do it but I was frustrated that I didn't know how to start. If only there had been a door marked "Show Business" with a list of vacancies posted outside. I had no way of knowing where to go. If there is such a thing as luck, that's where luck came in.'

Luck, in his case, came when his bicycle broke and he had to take the bus into work. On the top deck he met his schoolfriend, Frances Slade, who was now a student commuting daily to Hornsey College of Art. Somewhere between Cheshunt and Enfield, where Harry had to get off, Frances mentioned that the singer in the skiffle group her boyfriend Terry Smart was drumming for had just been called up to do his National Service and they were looking for a replacement. Harry's name had been brought up, apparently because Smart remembered from the school plays that he could sing. Harry indicated his interest and, the next evening, Smart came knocking at the front door of 12 Hargreaves Close.

Terry Smart was a year younger than Harry and had left school at fifteen to become a butcher's mate but he knew him from playing in the school's rugby football team and from playing the role of The Ghost Of Christmas Yet To Come in *A Christmas Carol*.

He had started drumming after seeing a trio playing at a wedding reception in the Flamstead End Community Hall. 'I sat watching the drummer and I thought that's what I want to do,' he says. 'I used to have a paper round and I bought myself a bass drum, snare drum and high hat with my earnings. Later I bought a twenty-inch crash cymbal. A friend of my dad's had played drums in an army band and he used to come round and give me lessons.'

News that there was a drummer living on the estate came to the attention of Dick Teague, a fairly serious-minded accounts clerk whose big musical love was traditional jazz. When his younger brother Mick left the navy and bought a guitar he was inspired to start playing skiffle in the front room of his family's home at 19 Kingsley Avenue, with their mother Kathleen joining in on a washboard.

It wasn't long before the windows and doors were thrown open and friends would sit on the garden wall clapping along to these informal concerts. Eventually a neighbour complained to Brox-bourne Borough Council who threatened the Teagues with eviction unless the music was halted at 10 p.m. each night.

By the time Smart was recruited in June 1957 it had become a fully-fledged skiffle group with the Teague brothers playing guitars, Terry Harness singing and playing guitar, Allan Crouch on washboard and Ken Simmons on tea-chest bass. An insurance salesman who was a friend of the Teague family heard the boys rehearsing and booked their first public appearance at a pub in Stoke

Newington, North London, after which Dick's father, Walter Teague, began to manage the group, getting them regular work at local youth clubs, fêtes, pubs, jazz clubs and carnivals.

Terry Smart took Harry to meet the rest of the group at Frances Slade's home in Churchgate. 'It was an audition in a very loose sense of the word,' remembers Dick, who never had a high opinion of his group's musicianship.

'It would have been very presumptuous of us to consider we were auditioning someone. Basically it was a question of finding someone who could sing better than we could and none of us could sing a bloody note. Everybody was doing skiffle in those days. You didn't even have to be good at it.'

Harry turned up wearing a brown duffle coat and seemed shy and lacking in confidence as he ran through a couple of numbers in the front room of the bungalow, but his singing was distinct and impressive.

'There was a very musical, pleasant quality to his voice even then,' says Dick. 'As a matter of fact it wasn't the best sort of voice for the material we were doing, which often sounded better with a jazz voice that was slightly raspy and unpleasant. But Harry made everything he sang sound good.'

On 19 September 1957 Walter Teague wrote in the group's engagement diary: 'Harry introduced to group and enlisted right away. Good luck to the group's additional member.'

The next day Harry signed his first contract, a handwritten note made out on a sheet of paper torn from an exercise book. It read: 'We, the undersigned (members of Dick Teague's Skiffle group) hereby agree not to leave the group to take an individual engagement with any other musical concern without previously discussing the matter with the full group and its controlling manager.' It was signed by Harry Webb, Dick Teague, Mick Teague, Terry Harness, Allan Crouch, Terry Smart and Ken Simmons.

British skiffle, which reached its commercial peak in 1957, had developed from a fascination with American folk blues and was pioneered by traditional jazz musicians like Ken Colyer (trumpet), who had spent time in New Orleans in 1952, Chris Barber (trombone) and Lonnie Donegan (banjo), which is why a jazzer like Dick Teague found himself getting involved. It was Donegan's 1955 recording of 'Rock Island Line' which triggered off the national craze when it became a hit.

'Rock Island Line' was the perfect skiffle number. It was frantic, it was easy to play and it was splattered with Americanisms. The story of how it was discovered by the American folklorist Alan Lomax, who picked it up from a convicted murderer called Huddie 'Leadbelly' Ledbetter in 1934, gave it absolute credibility in the eyes of the purists who liked to think that the best songs were written from the soul without any thought of posterity or financial reward.

Donegan, who played in Chris Barber's band, had initially been given a spot to play 'Rock Island Line' as a novelty interlude in Barber's programme of New Orleans jazz but by 1957 he was a major star in his own right with a string of top twenty hits including 'Lost John', 'Cumberland Gap' and 'Putting On The Style'.

Although the songs were inevitably American and skiffle was supposed to have started at rent parties (parties in rented buildings) in Chicago during the 1920s, skiffle in the hands of Lonnie Donegan and his friends was a peculiarly British phenomenon which appealed not only because it was vibrant and unstuffy at a time when young people were looking for an excitement that would lift them out of the sea of post-war blandness, but because you didn't need to be an accomplished musician to play it and the equipment was inexpensive and largely improvised.

You could get by with three chords, a song book and a lot of enthusiasm. An upright bass could be made out of a used tea chest, a broom handle and a length of string, while percussion was produced by dragging a thimble across the ribbed metal of a domestic washboard.

It wasn't rock 'n' roll but it drew from the same well of black American culture and appealed to young people. It created a ready-made audience for blues singers like Big Bill Broonzy, Sonny Terry, Brownie McGhee and Lonnie Johnson when they later came to England and led directly to the folk music revival of the early sixties.

It was also an ideal place for potential rock 'n' roll musicians to get started in Britain. Trade embargos introduced after the war meant that electric guitars weren't available in British music stores and few teenagers in this country had enjoyed the long exposure to black gospel music, country and western and blues that people like Elvis Presley and Chuck Berry had. Six months before Harry Webb joined Dick Teague, John Lennon had started singing skiffle with the Quarry Men, and was later joined by Paul McCartney.

Alan Lomax himself saw the movement in glowingly positive terms. In August 1957 he commented: 'Before skiffle, even three or four years ago, relatively few people in London made their own music. Singing and playing was for show-offs or professionals. Pub singers mulled over the dry bones of the Cockney music hall songs which had little meaning for the younger generation. Nowadays the young people of this country have songs they like to sing.'

Harry hated skiffle. It was too worthy and folkish for him and lacked the raw electric energy of Memphis rock 'n' roll. But he saw the sense in keeping his mouth shut about his personal musical preferences and regarding the job in Teague's group as his first step into show business. Maybe he could even introduce a little rock 'n' roll into the act, he even dared to think.

'For me it offered a way of singing,' he admits. 'Skiffle was just a vehicle to take me where I wanted to go. I couldn't have possibly sung like a skiffle singer. I didn't find it very exciting but I liked being able to sing in front of an audience. There wasn't another skiffle singer who looked like Elvis. I unashamedly used it to further my own ends.'

Once he had signed the contract he rehearsed every night, learning the words to songs like Woody Guthrie's 'Bring A Little Water Sylvie' and the Donegan hits 'Rock Island Line' and 'Don't You Rock Me Daddy-O'. The group's sources were mainly the singles by

Donegan and Ken Colyer's song book, *Skiffle Album*, which had the words and chords to such skiffle favourites as 'This Train', 'John Henry', 'Down By The Riverside' and 'The Grey Goose'.

Before Harry joined the group Dick Teague's opinion was that they were 'basically rubbish'. His revised opinion was that they were 'basically rubbish' but with an added 'bit of quality'. The speed at which the new singer could pick up songs amazed them all. 'We would pick a record we liked and work out the chords in rehearsal,' says Dick. 'Harry could come back the next day and he would know the piece inside out.'

One of the group's regular gigs over the coming months would be an 8.30 spot at the Flamstead End Youth Club during a Friday night jazz evening known as the Saints Rhythm Club.

'What used to happen was that while the jazz bands were on, the kids flopped round the hall looking bored,' says Dick. 'Then when the skiffle came on they would go mad dancing.' It was here, on 4 October, that Harry made his debut as the lead singer of a group.

With the departure of Terry Harness the group had lost a guitarist. Harry couldn't yet play guitar but he did like to strap one over his shoulder and have it hanging behind him as he sang, Elvis Presley style.

'He used to embarrass me with it,' Dick admits.

Two weeks later Harry roped in Brian Parker, a friend from Cheshunt Secondary School who had played violin in the National Youth Orchestra, to play guitar. Parker was to go on to become an important figure in the rock 'n' roll scene around Cheshunt and Waltham Cross, playing with Dave Sampson and the Hunters and the Parker Royal Five before forming Unit Four Plus Two with an old school friend and scoring a number one hit in 1965 with 'Concrete and Clay'.

'I knew him mostly through sport at school,' says Parker. 'Then because I had owned a guitar for a couple of weeks he thought I must be very proficient and so he asked me to join.'

Over the next three months the Dick Teague Group played an

average of twice a week and rehearsed furiously in between. A look at the date sheet meticulously kept by Walter Teague shows that they played Flamstead End Youth Club once a week and then usually played another local event such as a Boy Scouts' party, a dance at Goff's Oak or a function at Waltham Town Hall. The group's fee was one pound, raised to three pounds and five shillings for bigger events such as the one at the town hall.

At the same time they were entering local talent contests but finding themselves unplaced. On 22 October Walter Teague wrote rather proudly in his diary, 'Received confirmation of group's entry in Haileybury Boy's Club competition in Hoddesdon, which was a skiffle group contest with a first prize of a silver challenge cup autographed by Tommy Steele.'

On 2 November there was the forlorn addition: 'Played in competition at Haileybury Club. Not in first 4 out of 12. Alleykats 3rd.' The Alleykats were their main local rivals.

Skiffle inspired dancing and quiet appreciation rather than screaming, but Harry was consciously introducing a rock 'n' roll element to his act by dressing sharp in patterned pullovers and emulating Elvis's pelvic thrusts. Sometimes, after his set, he would go out on the floor and dance with the girls but the partner most of the group remember him dancing with was his pretty fourteen-year-old sister Donella, who now called herself Donna and was catching the eye of all the local boys.

Surprisingly, in view of his Victorian contempt for the modern world, Rodger Webb supported Harry's skiffling, seeing in it perhaps some of the same unsophisticated fun that he had enjoyed in India with his brother Tom when they had played old Irish and Scottish folk tunes.

June Pearce remembers that he would regularly stop her at work to tell her how well his son was doing with his music.

'We used to have mid-morning breaks in the canteen and Mr Webb would come over and say that Harry was playing at such-and-such a place last night and they got on very well. He was obviously very proud of him.'

Yet, at the same time, he seemed surprised to find that Harry could succeed at something. Maybe his expectations had been progressively lowered through examination failures or maybe, with his own status in the world diminished, it was important for him to see Harry as a dependent child.

Walter Teague was taken aback when Rodger told his wife Kathleen that he was worried that Harry would hold the group back.

'He came along to one of the boys' local appearances,' remembers Walter, 'and he started talking to my wife. He said, "If only my son had the confidence that the rest of the group had, they would go far. But I'm afraid Harry will never do any good because he is so nervous."'

He was indeed nervous. In his early shows he found it hard to look directly at the audience and preferred to slink away afterwards. Although he was friends with Terry Smart and Brian Parker, whom he'd known from school, he never got close to anyone else in the group and didn't socialize with them.

Kathleen Teague remembers him as 'reserved and shy. He wouldn't push himself forward at all.' Her daughter Sheila picked up the same impression from seeing him rehearse at their home. 'I remember him with dark hair, jeans and a leather jacket just standing there looking very edgy. He used to have a nervous cough. They would hang a microphone from the light fixture in the middle of the room and start playing. I was extremely impressed with this boy's voice though. It seemed to boom out and fill the room.'

At twenty-two, Dick Teague was five years older than Harry. Whereas Harry couldn't wait to leave his office job and saw music as the key to his escape, Dick was rather happy in the accounts office of a local chemical company and was set against anyone taking the group too seriously. It had started out as fun, he thought, and when it stopped being fun the group should end.

Yet although he wasn't serious about a musical career he was serious about the type of music he thought they should play. He insisted that they be a 'purist' group not swayed by pop or gimmick songs. Dick Teague was a man for whom even Lonnie Donegan was suspected as a heretic. He had about as much interest in rock 'n' roll as Harry had in skiffle and thought that Elvis Presley was 'a great greasy wop'.

By December 1957 Harry was pushing Dick to let him sing 'Heartbreak Hotel' and 'All Shook Up' in a special spot. The suggestion appalled Dick who saw it as a compromise with commercial pop. He wouldn't allow it. Already he was worried about Harry's swivelling hips and vocal 'uh-huh's which he found totally inappropriate for songs expressing the anxieties of rural blacks and dustbowl migrants.

'He had slightly long sideboards and he used to do himself up as a dead ringer for Elvis,' Dick remembers. 'When Harry started shaking himself about I got uptight about it because we were supposed to be a traditional jazz outfit. I was very old-fashioned for a young guy.'

In October, unknown to his sons, Walter Teague had written to the BBC requesting an audition for the 'Saturday Skiffle Club', an experimental half-hour show on the Light Programme, which was produced by Jimmy Grant and later turned into the highly influential pop and jazz show 'Saturday Club'. To Walter's surprise, a letter came back offering an audition at BBC's Studio 4, Maida Vale, on 13 January.

The first that Dick knew of the audition was when he arrived home from work and his father told him not to bother changing out of his office clothes as they were going straight out.

'All the others knew about it, but they knew I was a perfectionist. I thought the group was rubbish and that they were rushing to places I didn't want to go yet,' he says.

The group went to Maida Vale that evening and played 'Stackerlee Blues', 'Sporting Life', 'This Train' and 'This Little Light Of Mine' in front of a clerk from the variety booking section.

'It was ridiculous really. They asked us who the lead guitarist was but we didn't really have one,' says Dick. 'We were just a bunch of guys thrashing away on guitars. They asked who the lead singer was and so we stuck the mike on Harry and he took the lead while the rest of us stayed in the background churning out our rubbish. The woman who had auditioned us came down from her cubicle after we had finished and said to Harry, "You've got a very good voice. You ought to have it trained." That was the only comment she made.'

What no one else knew at the time was that Harry was already planning to leave. He hated the songs he was having to sing and could see that there was no scope for his plans to emulate Elvis with Dick Teague policing his movements. The only person he grumbled to though was Terry Smart who he found shared his grievances.

'We both found rock 'n' roll far more exciting than skiffle,' says Smart. 'A few times during rehearsals we had asked to try some of these new numbers but Dick didn't want to. He didn't like the sound.'

So they planned to form their own rock 'n' roll group which would rehearse on the evenings that they weren't needed to play skiffle, only breaking the news to Dick when they felt confident enough to get their own engagements. The most immediate problem though was that they were only a duo and neither of them could play guitar, even though Harry had recently bought one from a mail order firm and had been shown the rudiments by his father.

They tried to coax Brian Parker away from Dick because Parker was becoming recognized as one of the brightest guitar talents in the area. 'I can remember actually getting on a bus to go down to Hargreaves Close saying to myself, "Yeh, I'm definitely going to join this rock 'n' roll group",' Brian remembers. 'But by the time I arrived I'd changed my mind. I told him that I was going to stick with the skiffle group.'

Eventually they decided they'd pull in Norman Mitham, Harry's old friend.

'He came to me and said that if I could learn to play guitar I could be in his band,' says Mitham. 'Up until that point I'd never had a music lesson and really knew nothing about music at all.'

What he did have though was an uncle, Philip Spur, who had played professionally in dance bands and who was willing to give Norman and Harry lessons on his Gibson guitar.

'First of all uncle Philip told us what key Harry sang in and then we'd play the record we wanted to cover and he would work out the chords,' says Mitham. 'He'd teach us the chords, show us where the chord changes came and we built up a repertoire like that.

'We didn't have the musical ability to play instrumental breaks so we improvised with a sequence of chords. It was similar to what the skiffle boys did but Terry made it more rock 'n' roll by playing a definite beat. In the skiffle group he tended to play with brushes but now he was using sticks to play a more prominent beat.'

Dick Teague sensed that something was happening behind his back when Harry's legendary talent for picking songs up overnight seemed to disappear. He also noticed that Harry's friend Norman was now coming along to the group's gigs and studying his guitar chords.

Then one evening, while returning young Joan from a play session with his daughter Sheila, Walter Teague heard the sounds of a rock 'n' roll group rehearsal coming from the open windows of 12 Hargreaves Close.

'After telling Dick not to teach him how to play guitar,' says Walter, 'there he was playing as lively as you like.' A crisis meeting of the group was called for 17 January at which Harry argued that the skiffle group should include rock 'n' roll.

'The other guys said that they liked what we were playing,' remembers Dick. 'They thought that the type of material we were playing was most suited to the instruments we had. Rock 'n' roll required more competence.

'Then Terry Smart piped up that he also wanted to play rock 'n' roll. I said that there was no question about it. Either they played our sort of music or we had a split. Harry said he'd rather play rock 'n' roll but he'd prefer to do it with me because we had a good thing going. I said it wouldn't be with me.

'It wasn't unpleasant but it was a sort of agreement that the music we wanted to do was different and we just packed up that night. I just said to Terry, "Well, off you go", and I lost contact with both of them after that.'

Walter Teague solemnly recorded it in his diary: 'Harry and Terry left group after full discussion of all matters relating to future policy.' Coincidentally, the local paper ran its first feature on the group that evening beneath a photo of Harry singing at the Saints' Rhythm Club. The headline was, 'Local Skiffle Group Get BBC Audition'.

'Many people are saying that skiffle music is on the way out, but for a local group, Dick Teague and his Skiffle Group, it may well be just on its way in,' read the report.

'This local skiffle group had an audition with the BBC on Monday evening for the "Saturday Skiffle Club," which is heard every Saturday morning at 10am. The result of the audition will not be known for some time.

'Dick Teague commented afterwards: "The audition went very well, and I hope that we have passed it . . ."

'The group was formed just over six months ago, and its motto is "The surest way not to fail is to determine to succeed." Since its formation, the group has been rehearsing at every opportunity.

'For the first four months the group were in existence the instrumentalists sang the songs, but in September Harry Webb joined the group as their singer.

'In its early days the group entered for many skiffle competitions but was never placed. Now they have ceased to enter for them. Dick Teague explained: "At these competitions a group is generally expected to sing Lonnie Donegan style numbers, and we don't like them. We specialise in true traditional skiffle." '

A week later Walter Teague received a letter from the BBC letting him know that the Group had not passed the audition for 'Skiffle Club'. 'Heard from BBC re. audition,' he noted in his diary. '(No go).

If at first you don't succeed etc. Something attempted is something done.'

Harry's only response, when he saw the newspaper, was to think how much he looked like Elvis. His mind was already made up to leave skiffle far behind and concentrate on rock 'n' roll.

7

'Something told me he was going
to be really big'

For Harry Webb, 1958 was to be the last year of normal life; the last year he could walk along a British street without being recognized, go out on a date with the assurance that he wasn't being used for his social position, or have what most people refer to as a private life. It was also the last year he would have to worry about money.

He began the year as a shy young office clerk playing skiffle in Hertfordshire village halls, and ended it under another name as a national celebrity who girls wanted to paw and their boyfriends wanted to punch.

The speed of the transition was mind-blowing. Twelve months after his first appearance with Dick Teague he was closing the show on a major tour. Elvis Presley had to wait a year and a half after cutting his first single before he was on national television, and John Lennon, who started playing skiffle in March 1958, didn't become a celebrity until 1963.

The opening months of the year were charged with excitement. Not only had his picture appeared in the paper but he was rehearsing every night at home with his own rock 'n' roll trio.

Between them Harry, Terry Smart and Norman Mitham would buy the latest American rock 'n' roll singles on a Friday night and then Donna would painstakingly transcribe the lyrics while they worked out the chord changes. In this way they quickly learned to play 'Blue Suede Shoes', 'Heartbreak Hotel', 'Rock Around The Clock' and 'Blueberry Hill'.

His musical preferences were for the sweeter style of singers like Ricky Nelson and the Everly Brothers, rather than the vaguely-threatening screams and squawks of Little Richard and Gene Vincent. He even admired Pat Boone, a white boy from Tennessee who made his name by recording cover versions of black rock 'n' roll hits in the knowledge that in a society still racially divided they would sell to the conservative white audience.

Smart suggested calling the trio the Planets. It was a topical enough name—the space race had just been inaugurated with the launch of Russia's Sputnik-1 satellite—but Harry and Norman Mitham didn't think it was quite right.

They looked up 'planet' in the dictionary and found that it came from the Greek 'planetes' meaning 'wanderer' or 'drifter'. They toyed with the idea of being the Wanderers or the Drifters and it was the Drifters that stuck. They were unaware that an American vocal group led by Clyde McPhatter had been recording under the name since 1953.

'It sounds crazy now,' says Mitham, 'but almost as soon as we started playing we decided on the cover of our first album. We hadn't recorded a single song but we said that if we ever made an LP we could have a picture of us sitting on a toboggan driving into a snow drift.'

The Drifters made their debut in March 1958 at the Forty Hill Badminton Club, between Cheshunt and Enfield, where Harry and his parents were members. It was the annual dinner and dance and they played the cabaret spot, getting the then-enormous fee of five pounds.

'I was elated that all these people were applauding me,' says Cliff, 'but it probably gave a false impression because these were people who knew me and who I played badminton with every week.'

Harry's life was incredibly full and even though he was donning a suit and tie each day to go to work, the fact that he was singing in a group reassured him that he was somehow different from all the other people there. At least he had the hope of one day breaking out. He knew that British teenagers were starved of live rock 'n' roll. There had been Tommy Steele and Terry Dene but neither of them had successfully captured the American sound.

In his already busy schedule he now found time for romance. During his last year at school he was attracted to his classmate Janice Berry who, unfortunately for him, was wrapped up in a serious relationship with Brian Cooke. A bright pupil, Janice had become head girl and passed six O levels. She was working in a two-year secretarial job with ICI in Welwyn Garden City with plans to train as a teacher when she was eighteen.

'All the time I was going out with Janice I knew that Harry wanted to go out with her,' says Cooke. 'Then one day she told me that she wasn't going out with me any more and the next thing I knew she was going out with Harry. I think she must have had him in mind when she got rid of me.'

Janice admits as much. 'It was the day I finished with Brian that he [Harry] knocked on my door and that evening we went to the cinema in Waltham Cross,' she says. 'I have to be honest and say that it wasn't entirely a coincidence. He had heard about the break-up.'

When in later years Cliff was to talk about the 'couple of times' he really believed he had fallen in love, Janice was certainly included although he has never before mentioned her by name and Janice has never told her story.

In a fan booklet published in 1959 she was referred to as 'June', a 'sixteen-year-old brunette' whom he dated for five months. 'They quietly held hands at the local cinema,' it read. 'They went to teenage parties together (spending most of the time in a corner alone), and took long country walks.'

Four years later in an interview he spoke of 'Janet', the girl he had been 'courting steadily' before he broke into show business. 'I guess she was the most serious girl I ever had,' he said.

Today he says, 'If love came into it at all, that was the first time.'

She was a dark-haired girl who lived with her mother at 242 Turner's Hill, a fifteen-minute walk from the Webbs' home. She was an only child, and her father had died suddenly while she was still at school.

She had always been part of the close-knit gang that centred on the school drama group and had often been to Hargreaves Close for tea. 'She was a lovely girl,' says Cliff's mother. 'We were very fond of Janice.'

Their brief relationship in 1958 typified the teenage innocence of the time. They would talk over coffees at the Blue Bird Café, go off on country rambles, visit the cinema or just see each other at home.

When she came along to group rehearsals she would sit in a corner quietly listening and supplying them with cups of tea. They even used her front room to practise in, setting up in the bay of the front window and leaving a threadbare patch of carpet behind as a memory.

Once, while on an evening walk, Harry surprised Janice by vaulting over the wall of a garden and picking her a flower.

'There was a beautiful magnolia bush,' she remembers. 'It was at its peak and I just happened to say something about how beautiful it looked in the evening light and he leapt over the wall, picked this flower from the tree, leapt back and gave it to me. It was a terribly romantic thing to do but it wasn't typical. That's why I remember it!

'A lot of what we did together was built around the Drifters' rehearsals. We were the same as any other boyfriend and girlfriend really. It was a loving relationship. People in those days didn't leap into bed together as they do now. Maybe some people did, but we didn't and it wasn't something that the crowd of people I was with did.

'I was certainly in love with him and, I don't know . . . I can't answer for him. Maybe it was one-sided but we both seemed to be in love.'

Dates with Janice had to be fitted in between dates with the group.

They had been offered a spot at the Five Horseshoes, a pub up the road in Burford Street, Hoddesdon, where the publican was experimenting with live music during the week.

The stage was a small raised platform next to the door to the gents' toilet. There was no amplification and anyone who played had to compete with customers' chatter and the sound of darts thudding into cork boards.

When the Drifters took on the challenge one mid-week evening in March, a well-built local lad with a Tony Curtis haircut and a black leather jacket was standing at the bar. John Foster was, in his own words, a 'bit of a Ted' but he considered himself wise in the ways of rock 'n' roll because, unlike most young people in the area, he had visited the legendary 2 I's coffee bar in London's Soho. Once when he was there he found himself standing next to Terry Dene, who in 1957 had been touted as 'Britain's answer to Elvis Presley'.

What John Foster saw at the Five Horseshoes that evening impressed him deeply. It wasn't the musicianship—the group was barely mastering the most basic chords—but there was something about the singer that transcended all the failures of the act.

'I didn't look at Terry and I didn't look at Norman,' he admits. I looked at the singer in his white shirt and black trousers and I saw Elvis. Something told me, yes, he's going to be big. He's going to be really big. I don't know what made me do it because I was drinking with my mates at the bar, but I just walked up to the group and asked them if they wanted a manager.'

It was pure bluff. He had no experience of show business management and had never booked an act into the 2 I's. He was a driver employed on the local sewage farm. But he was on speaking terms with the manager Tom Littlewood, a former film stunt man who had the unusual business practice of paying groups to play in the cellar and then charging them a ten per cent commission for the privilege.

Being asked if you wanted to play at the 2 I's was like being asked if you would like your latest film to be shown at Cannes. For aspiring British rock 'n' rollers it was the place to play. It was where Tommy Steele and Terry Dene had been 'discovered' by their future managers and it had become the best-known coffee bar in Britain.

They did need a manager, especially one with such apparently good contacts. Foster even had a telephone in his home, something that neither Terry, Norman or Harry had.

'I knew I was being rather flash when I gave them my phone number,' he says. 'It was a rather impressive thing to do in those days.'

He promised them that if they met him that weekend he would arrange a spot for them at the 2 I's. No trouble.

'Foster told us to be prepared to go up to London on the 715 Green Line bus that Saturday,' remembers Mitham. 'He said it would be coming through at two o'clock and that he would be sitting on the nearside. We were to wait at the Old Pond bus stop in Cheshunt and get on when we saw him.

'We talked about it all week among ourselves. We didn't know if we were being taken for a ride. However, we turned up and waited and John was on the second bus that came, sitting up against the window. I think Harry had a lot more faith in him than I did. I didn't think he would be there.'

The 2 I's was at 59 Old Compton Street, not far from Shaftesbury Avenue. It was a small street-level coffee bar with live music in the cellar. It had been taken over in 1956 by two Australian wrestlers, Paul Lincoln and Ray Hunter, who bought it from the Irani brothers (hence the I of the 2 I's).

It was at a time when coffee bars were the latest teen sensation, providing a meeting space that was neither church youth club (where adults were concerned about your moral welfare) nor public house (which required that you be eighteen). The Gaggia machines which gushed and gurgled on the counters provided an exotic new beverage from the Continent known as 'espresso'.

At first the 2 I's had been a financial disaster. Then, on 14 July

1956, a young commercial artist called Wally Whyton dropped by and asked whether he and his skiffle group the Vipers could busk there.

'Paul Lincoln said it was OK, and within about three weeks the place was literally packed to the doors. Instead of letting us busk he charged a shilling admission and paid us two pounds a night each,' remembers Whyton. 'The basement had been a store room and when we became the resident group down there I went with Lionel Bart and a couple of others and painted designs on the walls.'

Even though they lived on the fringes of London none of the Drifters had ever ventured into Soho before. As they walked through its narrow streets they felt a frisson of excitement at the sight of the jazz clubs, foreign food stores and striptease clubs. Soho had not yet become the sleaze pit of the sixties but there was enough of an air of strangeness and naughtiness to cause a provincial lad's eyes to widen.

'I can remember someone pointing to some girls and mentioning that they were prostitutes,' remembers Mitham. 'We had never had anything to do with prostitutes and we couldn't believe that we were right in the middle of it all.'

They were met at the 2 I's by Tom Littlewood who listened to them perform two songs before telling them that they had passed the audition and could play their first show that night.

'We weren't the star attraction but at least we were on and got invited back the next day and then the day after that,' says Mitham. 'There was no screaming. The kids just listened.

'What we talked about afterwards was the fact that people had paid and they had stood there and listened. We weren't there as incidental entertainment like at the Five Horseshoes or the Badminton Club. People had paid to watch us and they seemed to like us.

'By the time I got home that night my parents were asleep but I actually woke them up to tell them that I had played at the 2 I's.'

John Foster's bluff had paid off. The audition had led to what was in effect a two-week residency during April 1958.

'It was all very exciting for him,' says Janice, who was by this time seeing even less of her boyfriend than before. He obviously wanted to succeed and the fact that everybody applauded at the 2 I's reinforced the idea that he was going to.'

During the first week a sandy-haired young man on leave from the RAF, where he was just finishing his National Service, came up to them and asked if they needed a lead guitarist to boost their sound.

He was Ian Ralph 'Sammy' Samwell and like Harry had been playing in a group—the Ash Valley Skiffle Group—while really wanting to play rock 'n' roll. What the Drifters were doing summed up everything he hoped to do.

'They asked me to audition for them on the Saturday afternoon,' says Samwell. 'That became my first group rehearsal and that night I played with them and effectively joined the Drifters.'

The same night Jan Vane, a teenager from Rainham in Essex, was visiting the 2 I's as part of a treat for her sixteenth birthday from her boyfriend Eddie. The cellar was so packed that they sat on a Coca-Cola fridge and craned their necks to see.

'I can't remember what he sang that night but I just thought that he was so unusual,' she remembers. 'He was so handsome and so different.

'He was young and exciting and I had never been anywhere like that before. I was caught up in the whole atmosphere of the evening; of seeing someone live and of thinking that if he was playing at the 2 I's he must be extremely famous.'

A chatty, confident girl, she stayed behind to get Harry's autograph. After asking the usual questions about how long he had been playing and where he usually performed she asked him whether he had a fan club. Harry laughed at the question. He explained that he had only been playing rock 'n' roll for just over four weeks and apologized for having to leave so soon to get the last bus home.

'I told him not to worry because we would run him home,' says Jan Vane. 'Eddie had a car, which was quite impressive in those days.

So that night we all squeezed into a small green Morris Minor and drove back to Cheshunt. The group all lived in different places too so we spent half the night finding their houses.

'The main point was that we exchanged addresses. I told him I would keep in touch to see what he was doing and I started writing. Sometimes he would write back to me and sometimes his mum would write back and eventually I got invited back home.'

This was to be the beginning of the official Cliff Richard Fan Club. It started with half a dozen members who Jan would personally write to with the latest information, and rose to a 42,000-strong membership which required a full-time staff of four.

Harry Greatorex was the closest thing to an agent to spot Harry Webb at the 2 I's. He was a 35-year-old dance hall manager from Derbyshire who scoured London to find talent worth promoting in the North.

He heard the Drifters during their second week and told John Foster that he could give them work at the Regal Ballroom in Ripley. He offered a fee of five pounds with an additional ten pounds for expenses.

There was just one thing that Harry Greatorex wasn't happy with. He didn't want to bill them as a group act, but as a singer with a backing group. He didn't think Harry Webb and the Drifters sounded convincingly rock 'n' roll enough. Foster assured him that the problem could be solved within minutes and he hauled the boys to The Swiss, a pub in Old Compton Street, to dream up a new name for Harry Webb.

It wasn't unusual for English rock 'n' roll singers to ditch their given names for something more evocative. Manager Larry Parnes had made an art of it—contrasting warm and friendly first names with tough and aggressive surnames: Tommy Steele for Thomas Hicks, Marty Wilde for Reginald Smith.

'All the American people had cool names anyway,' says Samwell. 'They were Chuck, Rick, Carl, Gene and things like that. None of them were called Ian or Norman.'

They started by playing on variations of Russ Hamilton, a British singer who'd had a couple of hits the year before, and came up with Russ Clifford and Cliff Russard before hitting on Cliff Richards. Samwell then suggested dropping the 's' as a tribute to Little Richard. John Foster then returned to Harry Greatorex and told him that it would be Cliff Richard and the Drifters who would be appearing in Ripley.

'I can remember him coming back home and saying that from now on he would like to be called Cliff and not Harry,' says his sister Jacqui. 'I don't think Dad ever called him Cliff but Joan, Donna and I started calling him it fairly quickly. Mum took a bit longer just because she kept slipping up. I mean, after calling your son Harry for seventeen years it is a bit difficult to call him something else overnight.'

The Ripley show, booked for Saturday 3 May, was their biggest engagement so far and their first outside London and Hertfordshire. They took a train to Derby and, on arriving, they were impressed to see posters announcing, 'Direct from the famous Soho 2 I's Coffee Bar—Cliff Richard and the Drifters'.

The Regal Ballroom was a converted snooker hall with a mock-Tudor frontage which Greatorex had taken over two years before and turned into a dance hall with events ranging from old-time dancing to skiffle. On the night Cliff and the Drifters played there was a 'top twenty record session' and support from Keith Freer and his Dixielanders.

'They had a stage with curtains which was quite something to us after the 2 I's,' says Samwell. 'The curtains parted, we were standing there and that night we really rocked. The place was absolutely jam-packed and the response was fantastic.'

After the show they had to bed down on hard benches in the venue because they were too late to get a train back home. 'It was a very exciting gig because it felt much more like the big time,' says Cliff. 'Suddenly I was fronting the band.'

Three weeks later Jerry Lee Lewis, one of the group's favourite American artists, played his first British concert. The tour was surrounded in controversy because news had leaked out that the new bride accompanying him was actually his fourteen-year-old cousin and he hadn't divorced his previous wife before the wedding.

Exposing the moral corruptness of a rock 'n' roll star was a job that the British press took to with great relish. They hounded Lewis during his stay in London and wrote editorials suggesting that the Home Secretary should deport him and teenagers should boycott his concerts.

Jerry Lee Lewis wasn't an avuncular figure like Bill Haley or a Southern gentleman like Elvis. With his narrow eyes and tight mouth he looked to be in a permanent state of mischief. His music was the look perfectly portrayed in sound—wild, sleazy, lustful, dangerous.

Cliff and the Drifters played 'Great Balls Of Fire' and 'Breathless' in their set and when they found that he was playing at the Kilburn State Theatre on Sunday 25 May they bought tickets as soon as they went on sale. The anti-Lewis publicity put out by *The People* and the *Daily Sketch* had its effect because on the night only a quarter of the seats had been sold.

'Jerry did a heck of a show that night to a poor audience,' remembers Samwell. 'There were one or two cat-calls and the people in front of us made rude noises when he stopped to comb his hair. John Foster, who was wearing his leather jacket, leant over and said, "One more peep out of you and that's your lot." They didn't make another noise.'

After the show John Foster thought of his greatest wheeze yet. He would take Terry Smart, Sammy Samwell and Cliff backstage so that he could brag about his future star. They found Lewis in his dressing room, wearing a ribbon tie and black gambler's jacket with leopardskin lapels, being photographed by a man from the *Daily Mirror*.

'I basically conned my way into the room by saying that Cliff was the latest British rock 'r' roll sensation,' says Foster. 'Of course, at that time he was nowhere near it. He'd hardly got used to the name Cliff Richard and had never been near a recording studio. Anyway, I asked if we could have our picture taken and we did, with Cliff standing right next to Jerry Lee.'

It was the closest any of them had come to a rock 'n' roll legend. Within a week Cliff was to have his own first taste of the fury and excitement that could attend rock 'n' roll.

Foster had booked the group into the Gaumont Teenage Show, a Saturday morning show at the Gaumont Theatre in Shepherd's Bush which mixed films, music, variety acts and celebrity appearances.

It was here that Cliff-mania began in a wave of frenzied screaming.

'We just weren't used to that sort of reaction from people,' says Mitham. 'It was the first reaction we had ever had to Cliff as a sex symbol. In Soho and Ripley you thought they were getting excited at the music but in Shepherd's Bush the audience was seated and they were screaming at Cliff.'

He had been playing rock 'n' roll for less than four months and had already stumbled on his natural audience. 'It didn't make sense and it felt unreal but I loved it,' he says. 'In those days the sound of girls screaming was the gauge of success.'

8

'I wanted a career so I got rid of the girlfriend'

On Saturday 14 June 1958 Cliff Richard and the Drifters returned to the Gaumont, this time as 'special guests' on a talent show.

Knowing that it was almost guaranteed to be another storming success, Sammy Samwell had been scanning entertainment newspapers to find an agent he could invite along. The names he saw meant nothing to him and so, at random, he picked on George Ganjou of George Ganjou Ltd. Entertainments, who regularly advertised on the back page of *The Stage*, and gave him a call.

What Samwell didn't know was that Ganjou was the least-likely agent to launch the career of a teenage rock 'n' roll group. Already in his late fifties he had spent most of his life in Poland before coming to England as part of an adagio act, the Ganjou Brothers and Juanita, and on retiring as a performer he had become an agent for several variety acts. He knew nothing about rock 'n' roll beyond the fact that he didn't like it. He proudly referred to himself as a 'square'.

Yet, to his credit, when John Foster and Sammy Samwell visited him at his Albemarle Street office on 6 June he agreed to come to the show despite the fact that it meant cancelling a weekend game of golf. He thought they were 'nice boys' and liked the looks of the singer whose photograph they showed him.

Ganjou suggested that Cliff and the Drifters should cut a demonstration record which he could play to his friends in the record industry. Early the next week they recorded two songs at a small studio above the HMV record shop in Oxford Street. They chose Elvis Presley's 'Lawdy Miss Clawdy', written by Lloyd Price, and Jerry Lee Lewis' 'Breathless', written by Otis Blackwell.

When they returned to the Gaumont that Saturday it caused an even greater storm than the debut. The audience was now primed and when Cliff hit the stage it was as if a dam had burst. His voice was barely audible above the screams and wails.

'As soon as Cliff started to sing, they all, especially the girls, went mad,' Ganjou remembered. 'They started to shout and rush towards him and after seeing this I decided, well, I'd better go back stage and have a talk to him.'

Ganjou's interest was aroused by show business common sense. Cliff looked good, seemed to have a pleasant personality and there was a demand for what he was doing. You didn't have to like rock 'n' roll to know you were on to a good thing here, and he had good connections with record companies through old dance band musicians who had gone on to become musical directors.

Samwell remembers being staggered when Ganjou came into the dressing room after the show and asked, 'Would you like to be on Decca or Columbia?' Samwell faked nonchalance and said his preference would be Columbia and so Ganjou said he would pass the demo disc to Norrie Paramor, a friend of his who was head of artists and repertoire for the EMI-owned Columbia label.

The scene in the dressing room that morning was a mixture of excitement and tension. There was a palpable sense that something very big was going to happen for them but also a slight fear of the teenage power that was being unleashed.

John Brunel, a reporter on the *Shepherd's Bush Gazette & Post* had been a judge on the morning's talent show (won by a local skiffle group called the Avro Boys) and described what he saw in his weekly column.

'Black-haired Cliff Richard had just been "sending" the fans and I found myself in a top floor room with the orders "Don't leave the building".

'No, I wasn't a political prisoner of the Rank Organization, but there were three hundred screaming fans down in the road below, the exit doors were being rattled and if we went out there it would have been like being thrown to the lions. So we stayed put, Cliff got out some buns (he had not had any breakfast) and we started the long wait.

'I asked a girl who introduced herself as the leader of Cliff's fan club how old he was. She did not know. Cliff ate another bun. The girls outside screamed more and we had to pretend we had left the building to kid them into leaving too.

'Who'd be a rock star? Not me.'

These experiences at the Gaumont convinced Cliff that something important was about to happen for him and he thought it was time to cool his relationship with Janice.

'I enjoyed being with her,' he says, 'but I can remember at that time feeling that I had to make a choice. I thought even then that if I was going to be a pop star my fans wouldn't want me to be married or to have a girlfriend. I could see how my sister Donna would quickly go off a pop star that she'd liked if she found out that they were engaged or married. The rock 'n' roll singer became a sex symbol and belonged to the fans.

'With Janice I had to make the decision that if I was going to go all out to be a pop star I didn't want any attachments. I didn't want anything to get in the way of me being famous and having loads and loads of girls chasing me all over the place.'

Janice had separately come to the same conclusion. She had too much self-respect to imagine herself as a bit-part player in a drama of rock 'n' roll and screaming girls.

'I can remember seeing mounted police outside the theatre and I had to stay inside while they got him out and it all worried me slightly,' she says. 'I remember thinking, well, this isn't me. I don't like this. I don't really like coming to these concerts.

'Cliff knew that if he was known to have a girlfriend it wouldn't be good from the point of view of his girl fans. It obviously looked better if he was a single fellow and available.

'So all these things meant that it was his and my decision that it was better if we separated.

'I remember the evening that it happened. He brought me home and we knew we were going to part anyway because we had been talking about it. We were standing in the porch of my house and he gave me the words of a song he had written for me. It said:

"When teenagers love
They love for ever
When teenagers love
It's bound to be true
I'm a teenager in love
A teenager in love
I'm a teenager in love with you"

'I was literally crying on his shoulder after he handed me the piece of paper. It wasn't me saying that I'd had enough of him, it was a joint decision that this was the only thing we could do.

'I wanted Cliff to be successful. I wanted him to do well because he wanted to and I could actually see that I was in the way. I could see that he was better without a girlfriend. I don't mean without me in particular but that he was better off being single.'

It was the first of many times that Cliff would consider the options and always he has made the same choice with the same measure of apparently dispassionate calculation.

'It was far easier than it might appear looking back,' he says of the end of his romance with Janice. 'I wanted a career, I didn't want a girlfriend. So I got rid of the girlfriend. That's as brutal as I can put it. It didn't mean I liked her any less but I just made the cold-blooded choice to go for that. That's what I wanted.'

Within days of ending the relationship he was sitting in Norrie Paramor's office in Great Castle Street under consideration for the

Columbia record label.

Norman William Paramor, known to everyone as 'Norrie', was forty-four years old and had been in the music business since leaving school at fifteen. He'd been a pianist, a band leader and, since 1949, a record company music director.

In common with George Ganjou he had no real experience of rock 'n' roll because he'd grown up in the big band era and, as a producer, was best known for working with old-style singers like Michael Holliday and Ruby Murray. His most recent hit was 'Lollipops' by a group called the Mudlarks.

Rock 'n' roll was still dubious music to these men who couldn't believe that the big band era was really over. They thought it was an American craze that would soon die out. Paramor had had a stab at producing the sound with Tony Crombie and his Rockets, Britain's first rock 'n' roll combo, back in 1956.

Older musicians who'd sweated through apprenticeships in dance bands and orchestras were angry at the new wave of guitar strummers and tea-chest bassists who were able to earn twice as much money with an eighth of the skill. The musical style that was liberating for a generation of teenagers was putting an older generation of professional musicians out of work.

Paramor was open-minded. He was a warm and gentle man with young daughters who were already dancing at home to the new music and he knew that in his position personal taste had to give way to market trends.

Although the acetate by Cliff Richard and the Drifters was crude and amateurish by professional standards, there was something about it which convinced him that they should be given a try. He took it home and played it to his teenage daughter Caroline.

'She flipped when she heard it,' Paramor wrote a year later, 'and she double-flipped when I showed her Cliff's photo. This photo was not of Cliff alone but included the Drifters and American star Jerry Lee Lewis.' He arranged a meeting with Cliff. 'When he eventually turned up he brought his whole group along with him, complete with instruments. My immediate reaction was that if this youngster could go to the trouble of bringing his group along, the least I could do was to listen to what they had to offer.'

The boys plugged in their guitars and played to Paramor in his office. He later claimed that he was 'instantly filled with excitement by this thrilling sound,' but if he was, he managed to contain it for the moment and told the boys that he would make a decision over the next two weeks while he went on holiday to Tangier with his family. Cliff has since described this period as the longest fortnight of his life.

It wasn't wasted time. John Foster made up reel-to-reel tapes of a Drifters' performance and hawked them around to anyone who cared to listen. He mostly faced indifference, sometimes hostility. One record company told him that Cliff would never be a singer in a thousand years. Tommy Steele's agent told him to advise Cliff not to give up his day job.

The group carried on playing and rehearsing. On 15 June they played at the Freight Train, a coffee bar at 44 Berwick Street owned by skiffle star Chas McDevitt and named after his 1957 hit with Nancy Whiskey. Sammy Samwell wrote a letter of thanks to the coffee bar's manager who was obviously absent for the show:

'Despite the late arrival of your staff they [the Drifters] thoroughly enjoyed the evening and were pleased by the most appreciative audience. Unfortunately playing for almost three hours proved rather too strenuous, this was, however, compensated by the addition of eight new members to our "Fan" club.'

A week later they were at the Tudor Hall, Hoddesdon, supported by the Missin' Links, their main local rivals, and on 6 July they played the Astoria in Ware, sharing a double bill with a Kim Novak film. On the nights they weren't playing they would meet at Cliff's home and run through new songs.

An amusing note in the Broxbourne Borough Council files from 1958 records that on 5 July the occupant of 11 Hargreaves Close complained to them that a 'skiffle group' was playing every night at number 12 until eleven o'clock and that they should 'ask them to stop these long noisy evenings'.

The council officer obviously relayed the message to the Webb family for beneath the entry of the complaint was added the handwritten comment, 'Son not willing to co-operate'.

When Paramor returned from Tangier in mid-July, the news was good. Franklyn Boyd of the music publishers Aberbach Music had sent him a song called 'Schoolboy Crush' which had been a hit in America for Bobby Helms and Norrie thought it was a good number for Cliff to cover.

In those pre-Beatle days most artists neither wrote nor chose their own material. The power resided with the publishers and record companies. In Britain during the late fifties there was a tendency to feed out cover versions of American hits. Terry Dene had made it with Marty Robbins' 'A White Sports Coat' and Marty Wilde, Britain's latest new Elvis, had just scored with 'Endless Sleep', originally recorded by Jody Reynolds.

'Schoolboy Crush' was not a great song. It was a formula number of teenage angst in which a young student tells his 'baby doll' that even when they graduate she will be his 'steady date' because she's more than a 'schoolboy crush'.

Cliff was sent an acetate and learned the song in a day. 'Then he phoned me and told me that he'd like to come in and sing it to me,' said Paramor. 'He came up the same day with the Drifters and gave a faultless performance of the song. It impressed me enough to offer him a contract with Columbia.'

Even though it was Cliff Richard and the Drifters who had passed the audition, it was Cliff who was awarded the contract. This meant that although the group's name would appear on the record label, they would not be getting a percentage of the royalties. They would only be paid a fee for taking part in the recording session.

The most immediate problem was to find something to put on the B side, the side of the record which wouldn't be getting radio play. The normal practice was to add a 'filler', a song with no real commercial potential. Because the 'mechanical' royalties (based on record sales rather than stage performances or radio plays) were the same as the A side, producers often made themselves extra money by knocking up throwaway songs for flip sides and publishing them under assumed names.

Fortunately Samwell had just written his first song, called 'Move It', and they played it to Paramor. 'The arrangement was pretty rough and Cliff was not sure of the melody, but they gave such a spirited performance that I wasted no time in fixing up a session which would include Samwell's "Move It", which was to be the backing of "Schoolboy Crush".'

At the time it was virtually unheard of for a British rock 'n' roll group to record a song written by one of its members. The closest was perhaps Tony Crombie's co-writer credit on 'Rock 'n' Roller Coaster' (1957) or the writing of 'Rock With The Caveman' (1956) by Tommy Steele's friend Lionel Bart. That the song should become an A side and then a national hit was unprecedented.

A rockabilly song with lots of American slang ('babe', 'honey', 'groove'), Samwell had written 'Move It' late in June while travelling from his mother's home in London Colney to Cliff's house in Cheshunt on a Green Line double-decker bus. He had wanted to create an authentic sounding rock 'n' roll song that would expose the pale British imitations. He sat upstairs in the back seat with his guitar on his knee and hit on the tune while deconstructing Chuck Berry licks to discover their secret.

The lyric was partly his response to a recent *Melody Maker* article by broadcaster and music writer Steve Race bemoaning the effect of rock 'n' roll on popular music. 'So rock-'n'-roll is dead, is it?' 37-year-old Race, a graduate of the Royal Academy of Music, had challenged. 'All right then. My funeral oration consists of just two words: good riddance.'

He went on to wonder whether ballads might be on their way back into fashion and concluded, 'As of early June, 1958, there is no clear sign about what the next craze will be. Indeed, there may not be another craze at all. The record-buying public has not shifted its allegiance to some other kind of music: it has merely stopped buying so many records. That, too, is all to the good. Perhaps now we shall see some sense of proportion returning to the pop music business.'

It wasn't an unusual rant for the time. There were many of his generation who were only too glad to leap in and write the obituary of rock 'n' roll. Samwell's response was:

'They say, it's gonna die: Oh! Honey please, let's face it;
They just don't know what's a-goin' to replace it.
Ballads and Calypsos, have got nothing on
real Country music that just drives along.
Oh! Honey move it.'

'By the time I got to Cliff's house the song was complete,' he remembers. 'I just played it to the rest of them, including my introduction. I had to rewrite the lyric out because it was full of bits and pieces and Cliff needed to be able to read it. I used to put the "ah"s and the "uh-huh"s in because you need to have every nuance there.'

Mitham became the first casualty of the new-found success. Samwell felt that his guitar added nothing to the overall sound and that it was a waste of money having three guitars when two would be adequate.

'Sammy was older than us and having served in the RAF seemed much more a man of the world, and he said that I was only duplicating Cliff's guitar work,' says Mitham. 'What you have to remember is that Cliff and I had been friends since we were nine or ten and we had gone through a lot together. Now it had got to the stage where an outsider had turned round and said, "I think you ought to get rid of Norman." I'm sure Cliff gave it a lot of thought but he told me that was what had been suggested and I said I agreed but it's not going to stop a friendship. Then that was it. I was out of the story.'

For the recording at EMI Studios in Abbey Road on 24 July Paramor hired two seasoned session men. His original plan had been to use the Ken Jones Orchestra, whom he had used to back Michael Holliday, but Cliff was insisitent on a group sound. In 1958 there could be re-takes of a song but no overdubbing or mixing because it was all recorded onto a single-track tape, and for 'Schoolboy Crush' and 'Move It' there was only three hours of studio time booked.

Norrie brought in Frank Clarke on double bass and Ernie Shear on electric guitar. Both men were in their early thirties and had a wealth of experience playing in orchestras. To them it was just another session, Cliff was a fresh-faced young kid, and rock 'n' roll was a new musical craze they knew they'd have to get used to if they wanted to stay in business.

'Schoolboy Crush', the first track of the evening, didn't really showcase their talents. It had no fire in its belly and was covered in a soufflé of background vocals from the Michael Sammes Singers. But on 'Move It' their talents combined to produce a sound that could have come straight out of Memphis, Tennessee.

The guitar introduction has become such a classic of early British rock 'n' roll that there have been arguments ever since about who invented it and how much they got paid for it. The truth is that the idea was Samwell's, and the execution was Shear's. Samwell was smart enough to know he didn't have the competence to play lead guitar on the single so he showed Shear the riff he'd come up with, and Shear then translated the sketch into a full-colour masterpiece. Samwell, meanwhile, played rhythm guitar.

'I think we just talked about it in the studio and it developed,' says Shear. 'It was really a busking session for us even though we read music. I didn't even have a solid-body electric guitar then so I used to use a Hoffner acoustic with a D'Armond pick-up which I bought in America. To get the top sound I used to push it near the bridge. I wanted to get the toppiest sound I could get.'

When the session started, Peter Bown had been engineering but he had to leave for an appointment at the opera and so he handed over to his assistant Malcolm Addey, a junior engineer who had only been with the studio four months. There were rule books at EMI Studios in those days which even went as far as stipulating the volume at which music should be recorded. Addey allowed 'Move It' to go over the limit, and this added to its authentic sound.

It was a great performance. British rock 'n' roll records up until this date had been insipid affairs that had none of the clarity and attack of the Americans. With 'Move It' there was, at last, a single that offered a challenge to the originators.

Hearing it for the first time some twenty years later Carl Perkins, author of 'Blue Suede Shoes' and a former Sun Records artist, commented:

'That sound could have been made in Sun Studios in 1954. It's basic rockabilly music. That guitar is doing what we did. He's got some echo and he's working on more than one string. He's getting three of the bass strings and he's doubling up on the bottom. That's very good.'

Paramor quickly had test pressings made up and circulated them to his contacts, and seven days after the recording Cliff was featured in a prominent *Daily Mirror* article written by record columnist Patrick Doncaster under the headline 'New Recruit For The Disc War'.

Although he committed himself to no more than the claim that Cliff had 'a personality that shines through the grooves,' and that 'he could succeed in Discland,' it was an impressive ammount of space for an office lad who had yet to release his first record.

Publisher Franklyn Boyd was also doing the rounds with test pressings because of his stake in 'Schoolboy Crush' and he wanted TV and radio exposure. His first contact was Dennis Main Wilson who was producing '6.5 Special'. Wilson liked the record but couldn't use Cliff for six weeks so Boyd contacted his opposite number on independent television, Jack Good, who earlier in the year had done two pilot shows of 'Oh Boy!' and was planning an autumn series.

Good was one of the geniuses of British rock 'n' roll whose

understanding of the medium was at least a decade ahead of its time. He cut an odd figure in the world of greasy-haired teenage school-leavers with tight jeans and James Dean scowls. He was a 27-year-old Oxford graduate with thick glasses and a booming voice, whose eyes would pop out with excitement when he heard something he liked. But his taste was impeccable and his faith in pure rock 'n' roll remained, and remains, unshakable.

Boyd made an appointment to see him and played a white label of 'Schoolboy Crush' on Good's office record player. Good listened politely but was non-committal. He recounted what happened next in his 'Sidetracks' column in *Disc* on 9 August, when he told the story of how he had just heard 'the most amazing first recording made by any teenage artiste in Britain'.

In a full-page article under the headline 'Just another beginner? No—this boy is really terrific!' Good wrote, 'Then he [Boyd] spins what he laughingly refers to as the "flip-side". Wham! This disc could sell 50,000 on its first eight bars alone.

'It kicks off with a forceful, dramatic guitar phrase that runs an electric shock down the spine. In comes the drum, driving a vicious beat right through the heart of the number. Then the voice rides confidently over this glorious backing—a voice with an amazingly "non-imitative" style, considering that this kind of music ought by rights to be foreign to anyone who is not a native of the Southern States.

'The diction is clear; the phrasing authentic, professional—there is a real feeling for this country-and-western style. If this disc had been a product of Sun records of Memphis, Tennessee—the original recording company of Elvis Presley and Jerry Lee Lewis—I should not have been surprised, but would still have rated it as important and good enough to be compared, though not, of course, on equal terms, with those two giants of the beat.

'But when one considers that this is the product of a 17-year-old boy from Cheshunt, Hertfordshire, the mind just boggles.'

Good was immediately eager to see the artist in the flesh. He couldn't believe that he would look as good as he sounded. He was sure that there would be some physical drawback and that 'Move It' was just a fluke of the recording studio. An audition was arranged for the following evening at Max Rivers Rehearsal Rooms at 10–11 Great Newport Street, just around the corner from Leicester Square underground station.

In a room on the third floor Cliff and the Drifters played while agent George Ganjou lurked hopefully in the corridor outside.

'I thought it was wonderful,' says Good. 'I thought he was a good singer but there was nothing special about his physical performance. He just bounced up and down adequately and I thought he looked a bit trashy with his sideburns.'

Good's recollection is that he agreed to book him there and then and walked Cliff down to the underground while explaining to him that the guitar and the sideburns would have to go before he made an appearance on 'Oh Boy!'. Boyd doesn't think he decided that quickly.

'Jack loved him but Jack's wife, Margit, didn't like him at all. So when we came away Jack said, "Look, I like him." So I said, "Are you going to use him?" He said he didn't know and that he would try to sort it out. But his wife was quite adamant that she didn't like Cliff. He then rang me a couple of days later and said, "OK, I'm going to use him but he's not going to be singing 'Schoolboy Crush'. He's going to be doing the B side."'

Margit Good can't remember the audition but says that it's quite likely that she was apprehensive. 'I tended to be the more pessimistic one,' she admits. 'Jack was always totally enthusiastic about everything. I would imagine that the fact that Cliff looked like a shy little boy, definitely non-show business, would have made me wonder—well, what on earth are you going to do with him?'

The day that Good's article hit the news stands, and alerted the music industry to the 'exciting newcomer', was coincidentally Cliff's last day working at Atlas Lamps. Ganjou, who was the sole entertainments booker for Billy Butlin's holiday camps, had offered him a two-week contract singing at their 2,000-capacity Clacton camp and the only way to fulfil the engagement was to leave his job and turn professional.

Cliff had only ever spent one night away from his mother and father. Most young people in the fifties were naïve compared to later generations but Cliff struck those he met as having been particularly protected. Tulah Tuke was a young actress employed by Radio Butlin and recalls that her chalet mate who was known as Randy Rene made a play for him one night.

'He was very young and very unsophisticated and didn't know what on earth was happening. She managed to get Cliff back to the chalet but I think he brought John Foster with him as protection. I remember thinking that he was very young even for his age. He was seventeen but I thought of him as sixteen.'

Foster remembers it as a time of good clean fun. Only he and Samwell smoked (which is why they had to share a chalet), none of the boys were big drinkers and no one had time for girlfriends.

'In those days it was big news to sleep with a girl,' says Foster. 'You didn't want to set up a lasting relationship with someone who slept around. We were still all innocent boys and women were up on a pedestal somewhere.'

During the first week the camp's entertainment manager moved them around because he couldn't find the right venue for a rock 'n' roll trio. Drinkers in the camp pub, The Jolly Roger, weren't the right generation to appreciate Cliff Richard and the Drifters and they didn't contribute to the ambience of the Hawaiian style cocktail bar, so they were finally assigned to the Rock 'n' Roll Ballroom.

A poor-quality tape recording of one of their sets survives. It was made by Stan Edwards, a fellow Red-Coat entertainer, who set a reel-to-reel tape recorder on a chair in the middle of the ballroom. The guitar sound is unsurprisingly thin and limited but Cliff's vocals are already well developed although hampered by an obvious affection for Elvis. He puts a little too many 'uh-huh's into every song and doesn't yet have the confidence to match the looseness he's striving for.

The set list is dominated by songs made popular by Elvis and Jerry Lee Lewis. He starts with Eddie Cochran's 'Twenty Flight Rock', then sings 'Move It' and 'Breathless'. This is followed by five Elvis songs—'Money Honey', 'Heartbreak Hotel', 'Hound Dog', 'I Got A Woman' and 'Milkcow Blues Boogie'—before closing with 'Move It' and 'Whole Lotta Shakin' Goin' On'.

On 'Milkcow Blues Boogie' he even follows the pattern of Elvis' Sun Records recording where the song is started as a lazy blues before Elvis stops the musicians and says, 'Hold it fellows. That don't move me. Let's get real real gone for a change' before launching into a rocked-up version. In a jive American accent Cliff can be heard saying, 'Wait a minute fellows. That don't move none. Let's get real real gone for a change, huh?'

Pre-release copies of 'Move It' had been sent by EMI to Radio Butlin which broadcast throughout the camp.

'When Cliff's acetate came in I was just grateful to have something that I could chat about,' remembers Tulah Tuke. 'I could say that he was playing on site and announce the venue. I gave the record a great plug and the next thing I knew was that Cliff and John Foster were standing at the door saying "That's the first time we've heard it. It's great. Thanks a lot. Can we hear it again?" So they came in to my studio and I played it to them. That must make me the first person ever to play a Cliff Richard record to the public. I was certainly the first person to play a Cliff Richard record to Cliff.'

It was also while at Clacton that the group first heard the record on Radio Luxembourg. 'It was unbelievable,' says Foster. 'They may have played both sides of the single but I definitely remember "Move It" and after that they started to play it quite regularly.'

When they returned home from Butlin's there was more good news waiting for them. Mark Forster, who worked for top promoter Arthur Howes, was offering them a spot on an October tour of Britain headlined by the Kalin Twins. Their fee would be two hundred pounds a week, the most money they had ever earned.

Then there was a letter from Jack Good, who had auditioned Cliff and the Drifters for 'Oh Boy!'. They would be needed the next day, Sunday 7 September, for the first rehearsals of 'Oh Boy!'

9

'I didn't want the real Cliff Richard. Real people on television are boring'

J ack Good invented rock 'n' roll television. He was working as an actor understudying Wilfred Lawson on a 1956 television drama when he went to see the film *Rock Around The Clock* one afternoon when he wasn't needed at the rehearsal room in Islington. The experience was to change his life.

Whereas the film *The Blackboard Jungle* had simply used Haley's song in the soundtrack, *Rock Around The Clock*, directed by Sam Katzman, was chock full of rock 'n' roll. There was not only Bill Haley but Little Richard, the Platters, and Freddie Bell and the Bellboys. For Good it was an experience of pure primitive theatrical excitement.

'I had always hated pop music,' he says, 'and therefore this rock 'n' roll appealed to me in a perverse way because I immediately realized that Frank Sinatra would hate it, and I loathed Frank Sinatra. Rock 'n' roll had a raw excitement and that was what I liked about theatre.

'To me, Laurence Olivier was an exciting actor, and Shakespeare done right was exciting. There was nothing like it. It seems ridiculous to say it, but there was something electrifying in good rock 'n' roll, and that's what I liked.'

Shortly afterwards he abandoned his short-lived career as an actor to work for the BBC where he thought there might even be opportunities to translate the excitement of rock 'n' roll into television.

His chance came when he was paired with Josephine Douglas and asked to come up with a winning formula for a teenage programme that would fit the space immediately after six o'clock in the evening which had up until then been left 'dark' so that parents could use the time to put children to bed. What they came up with was the '6.5 Special'.

The first show was broadcast in February 1957 but there were too many compromises for Good's liking. There was a bit of rock 'n' roll—a duo he had discovered on a United States Air Force base, called Bobby and Rudy, singing 'I'm Gonna Teach You To Rock', and a clip of Little Richard from the film *The Girl Can't Help It*—but there were a lot of features that certainly weren't rock 'n' roll: a boys' choir, a team of Hungarian acrobats, trumpeter Kenny Baker and Pouishnoff playing Mozart.

There was a conflict of ideas between Josephine Douglas, who wanted healthy Boy Scout type features on hobbies such as stamp collecting and mountaineering, and Good who wanted to terrorize adults and excite teenagers with his vision of wild abandon.

Realizing that he was never going to have his way with the BBC, who were warning that rock 'n' roll was on its way out, Good left and joined the independent television company ABC. They allowed him to produce two trial live rock 'n' roll programmes at the Wood Green Empire in June 1958. Good called the shows 'Oh Boy!' after Buddy Holly's song.

These two half-hour shows were topped by Marty Wilde, a lanky South Londoner who had shot to prominence after an appearance on '6.5 Special', and they moved faster than anything seen before on British television.

'I wanted pace, attack and no chat,' says Good. 'I hated light entertainment. I wanted next number, next number. I'm bored with that, next number . . . so by the time you were sick of somebody they were off and the next act was on—flash, flash, flash! I wanted it to jump. I wanted action. I wanted the lights to go on cue, the music to go on cue and the audience to go up in the air and everything to be like a Cadillac zooming down a freeway.

'The lighting was very important. I had seen a photo of Ricky Nelson standing in a strong spotlight which was circled on the floor, and that shot was seminal to the look I wanted. Also there was a company called Theatro Nationale Populaire who put on Shakespeare but they did it all with black and white lighting and very little in the way of sets.

'At the time I was into the psychological effect of rhythm and lights. I was into all sorts of strange books about brainwashing and the effects of voodoo. I thought I was doing the public a favour by introducing these things to television. William Sargent's book *Battle For The Mind* (subtitled 'A Physiology of Conversion and Brain-Washing' and first published in 1957) was very influential.

'I wanted to create tremendous tension and excitement which I justified in my mind as being a form of catharsis as described by the Greeks. I thought that the kids would let off steam in the theatre and would then be peaceful and passive when they went back on the streets. Absolute rubbish! It worked quite the other way. I should never have been let loose.'

It was a powerful concoction and knocked spots off '6.5 Special', which was cosy and amateurish in comparison. ABC knew they were on to a winner and gave Good a spot between 6 and 6.30 each Saturday evening beginning on 13 September 1958 and lasting for as long as they could see.

Good began pulling together a show that would be transmitted live from the Empire Theatre in Hackney. He planned to keep the line-up that he'd had at Wood Green—instrumentals from the John Barry Seven, vocal harmonies from the Dallas Boys and the Vernons Girls, a Fats Domino style rhythm blast from Lord Rockingham's XI led by Harry Robinson, Hammond organ music from South African

Cherry Wainer and solo spots from Marty Wilde, Bernice Reading and Ronnie Carroll. The last-minute addition, made after hearing 'Move It', was Cliff Richard and the Drifters.

Rehearsals for 'Oh Boy!' were intensive. Cliff was needed for a full week to go through 'Move It' and 'Don't Bug Me Baby' because Good wanted to plan every move and build a persona for Cliff that would make him instantly recognizable in a crowded market-place.

His plan had swung into action the first evening they met when he told Cliff that the obvious similarities with Elvis would have to go. 'Although we were keen to have someone on "Oh Boy!" who would have the impact that Elvis did, we didn't want an Elvis impersonator. Also, Cliff clearly couldn't play the guitar very well and this would prove very limiting for the shots.'

Having eradicated the most obvious of the Elvis traits, Good set about building Cliff Richard. He was to be a young naïve teenager surging with sexual energy, but apparently unaware of it.

'He was very slim and innocent looking,' says Good. 'We presented him as if it was beyond him not to smoulder and yet he didn't mean to. That was the excitement. Elvis looked as though he'd knocked around a bit and he would bump and grind and sneer. Cliff didn't do any of that. He would be withdrawn, and the audience would come to him.'

Every day for the week before the first show Cliff would go to the 'Oh Boy!' rehearsal room at the Four Provinces of Ireland club in Canonbury Lane, Islington. Vernons Girl Maggie Streader remembers him coming in looking like a little boy lost, obviously overawed at being surrounded by hardened professionals, television executives and music business hangers-on.

'He was so sweet,' she remembers. 'He was around the same age as us but when you saw him you just wanted to look after him. There was no brashness. He wasn't "of the business" as it were. I think we girls were a bit overpowering for him.'

Good would work through the songs with Cliff line by line. Cliff was so self-conscious that he had to be tutored in a room away from the rest of the cast. Good taught him to hide the pointed tooth that still bothered him, to tilt his head at the camera and raise his eyes up and, most effectively, to suddenly grab at his arm 'as if stuck with a hypodermic syringe' at key emotional points in the songs. The word 'sex' was never mentioned.

In February 1959 Good wrote about these rehearsals in his *Disc* column.

' "Move It" ' was probably the most difficult number I have had to produce so far,' he said. 'Cliff and I spent some hours getting the thing absolutely right for his first TV appearance ... Every blink, every change in the pose of the head, every gesture, had to be worked out and made meaningful.

'The whole song was broken down into fragments. At last, each fragment was right. Then came the very difficult job of putting all the component parts together and creating not a mass of details, but a complete and meaningful whole. Above all, the finished product must not seem to have been worked over to the nth degree. It has to seem quite fresh and unconsidered.'

For stage wear Cliff had a pink jacket and black tapered trousers (which he had made to measure by a tailor in Dean Street, Soho), pink tie, black shirt and pink socks. It was his decision to develop this image although the idea wasn't original. Elvis had been buying pink and lime-green jackets from Lanksy Brothers clothing store on Beale Street in Memphis and wearing them with black peg-legged trousers. But, in those grim post-war days when most fathers were still wearing the black or grey suits they had been issued with on leaving the armed forces, it was a fashion statement which excited the young and worried the old.

'If a woman wore shocking pink in those days it was considered quite brave,' says *Observer* journalist Janet Watts, who saw Cliff in concert in 1958 when she was a teenager. 'For a man to wear pink was alarming! For us it was liberation. It was a splash of fun and colour into what had become a very grey world.'

On the day of the broadcast there were two further rehearsals—

one in the morning for vision only, one in the afternoon for sound and vision. The director was Rita Gillespie, a woman in her mid-twenties who had little experience of rock 'n' roll but saw it as an opportunity to experiment with television. It was from her carefully-prepared camera scripts, based on listening to the songs, that Good developed his stage directions.

'Cliff was very inexperienced and he wanted to be told what to do,' says Rita. 'I loved shooting him. He had the perfect face for television. I never tired of close-ups and profiles of him.

'Once, by sheer accident, I caught him singing something with a "t" or an "s" in it and his spit was highlighted by the arc lights as a glittering tiny speck. After that I kept waiting for it to happen again.'

It would complete the fairy tale to say that Cliff tore the house down on his TV debut, but the response was muted. The screams were reserved for Marty Wilde, already a TV star, who was at four in the charts with 'Endless Sleep'. But the effect of the national exposure was undeniable. The following week he returned to sing 'Schoolboy Crush' and by the week ending 27 September 'Move It' had entered *Melody Maker*'s top twenty chart at number twelve.

Good's coaching had paid off. The reserved boy from Cheshunt was now regarded as both 'moody' and 'sexy'. Before the year ended he would be accused of 'crude exhibitionism' and 'short-sighted vulgarity' by *New Musical Express* (in an anonymous attack by its publisher Maurice Kinn) and the *Daily Sketch* would ask, 'Is this boy TV star too sexy?'

Good just used to laugh at these stories, and Cliff took up Elvis' argument that he meant no harm—it was the beat that made him do it.

'I can't help it if people say I'm too sexy in my singing,' he said. 'I can't help it. I don't push it, believe me. I just get carried away. It's just that I do exactly what the songs tell me inside I gotta do.'

For the Kalin Twins' tour new musicians needed to be drafted in to work with Cliff. They had met a guitarist called Ken Pavey at Butlin's who had filled in for them but he'd been offered a residency in a pub in Wood Green and didn't want to pass on what looked like a secure job for the sake of a rock 'n' roll tour. This left Cliff with Samwell now playing bass, Smart playing drums and a tour due to start on 5 October.

Foster went down the 2 I's to find a replacement.

'I went to meet Tony Sheridan, a very good guitarist. While waiting for him I met Hank Marvin who got his guitar out and and played a few Buddy Holly riffs and something by Ricky Nelson's guitarist James Burton. It turned out that he was already on the tour playing for the Most Brothers so I asked him to double up by playing for us as well. Hank agreed to it but he wanted to bring his mate Bruce Welch who played rhythm guitar.

'The next I heard of Tony Sheridan was when he cut his first single in Germany with the Beatles as his backing group.'

Hank Marvin and Bruce Welch were two sixteen year olds who had come to London from Newcastle to play in the finals of a talent contest with their skiffle group the Railroaders, and had never returned.

Their recent past was remarkably similar to Cliff's. They had both started playing skiffle in 1957, flunked out of school with no qualifications, changed their names to sound more American (Hank's real name was Brian Rankin and Bruce's was Bruce Cripps). Both had played rock 'n' roll and headed for the 2 I's because they had heard that this was the place where things happened.

When they arrived in London in April 1958, Cliff was already playing at the 2 I's but they didn't catch sight of him until July when Welch, who took a job in the coffee bar working the orange juice machine, went back and told Hank about the most exciting British rock 'n' roll singer he had ever seen.

Hank was by then playing in the Vipers, the one-time skiffle group which Wally Whyton was updating to meet the challenge of rock 'n' roll by adding drums and electric guitars. What Whyton didn't know was that he was creating the Shadows in embryo. Besides Hank on guitar he had Tony Meehan on drums and Terence 'Jet' Harris on bass.

'We went out and had a bit of a disastrous tour,' remembers Whyton. 'We had new amplifiers which blew up and at that point I decided I didn't want to be involved with electric music. So I went off busking in the South of France and the lads asked me if it was alright if they went out with Cliff who was touring for three weeks. I said, "Do exactly as you want."'

The first rehearsal of the new Drifters was at 12 Hargreaves Close. Cliff, Hank Marvin, Bruce Welch, Terry Smart and Sammy Samwell worked through a set of 'Baby I Don't Care', 'Don't Bug Me Baby', 'Blueberry Hill', 'Move It', 'Whole Lotta Shakin' Goin' On' and 'King Creole'.

'The drum kit was set up in the living room,' remembers Hank. 'The rest of us played electric guitars through amplifiers that were the size of cornflake packets which meant that it wasn't particularly noisy. But we could see straight away that Cliff really had something going for him.'

Two days before the tour, Cliff recorded another Samwell song at Abbey Road, 'High Class Baby'. Again Paramor hired Frank Clarke and Ernie Shear to beef up the sound, but this time the combination didn't work. It wasn't their fault. 'High Class Baby' was a colourless song.

When Cliff got home that evening he broke down and cried. He thought his career was over, that everything he had attained had been through a recording fluke. 'I thought that was it,' says Cliff. 'It just didn't compare in any way to "Move It".'

The Kalin Twins tour began on 5 October at the Victoria Hall, Hanley and Cliff Richard and the Drifters were booked to open up the second half of a show that started with sets from the Most Brothers, the Londonaires and Eddie Calvert.

Calvert was an old-time trumpeter, produced by Norrie Paramor for Columbia, who'd had several hits (including two number ones) since his chart debut in 1953 with 'Oh Mein Papa', the Londonaires were a jazz-based trio and the Most Brothers were, according to Mickie Most, 'an Everly Brothers with bad harmonies'.

At the time the Grade Agency booked the tour, the Kalin Twins had a number one single with 'When' but it had since fallen while 'Move It' was still climbing. This put the Kalins in the unenviable position of closing the show after a set by one of the hottest acts in the country.

Hal and Herbie Kalin were not a rock 'n' roll act. They were twenty-four years old at a time when pop stars were expected to be teenagers, and had started out singing Frankie Laine and Johnnie Ray songs. What made them acceptable to a rock 'n' roll audience was the fact that they looked younger than they were, they had a hit record and they were American.

The Kalins had come to Britain expecting to discover that Cliff Richard was a nice-looking boy who couldn't sing. They had worked in America with Fabian, a handsome Italian who had trouble holding a tune in his head or keeping to the beat. But what they saw on stage in Hanley on that opening night made them realize that Cliff not only had a hit but had a voice to carry it off on stage.

'He tore the house down,' says Hal Kalin. 'Then the audience would have to go from that to, "And now ladies and gentlemen—the Kalin Twins" and you'd hear a five-piece jazz band trying to outdo what the Drifters had just played. Our volume alone was half theirs! It was a constant battle.

'Then there was a shift during the last four or five dates when they arranged to put Cliff on last because it was obviously not working out with us. There was no way we could compete with an up-and-coming seventeen year old. It had become a nightmare for us.'

The second night of the tour, at the Odeon, Blackpool, was reviewed in the *West Lancashire Evening Gazette* by someone who, in common with a lot of show business correspondents of the day, persisted in evaluating a rock 'n' roll performance as if it was a new music hall turn.

'The package, tied up by wisecracking, crewcut compere Tony Marsh, contained a collection of "pop" musicians to the exclusion of comics, jugglers and tumblers who used to be measured amongst the choice of the music hall,' wrote the anonymous critic.

'The show pleased teenagers, but there were not enough there to fill more than a third of the house.

'The American Kalin Twins, whose disc "When" has only just slipped from the top rung of the hit parade, made the boys and girls yell for more. And Cliff Richards [sic], a new British recording star, generated almost as much excitement as he rocked and roared in a "shocking pink" jacket, surrounded by four bandsmen, dressed in sinister style in black shirts and wearing sunglasses, and the jumble of wiring and amplifiers which transmit the latest sound.'

Standing in the wings as Cliff and the Drifters played those opening nights was Jet Harris, Wally Whyton's nineteen-year-old bass guitarist who had been picked up for the tour by Mickie Most.

'I still maintain that "Move It" was the turning point for British rock and roll,' he says. 'It certainly shook me because I was a staunch jazz man. Then, part way through the tour, Cliff asked me if I'd like to beef up the sound by playing bass with the Drifters. I said "yes" straight away.'

Jet was not only older that the rest of the group but he was more worldly-wise and more experienced as a musician. Whereas Cliff and Hank looked like home-loving lads, Jet with his bleached blond hair kept in place by Vitapointe and his permanently dangling cigarette could have been the member of a street gang.

He had started playing clarinet in jazz clubs at the age of fifteen and had then switched to double bass and worked with Terry Dene, Larry Page, Tubby Hayes, Ronnie Scott, Don Lang, Wee Willie Harris and Tony Crombie. It was the jazz drummer Crombie who suggested that he switched to a bass guitar.

'He played a Framus with a thin semi-acoustic body which sounded great at a time when everyone else was playing stand-up bass,' says Hank. 'He was also a very driving player who liked to turn up the volume and give it a lot of bottom end.

'He'd been around a lot longer than we had and had a concept of advanced chord sequences and how to play against them. To us he was like the old man of music.'

His image was that of the brooding bohemian and he added a neat rebellious hint to the Drifters. Where Cliff abstained from alcohol, Jet would drink it until he fell down. Where Cliff seemed unfazed by female attention, Jet was never without a woman. Where Cliff went home to life with mum and dad in Cheshunt, Jet returned to a basement flat in Eccleston Square, behind Victoria Station, which he shared with a collection of musicians, a fox, two monkeys, a dog, a cat and a skunk called Sam. His bedroom was carpeted with newspapers, had a broom handle fixed in the doorway as a wardrobe and was lit with a single bare light bulb.

'He looked incredible,' remembers Cliff. 'He had a quiff, he was gaunt . . . he was everything I wasn't. Jack Good once described him as "the moody, magnificent Jet Harris" and said that only Cliff Richard could ever stand in front of him.'

Even at the age of nineteen Jet had a reputation for being edgy and unreliable. Wee Willie Harris, an eccentric piano player who was dyeing his hair pink in 1957, employed Jet and found him difficult to be around.

'He was always a bag of nerves,' he says. 'He used to drive me mental. Whenever we shared a dressing room he would be up and down like a yo-yo pacing backwards and forwards. Just watching him would get me going.'

In 1958 touring conditions were primitive. All the artists travelled in an unheated Bedford coach driven by Ron King of Timpson's Coaches, and everyone but the headlining act had to find their own accommodation on arrival.

'They all had to pay for their own digs out of their wages,' remembers King. 'They would take the cheapest digs they could find even if it meant sleeping on the bus, which they nicknamed the "Hotel Bedford".'

The sound for performances was normally fed through two house speakers which would be positioned high up at either side of the stage. The drums wouldn't be miked and so the only sound worth checking was the sound made on the stage.

'There were no PA systems as such,' says Bruce Welch, 'and as for lights, it was just a matter of whether you wanted them on or off.'

Performances were brisk—the closing act was only on stage for eighteen minutes—and backing musicians were shared around to cut costs. Eddie Calvert's band supported the Kalin Twins and Hank was putting in performances for all the acts except the Londonaires. Jet was now playing for the Most Brothers and Cliff.

After playing Manchester on 10 October Cliff returned to London to appear on 'Oh Boy!'. He was in Liverpool on the 12th, where in the audience was a sixteen-year-old local boy called McCartney. 'My dad had a mate who used to work on the stage door,' says Paul. 'And I can remember he got me Eddie Calvert's autograph.'

Two days later, at the De Montfort Hall in Leicester, it was Cliff's eighteenth birthday. The fans threw birthday presents on the stage and the whole audience of 2,500 sang Happy Birthday to him. On 19 October, at the Colston Hall, Bristol, the tour came to an end. 'Move It' was now at number four in the charts.

10

'The kids liked him, but he didn't have an act'

G eorge Ganjou, who had been used to booking variety acts, was already finding himself out of his depth as an agent. John Foster, not as good at business as he was at bluff, stood no chance at arm wrestling with the power brokers of British show business.

Norrie Paramor spoke to Cliff and his father about the situation and recommended Franklyn Boyd, the publisher of 'Schoolboy Crush', as a man to manage Cliff's career as he was older and well-connected in the music industry.

Franklyn Boyd had the advantage of having been a singer himself. He had left the RAF in 1946 and worked with Teddy Foster's Orchestra for three years, later singing with Oscar Rabin and Eric Winstone. He agreed to handle Cliff's affairs as long as he didn't have to leave his job with Aberbach Music. John Foster was retained as road manager and put on an uncontracted salary of twelve pounds a week.

Then there was the question of the Drifters. Cliff was well satisfied with the addition of Hank and Bruce Welch but he was aware that their proficiency now exposed the weaknesses of Samwell and Smart. He knew that eventually they would have to go, and first of all he decided to get rid of Sammy.

He wasn't told right away. After the Kalin tour there were no immmediate dates to play and Samwell took a break. What he didn't know was that although the Drifters weren't playing, they were hard at work practising and that his replacement on bass guitar was Jet Harris.

It was only when he turned up with a new song that he realized he had been ousted. Still he wasn't told by Cliff. 'I think it might well have been John Foster who had to break me the bad news,' he remembers.

'Even though I didn't have to do the telling, it was a hard decision because Sammy was a friend,' says Cliff. 'This sort of thing never becomes easier but I have to be single minded when I want something new. In 1958 the decision was based on the fact that Hank was the bst guitarist, Jet was the best on bass, and that meant there was no room for Sammy.'

Cliff was now becoming the star of 'Oh Boy!', much to the chagrin of Marty Wilde's manager Larry Parnes who had seen the show as the perfect showcase for his boy and others, like Vince Eager, who he was currently grooming. While Cliff and Marty remained friends, sang together on the shows and admired each other's work, Larry Parnes tussled with Jack Good over the lack of attention he felt his protégé was getting.

Parnes was the most important rock 'n' roll manager in Britain and was determined to control as much of the scene as he could. He was born in north-west London to a Jewish family in the clothing trade. After school he managed women's clothing stores before being attracted to the theatre, where he invested a small amount of money in a touring play.

His big break came in September 1956 when John Kennedy, a publicity agent, told him about rock 'n' roll and introduced him to Tommy Hicks, a merchant seaman he'd seen playing at the 2 I's. The two men took over his career, and as Tommy Steele he became Britain's first rock 'n' roll star. Marty Wilde was their second discovery.

The battle that Parnes was creating between Marty and Cliff was partly built out of resentment that Cliff didn't belong to him. A major-league rock 'n' roll star had developed in Britain and he didn't have a share of him.

On 18 October this resentment spilled over into a full-blooded row. Both Cliff and Wilde were scheduled to appear on the show and Marty turned up in a steel-grey mohair suit which Good said he couldn't wear because it wouldn't work with the lights.

'When I told him that, Parnes flew into a rage and threatened to pull him out of the show if he couldn't wear the suit,' says Good. 'In the end I had to call a security guard to usher Parnes out of the theatre.'

Wilde did the show but Parnes pulled him out of the series and didn't allow him to come back until 7 February 1959. By this time he had been eclipsed by Cliff who was now in such demand that he didn't have the time to appear regularly on 'Oh Boy!'.

Wilde then lost out on the role of Bongo Herbert in *Expresso Bongo* which Cliff was eventually offered. The reason was mainly because producer Val Guest thought that Wilde, who stood six feet three inches tall, was 'too big to feel sorry for'. Parnes put an amusing spin on the rejection when he told the press that he thought it was 'a suitable part for a smaller talent than Marty'.

The Cliff versus Marty feud made great newspaper copy and kept both their names alive.

'The "Oh Boy!" row was the best thing that ever happened to Cliff Richard and the biggest boost to his career,' says Franklyn Boyd. 'It made the front page of the *Daily Mirror*. It was unbelievable. Cliff was immediately a big star because he made the front page of a national newspaper. Having a number one record doesn't make headline news but this hullabaloo did.'

What concerned Boyd was Cliff's inexperience as a performer. Television and radio commitments were keeping him in London during the week and he was only playing out of town on Sunday nights.

'Cliff was terrible in those Sunday night concerts,' he admits. 'You had people like Rory Blackwell who had come out of the jazz clubs and they were killing him. Cliff was top of the bill but all these other stars knew what to do on stage and it killed him. I mean, the kids liked him but he didn't have an act. He didn't know how to come on and off stage. He didn't know how to take a bow.'

So Boyd booked him into three weeks of variety shows during November and December—a week at the Metropolitan, Edgware Road, a week at the Chiswick Empire and a week at the Finsbury Park Empire. Cliff was to stay with Boyd and his wife Daphne at their apartment in Barons Court. He would rehearse his 'Oh Boy!' shows during the day and then give two performances a night with the Drifters at 6.15 and 8.15, the aim being to give him an intense forty-two-show crash course in stagecraft.

The variety bills make strange reading today. At the Metropolitan, for example, Cliff shared the stage with Little Beaver and Maree, a roller-skating tap dancer called Checker Wheel, someone called Bernard Landy who mimed to records, comedian Michael Roxy, multi-instrumentalist Michael Hill, puppeteer Janet Fox and comic double act Roy Hudd and Eddy Kay.

It wasn't a happy mix. The rock 'n' roll fans weren't interested in tap-dancing roller skaters and didn't take up their seats until Cliff appeared, and the admirers of old-time variety hall acts found rock 'n' roll too loud and brash.

'If there is one thing that the appearance of Cliff Richards [sic] demonstrates at the Met this week it is the deep gulf that exists between teenage taste and the conventional variety act,' reported *The Stage*.

'It is not unbridgeable, for the youngsters often appreciate the novelty of variety, but if the bridging is to be done I do not think this bill is going to do it. It provides, in fact, a strong argument against mixing the old and the new. Young Cliff Richards [sic] is an advanced example of his kind, an acquired taste that is quite as likely to antagonize as it is to please.

'I found his almost savage approach, backed by an overloud

battery of guitars and drums, most impressive and without, so far as I know, being "sent" anywhere in particular, I quite enjoyed the demonstration. But one needs to be teenage, I think, really to know what it is all about.'

Tulah Tuke, back from her stint at Butlin's, saw one of the Metropolitan shows and remembers how unpolished it seemed.

'The Drifters went on stage with their chords written out and sellotaped to their guitars. Cliff seemed very inexperienced. He was only eighteen and here he was topping the bill on a variety circuit.

'Kids weren't as street-wise as they are today anyway and Cliff's background was even more protected than most. When he became a star he hadn't had the experience of knocking around Liverpool and Hamburg that the Beatles had had by the time they started having hits.' (By the end of the Kalin Twins' tour, Cliff had been on stage fewer than a hundred times in his whole career to date. The Beatles, by contrast, played the Cavern Club alone 292 times before recording their first single.)

The reviewer who caught him at the Chiswick Empire was even more disdainful. After chiding a duo called Reggie Redcliffe and Desmond Lane, who had apparently moved around a bit too much on stage, he went on to deal with 'young Cliff Richard' who he said, disapprovingly, was 'another young artist in the long line of those who find it necessary, in order to express themselves, to jerk a leg or wave an arm as they string together a succession of extraordinary words and phrases, often repetitive, each jerk or wave producing more or less non-stop screams from youthful fans who hang on to his every word and gesture. Master Richard is backed by his Drifters—drums and electric guitars which, to the uninitiated, appear to be grossly over-amplified.

'How pleasurable, therefore, to sit back and watch someone who restricts movement to a minimum—Vendryes, who silently produces a succession of doves seemingly from thin air ...'

Because he was so obviously popular with the girls, the boys were becoming jealous. They didn't like this pretty, smooth-skinned boy who was becoming an icon to their girlfriends. He particularly wasn't liked by Teds and Rockers who fancied themselves as hard men.

At the Finsbury Park Empire a group of Rockers turned up threatening to cause trouble.

'They were the yobs of the time,' remembers Stan Edwards, who hadn't seen Cliff since they worked together at Butlin's. 'Cliff invited them to come and meet him. We were in the dressing room and these guys arrived in heavy leather gear and they turned out to be really great blokes. So they said, we like you and we'll make sure no one gets on stage. They had come as the aggressors and became the defenders!'

By this final week of concerts Cliff was flagging. He was now not only rehearsing 'Oh Boy!' and doing two concerts a day but was playing a small role in *Serious Charge*, a film being shot in Borehamwood. He wasn't used to working under such pressure and was clearly suffering from exhaustion.

'When it came to the last night Cliff just couldn't go on stage,' remembers John Foster. 'He came off after the first show and he just couldn't talk. So I threw everyone out of the dressing room, made him sleep and gave him honey and melted butter.

'While I was doing this Franklyn Boyd knocked on the door and when I opened it he asked, "How's my boy?" I said, "Look, get in your car, drive to Piccadilly Circus, go to the all-night chemist and get 'your boy' something for his throat because you're murdering him." I threw him out.'

He stayed in bed at home for a few days and his father began consulting Ray Mackender. He was then a fringe character in the music business, whom Cliff had met at a party thrown by Cherry Wainer, one of the cast of 'Oh Boy!'.

Ray Mackender was a handsome 26-year-old bachelor with thick wavy hair and a public school accent. By day he worked as a non-marine broker at Lloyds of London and by night donned a pair of jeans and headed down to Battersea Town Hall where he organized a rock 'n' roll dance night.

He desperately wanted to be part of the scene but hadn't yet found a role. He wrote some features for *New Musical Express*, became a disc jockey at the Poplar Theatre, and befriended many of the 'Oh Boy!' stars.

On Sunday mornings he organized coffee parties at his flat in Danvers Street, Chelsea, where the cream of Britain's young talent would gather for chat and drinks. In his visitors' book from that period are the names of Vince Eager, Jess Conrad, Sammy Samwell, Cliff Richard, Jimmy Page (later to form Led Zeppelin) and Gerry Dorsey (later to be renamed Engelbert Humperdinck).

'It was the fact of getting together in those days that was so exciting for us,' says Jess Conrad. 'We weren't drinkers. We just liked meeting and playing records and back then you really had to go somewhere else to play your records because your parents complained too much about the noise if you played them at home.'

Cliff's parents warmed to Mackender. Rodger, who was forever believing that his son was being exploited, was impressed with Mackender's position in the City and started calling him up for business advice.

'Rodger saw me as a complete God-send at that time,' Mackender admits. 'He confided that he was thinking of getting rid of Franklyn Boyd and he thought he could become Cliff's manager if I was willing to help him out.

'Initially I thought I could but, after a few meetings with the accountants, I realized it was a much bigger job than anyone could manage part-time. I was also reluctant to give up the security of my job with Lloyds.'

Rodger Webb went ahead anyway and sent a letter of dismissal to Franklyn Boyd, who had never signed a contract. The next day the story was splashed over the newspapers: 'Cliff Richard In Rumpus—Father Gives Manager The Sack'.

'I never had any quarrel with Cliff or his mother,' says Boyd. 'It was his father who was a pain in the neck. I think Cliff should have been strong enough to say, "Look Dad, I know you're my father but this is business." But he never said it.

'I knew he was struggling a bit rehearsing and doing the variety shows but I knew he had to learn show business very quickly. If he had stuck doing Sunday concerts it would have taken him a year to get the same experience. I knew he would have a hard time but everyone goes through that.

'His father was working in a rather dull office, cycling eight miles to work each day, and now show business managers had started to wine and dine him. He was becoming quite impressed with it all. Tito Burns, Cherry Wainer's manager, had been sending limousines up to Cheshunt to bring his mother to shows. In other words, everyone was winning the parents over because they could see the pound signs in Cliff Richard.'

Boyd left at around the same time that it was decided that Terry Smart, Cliff's last link with the original Drifters, was going to have to go. It wasn't a difficult decision to make because Smart knew that he couldn't keep pace with the professionals and he was keen to join the Merchant Navy when he was eighteen anyway.

The obvious first choice as his replacement was Tony Meehan, the drummer who had worked with Hank and Jet in the Vipers.

Although only fifteen, Meehan had been drumming since he was thirteen, playing in small dance bands in the Irish belt of North London and then graduating to Soho where he played in backing groups for Adam Faith, Vince Eager and Vince Taylor. He had been to see Cliff and the Drifters at the Metropolitan, Edgware Road.

'I went because they were complaining about how lousy their drummer was and they felt they just couldn't handle it any more,' he says.

'They were putting out feelers to see if I would be interested. So I saw him and I was impressed with what I saw. I thought he was terrific. He really was hot at that time and I was stimulated.

'Terry Smart was a real sweetheart but not a great player by any stretch of the imagination. It was a big wrench for Cliff when he left but he was quite ruthless about getting on. He was very determined. He knew that he couldn't put friendship before business.'

It was a hard time for Cliff because he was having to learn his stagecraft in the full glare of the national media and thousands of adoring fans. He was being projected as a star, yet he still found it hard to look directly at an audience. It took Cherry Wainer to coach him in the art of holding a microphone, and Franklyn Boyd to tell him how to take a bow.

By the end of 1958 he was starting to put it all together. With the addition of Tony Meehan, he had an experienced group behind him who could help paper over some of the remaining cracks.

11

'I worried for his life. I didn't want anything to happen to him'

A s his life as a star expanded, so he became less and less an ordinary boy from Cheshunt. He could no longer travel on the bus or walk out alone without being surrounded by fans. Girls turned up and sat outside his home in Hargreaves Close and he often had to spend hours waiting inside the Hackney Empire until crowds dispersed. Then there was the additional threat from the Teddy boys and the slighted boyfriends.

'He didn't seem to know what had hit him,' remembers Tulah Tuke. 'When I saw him at the Metropolitan he seemed amazed and somewhat horrified that there were these little girls screaming outside. I think he was knocked back by it. He was as excited as any teenager would be but there was also that frightening dimension of not knowing exactly what might erupt.'

One night in Romford, while the girls stood outside the dressing room windows yelling for Cliff, a mob of boys started throwing bricks through the windows of the tour bus. Cliff had to be smuggled out of the building though a toilet window and driven to a rendezvous point on the road back to London.

At the Chiswick Empire some lads threw a fire hydrant from the balcony and two girls in the stalls were injured. At the Lyceum, off the Strand, he was forced to abandon a concert after being pelted with vegetables and coins with sharpened edges.

'If one of those things hit you it would take your eye out or give you a nasty cut,' says Tony Meehan. 'We tried to play on and then one of these things came right across my cymbal and I said, "Right, that's it." So, after three numbers, we pulled the plugs. I think that was the only time we ever stopped a show. There was absolute uproar. There were hundreds of people squashed against the stage and there didn't seem to be any control. Then these people at the back started breaking up chairs and hurling them through the air. It was a horrible, horrible atmosphere.'

Events like this began to trouble Cliff's mother.

'I never worried about him being a rock 'n' roll singer but I did worry about what could happen to him. I used to try and go everywhere with him. Rodger wouldn't come. He said I was daft. But I told him that these people were doing rotten things to him and I could save him.

'There used to be rows of policemen linking arms trying to protect him from the crowds. These boys would be shouting, "Kill him! Kill him!" It was dreadful. I used to go to all these shows because I didn't want anything to happen to him and me not to be there. I used to go everywhere.'

Within months of his first hit single being released he was adapting to the abnormal lifestyle of the rich and famous. His earnings were phenomenal by the standards of his contemporaries—£15,000 for a thirty-week contract with the Grade Agency in March 1959—but there was no time to spend it and few places to go. At the age of eighteen he was hermetically sealed into a way of life that he has never been able to escape.

His old schoolfriends gradually fell away, partly through their own inability to deal with his fame, partly through Cliff's unavailability. His new friends and acquaintances were from the world of show business: people who lived the same hours and experienced the same problems. From the cast of 'Oh Boy!' he became particularly close to Cherry Wainer, who responded to this 'little boy lost' by taking him under her wing.

Cherry was something of an oddity on 'Oh Boy!'. She was neither from the same musical background nor the same generation as the regular stars of the show. She had come to Britain from South Africa late in 1957 with her drummer Don Storer and Jack Good had spotted her playing at a US Air Force base.

'Cherry always seemed so worldly wise,' remembers Maggie Streader from the Vernons Girls. 'She was older than all of us. She was a star! She knew everybody, knew everything and called everyone "darling".'

She met Cliff at his first rehearsal and began gently to coach him and advise him on how to handle himself in the business. She saw him as vulnerable and easily exploited.

He began to share his hopes and fears with her and together with John Foster and other performers from the show he would spend evenings with her at the Lotus House, a Chinese restaurant in the Edgware Road which was a late-night hang-out for the 'Oh Boy!' crowd. Because Cliff had no means of transport and no telephone at home she also began to chauffeur him around and take messages.

Through Cherry Wainer's influence Cliff was brought together with her manager Tito Burns, who was then introduced to his parents over a meal at the Lotus House.

'His mum and dad knew nothing about show business,' says Cherry. 'Cliff became so big so fast and everywhere he went people were trying to get at him. I think he was thankful and grateful that it was happening, but it bothered him.'

Tito Burns was everything that the Webbs could have imagined a show business manager to be. He had slicked-back hair and a Groucho Marx moustache, smoked cigars and liked talking about 'wheeling and dealing'.

He was born Nathan Burns in the East End of London and had joined a dance band on leaving school. *Melody Maker*'s annual polls voted him Britain's top accordion player, and he was also a good enough comedian to play support to Alma Cogan.

Unlike Cliff's previous managers, he already controlled several acts he could use as bargaining tools. George Ganjou had now been shunted on to the sidelines. He was still paid his ten per cent in line with the contract signed when Cliff was seventeen, but he no longer played any active part in Cliff's career.

Burns made no secret of the fact that he had no love for rock 'n' roll. He saw it as a short-term phenomenon and thought that the best insurance policy Cliff could take out would be to distance himself from the Drifters and introduce more classic cover songs into his act. Whereas Cliff had always seen himself as Elvis, Burns saw him as Frank Sinatra.

The move away from rock 'n' roll was eventually to come through Lionel Bart, Tommy Steele's songwriter. He had been approached by film producer Mickey Delamar to write songs for a film version of *Serious Charge*, a British play about a vicar who helps a juvenile delinquent who then tries to frame him on a charge of indecent assault.

At the time homosexuality was a risqué subject for cinema, and Delamar wanted a rock 'n' roll soundtrack to broaden its appeal. 'He asked me if I knew of an English kid who was an Elvis clone,' says Bart. 'I put Cliff's name forward.'

The director was 43-year-old Terence Young, later to make his name with the early James Bond films. 'I think we thought that if we put a few kids in it would draw a younger audience,' he admits. 'Otherwise it would have been strictly a television sort of audience. So the part of Curly was added for the film version.

'There were two or three singers that I went to see. I saw Cliff at the Chiswick Empire and I was sold on him right away. He seemed terribly self-assured and had a very good stage act. I thought if he could do that, then he could act.'

The film had a strong cast with former child star Andrew Ray playing the teenage delinquent, Anthony Quayle the vicar and Sarah Churchill, daughter of Sir Winston, a middle-aged parishioner with marriage on her mind. Cliff took the part of Curly, the delinquent's younger brother.

Filming took place at MGM's studios in Borehamwood and in the new town at Stevenage. Andrew Ray calls the film 'a poor man's *The Wild Ones* set in Stevenage'.

Cliff didn't have many lines and the ones he had he spat out of the corner of his mouth in a pseudo-hip accent that was far removed from his innocent looks.

'I remember Cliff was a lovely fellow,' says Ray, 'but he was very nervous about acting. He really wanted to get on with the songs in the film.'

While filming was going on, Tommy Steele, still the reigning King of British rock 'n' roll with eleven top thirty hits, paid an unexpected visit to the set. He asked to see Cliff in his dressing room. Jess Conrad, who was playing the leader of a local gang which disrupts the vicar's youth club, remembers the tense scene as the King met the pretender to the crown.

'There wasn't friction, but Tommy was the established star and now this new boy was coming up and he asked Cliff if he had ever played "knuckles", where you had touch knuckles and if you couldn't move away fast enough you got hit.

'Tommy was very good at it and very fast. He cut Cliff's hands to ribbons. I'll never ever forget it. It was the most devious thing I had ever seen because Tommy had decided that he wanted to draw blood from the new idol. It was really awful. Cliff could never get out of the way quick enough and it went on and on. Cliff kept saying he'd play on, and yet his knuckles were red raw where Tommy had been whacking and whacking him.'

Steele had learned the game as a merchant seaman on board the liner *Mauretania*.

'To lose at "knuckles" on that ship was as bad as walking the plank,' remembers Steele. 'A young man intent on entering the arena needed to be strong, sly and very quick—Cliff was not very good at it.'

One of the songs from Lionel Bart's soundtrack was 'Living Doll'. He had written it one Sunday morning in October 1958 while reading the *Sunday Pictorial*.

'I was looking at the back pages and there was a small advert for a doll which could apparently do everything,' Bart remembers. 'I wrote the song in ten minutes.'

The advert that caught his eye was for a 99/6d 'Darling Doll' which was said to 'kneel, walk, sit and sing'. He linked this idea with the Mills Brothers' wartime hit 'Paper Doll', in which the singer asks for a cut-out paper girl because others wouldn't steal her, and she would be easier to be with than a 'fickle-minded real live girl'. Bart added his own twist to the tale.

As performed for the soundtrack, 'Living Doll' was a fast song in four-four time which Cliff hated singing. Paramor tried to thwart its release as a single by writing a song with a similar title, 'Livin' Lovin' Doll', which Cliff released in January 1959. So that no one would detect the ruse he used the pseudonym Johnny May and his friend Bunny Lewis was credited as Jim Gustard. (Paramor and Lewis went on to write Cliff's 1960 hit 'A Voice In The Wilderness', this time not hiding their identities.)

But the public was not satisfied with 'Livin' Lovin' Doll', and it only reached number twenty in the charts. There was demand for a soundtrack EP from the film and so, at the end of April 1959, Cliff re-recorded the songs.

'We told Norrie that we didn't like "Living Doll" the way it was,' says Cliff. 'We were at Sheffield City Hall doing a sound check one afternoon [14 February 1959], sitting around thinking what we could do with the song, when Bruce started strumming his guitar and he said, "What about having it as a country song?"'

Since 'Move It' had reached number two in the charts and stayed around for over four months, Cliff had been struggling to maintain momentum as a singles' artist.

He tried to achieve this initially by recording more rock 'n' roll numbers, but after 'High Class Baby' reached number seven his chart positions wavered. 'Livin' Lovin' Doll' only just made the top twenty and 'Mean Streak', because it was competing in the charts with its own flip side 'Never Mind', stalled at ten. The number of records sold had slumped to below 200,000 from a high of well over half a million.

His first LP, recorded days before the concert at Sheffield City Hall, was to be the last all-out burst of rock 'n' roll. Paramor wanted to capture the feel of those early live performances, but to do it in the controlled environment of Abbey Road's studio two. Cliff and the Drifters played to an invited audience on a make-shift stage beneath the control room.

Over two nights, Cliff belted out his favourite hits, including 'Whole Lotta Shakin' Goin' On', 'Be Bop A Lula', 'Donna' and 'That'll Be The Day'. The result was *Cliff*, which went on to reach number four in the LP charts.

The slowed-down version of 'Living Doll' became his most important recording since 'Move It'. It redefined him as a singer, was his first number one and sold almost two million copies.

'It wasn't an out-and-out rocker. But by then I was coming to see that rock wasn't a tempo but a musical culture, and that a song like "Living Doll" fitted into it,' Cliff says.

'What we were discovering was that rock 'n' roll seemed to be fairly limited as a beaty form of music because the public weren't buying it in hundreds of thousands. We were the first rock teenagers and ten year olds had no money to spend so in the end records like "Living Doll" sold because they appealed to parents who had money.

'We helped the audience to grow. By the time the Beatles came along those ten year olds were fifteen and had money. They could make a stand for rock 'n' roll. The Beatles had the benefit of all the groundwork that we had put in.'

At around the time that Cliff hooked up with Tito Burns he moved away from home for the first time, renting a three-bedroomed flat at 100 Marylebone High Street.

At first he shared with John Foster but it soon became a crash pad not only for the Drifters but for singers such as Billy Fury, Dickie

Pride and Vince Eager. Comedian Jimmy Tarbuck often used the small spare bedroom.

'I didn't have a thing to my name back then,' says Tarbuck. 'Cliff used to let me stay at his flat when I was in London.' Cliff's mother and sister Donna would come up regularly to keep it clean and Donna would often stay for extended periods.

'We were on our own a lot of the time,' says Foster. 'We weren't really meeting new people. There weren't clubs like Tramps which you can go into today in London and he had become so big so fast that he couldn't go anywhere. He couldn't even walk out on the street.'

The move had to be made because in 1959 Cliff started what was to become a familiar pattern of one-nighter shows which would almost always start with everyone being collected from a pick-up point in Marylebone—either Great Cumberland Place or Allsop Place—and it was too much to travel in from Cheshunt continually, especially as he didn't yet drive.

In February and March he toured the Granada circuit as part of a package which included Wee Willie Harris, Tony Crombie and Johnny Duncan with Jimmy Tarbuck as compère.

'Cliff was top of the bill,' remembers Tarbuck. 'They were fun days but the tour was so disorganized. You might be in Hull one day, Bournemouth the next and then Glasgow after that, and all of it done by coach.'

During one show Cliff lost his voice again and Wee Willie Harris had to be positioned at the back of the stage to sing the songs while Cliff mimed.

'It just shows you what it was all about in the fifties,' says Harris. 'I don't think the girls were bothered who was singing. Every time he made a sexy movement with his legs they screamed even though I was singing in full view of the audience.'

In April Cliff played for a week each at the Birmingham Hippodrome and the Chiswick Empire. It was while in Birmingham that he sent away for Hank's Fender Stratocaster, the first solid-body electric guitar to be sold to anyone in England.

Hank had been playing an Antoria, but the neck was bent and the tuning suspect. Like Cliff he admired the playing of James Burton, whose guitar breaks on Ricky Nelson's records epitomized American rock 'n' roll. Hank knew that Burton's instrument was made by Fender Instruments of Fullerton, California.

Hank and Cliff acquired a catalogue, pored over it and decided that Burton must have been playing a Stratocaster. It was the most expensive of Fender's guitars and had revolutionized the guitar industry when it was introduced in 1954. Cliff offered to buy it for Hank (the cost was about five weeks of Hank's salary in 1959), and wrote to Dave Lilley, Ray Mackender's flatmate, to ask if he would order it:

'Dear Dave,
We've decided to have the "Red" Fender Guitar. With
A. Three pickups.
B. With tremelo lever.
C. Gold platted [sic] Hardware
The guitar is a "Stratocaster". Have marked in catalogue. When you send for it please order spare set balanced strings and also a "Fender Case".
Well Dave thanks a million.
All the Best, Cliff.'

Hank remembers it arriving.

'A magnificent flat case with plush red lining came, and inside it was this magnificent guitar—flamingo pink with a maple finger-board. You didn't have to play it. You just had to hang it around your neck and the audience would be totally impressed.'

The guitar, which was at the time considered to be very strange looking, changed the image and sound of the group. It was much easier to play, there was greater tonal versality and with the tremolo arm Hank was able to 'bend' notes. Within a few years solid-body guitars would be standard equipment for all rock groups.

At the Chiswick Empire, Jet met a sixteen-year-old girl in the bar. Her name was Carol Costa, and she came from Hounslow.

'She was with a chap but he wasn't her boyfriend,' remembers Jet, 'and I thought she looked terribly Brigitte Bardot-ish.' A relationship was started and the two of them moved into the spare bedroom at Cliff's flat.

It was to be a stormy relationship. Carol looked like a starlet but she was also physically tough. It was said that her father had wanted a boy and brought her up to defend herself and to mend cars. She rode a motor scooter without a licence and wasn't past landing a punch on anyone if they rubbed her up the wrong way.

The moment she saw Cliff she fell for him. The move to the flat suited her. Here she could officially be with Jet while seeing how far she could get by flirting with Cliff. Years later she confessed to Jet that she had only become his girlfriend so that she could get close to Cliff.

They started eyeing each other at the flat. They would even hold hands discreetly at the cinema, even though Jet was sitting on Carol's other side. Then there would be parties at Carol's home in Cedar Road, Hounslow, after which everyone would crash out overnight on the floor and again there would be looks and touches between her and Cliff.

'I had always fancied Brigitte Bardot,' Cliff says. 'When I was a teenager I had a poster of her on my bedroom wall which was made up of three parts given away in *Reveille* magazine. Bardot wore eyeliner and I remember Carol being like that.

'I fell for her. It was a strange time. It was the period I refer back to when I say that all my friends got married really young. All the Drifters were going steady with girls they would marry, and there was great pressure on me to get married. That must have played a great part in our relationship, brief though it was.

'I think Jet must have been aware that she fancied me. I don't think we were as discreet as we could have been really but at that stage it was only looks and glances.'

Cliff's mother began to suspect something was going on when she visited the flat one day to clean. She discovered that Carol had slipped a letter beneath Cliff's pillow before going out. Cliff told his mother that he was frightened of her and that he didn't like what was happening, but that was only half of the truth. The other half was that he was developing feelings for her. The fear came from the fact that she was the girlfriend of one of his closest friends.

What he didn't tell his mother he poured out to Cherry Wainer in long emotional conversations. He told her that he was very fond of Carol but that he didn't want to do anything that would hurt Jet or hurt his career.

'I think Carol was prepared to break off with Jet if she knew that she could have gone with Cliff,' she says, 'but at that time Cliff's mother didn't want anything to happen to him that would affect his career. I think although he felt very deeply for her, he didn't want to argue with his parents—to say, "Yes, I'm going to do this." So that's why he stayed put.'

At that time it was important for a young male singer to preserve his single image. His fans, who were mostly female, needed to be able to nurse the fantasy that they could be his dream girl. Terry Dene married in July 1958 and never had another hit. Marty Wilde put an end to his career as a teenage idol when he married one of the Vernons Girls in 1959.

'Without a shadow of doubt my marriage affected my record sales and my popularity,' says Wilde. 'Directly after that I really struggled. You had to change your career to survive. But we knew that would happen. I had a long meeting with my manager and he said, "I'll leave the decision to you, but you must know what you're up against."'

Cliff had thought right from the start that marriage would limit his career but an incident in 1959 confirmed it for him. He was dating a dark-haired girl called Jean who worked in a bowling alley in Wembley and had got on well enough with her to be taken back to meet her parents. Jet Harris remembers her as 'the most gorgeous girl'.

She came along to several concerts with Cliff and after one show, at the Finsbury Park Empire, she left the theatre with him and sat on his lap in the waiting car. Cliff looked out of the car window long enough to see that his fans were in tears and some of them had thrown their concert programmes into the gutter and were grinding them in with their heels.

He was shocked at the intensity of their feelings. 'When I started seeing Jean I thought, well, perhaps I can have a girlfriend but this experience underlined the fact that I couldn't,' he says. 'The fans wanted to own me, and I was happy with that.'

Franklyn Boyd reckons that early in his career Cliff's mother was also influential in keeping him single.

'She always told him not to get romantically involved with girls because it would be the end of his career.'

There can be no doubt that his image as a lonely boy just waiting for Miss Right to come along helped his career. One of the most popular magazine story ideas of the time was 'Cliff's Ideal Girl'. Cliff would always say that he liked plain-looking girls who wore no make-up and weren't too forward. In this way even the most ordinary-looking fan could think that she fitted the bill.

A typical story (featured in a romantic comic for girls) was headlined 'Cliff Richard Reveals—If Only I Could Find The Right Girl' and began, 'Although I meet pretty girls wherever I go—I haven't got a girlfriend'. What sort of girl would he like? Of course she must like rock 'n' roll, cowboy films and Chinese food but 'I like a natural looking girl . . . a girl who can let herself go without worrying if her hair is going to lose its curl in the rain, or her nose get shiny.'

Later the same year he told a fan magazine that the girl he would marry (at twenty-seven), 'needn't be too good-looking, as long as she's got a personality of her own'.

His ideal, he told *Boyfriend* in May 1959, was Hollywood actress Carol Lynley, who had been in two teen films, *Blue Jeans* and *Hound*

Dog Man, because 'she seems so wholesome ... so quiet. She's not specially good-looking. But in her very plainness there's a special kind of beauty.'

He couldn't have put it better if he'd been handed a script by a marketing executive. He was the boy with everything, surrounded by beautiful women, and yet all he wanted was a good old-fashioned plain girl who could cook him a meal and listen to records. Everyone was in with a chance. The challenge had been laid down. Even the prettiest of girls could leave off her make-up, tousle her hair up and affect just the right degree of plainness.

Jack Good was right. Cliff was too innocent to suggest the pleasures of forbidden fruit in the way that Elvis did. He was more suited to offering the promise of a romantic meal, a night at the 'flicks' and a kiss on the doorstep that was guaranteed not to go too far. Whereas a lot of parents might have had a hard time adjusting to having Elvis around the house, Cliff was the ideal boy to invite back home: traditional but not fogeyish, proper but not prim.

Interviewed in 1964, Sammy Samwell suggested that Cliff's broad appeal was because he was a rock 'n' roll star whom parents were comfortable with and that was more important in Britain at the time than it was in America.

'In England not every home has a record player,' Samwell said. 'In many of the homes that have one, it is still something of a prized possession and if the youngsters want to play a record on it which annoys the parents, then there is trouble.

'Cliff broke this down by having the clean-cut "wouldn't mind having him for my son" type of thing. His records in this way became acceptable, so the kids were free to buy his records and play them, and still retain their own private inner image of Cliff, different from that of their parents.'

When Cliff went away in the summer of 1959 it was his first holiday since the days when he visited his grandfather in Lucknow and his first time out of England since arriving in 1948. In *It's Great To Be*

Young he wrote, 'Ronnie, a chum of mine from the old days, was going out [to Italy] in his car and wondered if I'd like to join him. Would I? I jumped at it.'

Ronnie was Ronnie Ernstone, a 21-year-old car mechanic from Notting Hill Gate who had met Cliff at an EMI Studio's party. They probably wouldn't have got so close if Ronnie hadn't had a car and promised to run him back to Cheshunt.

He was soon giving Cliff driving lessons. When, in April 1959, he wanted a Lambretta motor scooter Ernstone ordered one from friends in the motorcycle business and had it sprayed nasturtium, which was the colour of the moment. Much later, in August 1959, he organized the purchase of Cliff's first car—a grey Sunbeam Alpine with red leather seats.

Ernstone's other useful connection was clothes. His father was a textile importer and it occurred to Ernstone that if there could be Fred Perry shirts there could also be Cliff Richard shirts.

'In those days people were wearing striped cotton shirts in bright colours,' he says. 'As it happened my father had just bought in some material like this. I showed it to Cliff and asked him what he thought about having some shirts made up.'

'He thought it was a good idea so I had some samples made up. I got Cliff wearing them, had him photographed, and did a deal with Tito Burns whereby Cliff got a royalty. I interested some teenage magazines in what we called the "Cliff Richard Shirt Offer", which was a shirt in either small, medium or large, presented in a box which had a picture on the lid of Cliff wearing one of the shirts.'

The holiday in Italy came about spontaneously. Cliff had a break in his work schedule and Ernstone suggested driving on the Continent, something he had been doing with his parents since he was a child. Both Cliff and Tony Meehan agreed to go and Ernstone brought along a platonic friend called Pam who looked like Audrey Hepburn.

They drove down through Belgium, Germany and Switzerland in Ernstone's red and grey Morris Oxford Estate. Meehan sat in the front seat and navigated and Ernstone drove while Cliff sat in the back with Pam, who attempted to snuggle up to him but was apparently kept at arm's length. They made it to Virieggio on the coast of Italy in thirty-six hours.

They checked into the Hotel Regina, an old seafront hotel with creaky wooden floorboards and a grand marble staircase. After crashing out for a few hours they went out for a meal of Steak Bismarck (steak with eggs) in a local restaurant, washing it all down with a large bottle of Chianti. 'We were all eighteen then and felt we were really great,' says Ernstone (actually Meehan was still only sixteen). 'We were really putting the steak and wine away, and the truth is that we all got absolutely paralytic. We staggered back down the main street swaying all over the show and feeling as sick as dogs.'

'It was the first time for all of us,' says Meehan. 'Cliff threw up. I sat outside the hotel with my head in my hands feeling absolutely smashed. It was a beautiful evening and somehow I didn't get sick.

'But when I got back to our suite Ronnie and Cliff were just vomiting into the sink. They were very badly sick. Then they had to keep going into the shower. I cleared off out again because I couldn't stand the smell. The next day we all felt pretty fragile.'

For the next twelve days they sunbathed and swam, and listened to the music in the Italian pop charts. One night they went to a cabaret club where Cliff was pulled out of the audience and asked to sing a song. The owner, a friend of Ernstone's parents who therefore knew who Cliff was, handed him a guitar and said, 'Now, ladies and gentlemen. From London England—Richard Cliff!'

Cliff remembers it as a wonderful experience. In one way it was the last time he could be a lad among lads and spontaneously elect to drive off. In another way it was the start of his globetrotting.

'It was the beginning of it all,' he says. 'It was the first holiday I had ever afforded. I can remember we stopped to clean our teeth in a Swiss mountain stream on the way down. It was my first feeling of real freedom. I was not only able to leave my family and go off on holiday but I could afford to go to another country.'

Ever since his first press interviews Cliff had said the same thing when asked what his personal ambition was. It was 'to meet Elvis Presley', and it was on his way back from Virieggio that he made the first of several attempts.

Inducted into the US Army in December 1957, Elvis had left America in September 1958 to join the Third Armored Division in West Germany and was eventually posted to the small town of Bad Nauheim, north east of Frankfurt, where he rented a three-storey white stucco house, Goethestrasse 14.

It was well known that Elvis lived in Bad Nauheim but Cliff and his friends knew no more than that. They decided to give it a try, to drive into the town and ask around to see if they could track down the king of rock 'n' roll.

'We got to the army camp and told one of the guards that we had come to see Elvis Presley and they told us where we could find him,' says Ernstone. 'I seem to remember that his house was the third one on the left and we pulled up outside and then we just sat there in the car for about ten minutes deciding who should be the one to go and knock on the door. Tony wanted me to go and I wanted Tony to go and then I said I thought it should be Cliff who went first because he was the rock 'n' roll star.

'In the end we voted and it was decided that Cliff was going to be the one to do it. I said, "I'll tell you what. If you go and knock on the door I'll film you with my cine camera and then when he comes out and shakes your hand, we'll have a record of it."'

The footage has been exhumed after twenty-four years in Ernstone's mother's attic. It shows Cliff, dressed in a striped shirt and jeans, walking slowly to the white wooden gate. He goes up a short flight of steps on the left side of the house where he drags his fingers through his hair and presses a door bell.

The door is answered by a friend of Elvis' who tells him that unfortunately Elvis is on leave in Paris but that he'll pass on Cliff's good wishes. A dejected Cliff comes back down the steps and then the camera pans along the wall in front of the house where girls have scribbled their messages of love. The picture ends up on Elvis' parked car.

'It was very disappointing for all of us,' admits Meehan. We were very keyed-up and thought it had been quite a feat for us to find his house. The guy who answered the door said that if Elvis had been around he would have loved to have met Cliff. It felt like a big let-down.'

'It would have been a great time to have met him because that's the Elvis I remember,' says Cliff. 'The second Elvis, the big fat Elvis, was not the one I wanted to meet.'

What Cliff didn't know was that Elvis was away meeting Franklyn Boyd in Paris at the time. 'I spent ten days with him there with his Memphis friends Charlie Hodge and Lamont Fike,' says Boyd. 'I'd had a call from my boss in the States, Jean Aberbach, who told me to meet Elvis at the Gare de Lyon in Paris. I talked Elvis out of coming to England. He wanted to come and I told him that he'd never get out of his hotel.'

On the same day, nineteen-year-old Terence 'Jet' Harris was marrying seventeen-year-old Carol Ann Costa at St Paul's Church, Hounslow Heath, in London. Even though Cliff must have realized that nothing permanent could have come of his flirtation with Carol, he still wasn't ready for it to end.

'I knew it was going to happen,' says Cliff. 'I must have been disappointed but I don't think I'm cut out to be married. I think I wanted the trimmings but I didn't want marriage. So, in point of fact, it was probably a good "out" for me.'

12

'America was a real eye-opener for us'

Within a day of returning from Italy, Cliff plunged into a string of concerts around Britain. Travelling on the tour was Royston Ellis, an author who had been commissioned to ghost-write a book for Jet Harris called *Driftin' With Cliff*.

Ellis was Britain's first teenage pundit. He'd started by writing poetry about coffee bars, motorcycles and rock 'n' roll and the newspapers seized on him as an erudite beatnik, an Allen Ginsberg of suburban London. The fact that he wore a beard and had worked as an office boy, duster salesman, gardener, milk-bottle washer, building labourer and farm hand by the age of eighteen helped confirm the image.

'I guess you'd call the boy in the picture a weirdie,' said the *Daily Mirror* in 1959 below a photograph of him dressed in a fur-collared jacket. 'And you'd be right. He's strictly, as they say in beatnik language, from Weirdsville.'

His first volume of poems, *Jiving To Gyp*, was dedicated to Cliff and he was soon asked by television programmmes to explain what teenagers were all about. He ended up with his own series, 'Living For Kicks', in which he explored the controversial issues of the day such as pep pills, and sex before marriage.

A cogent musical commentator—his 1961 paperback *The Big Beat Scene* still stands up as an appraisal of early British rock 'n' roll—he was soon to meet the fledgling Beatles (in May 1960) and show John Lennon and Paul McCartney how to break down a Benzedrine inhaler and sniff the strips inside to produce a mild high. This was, Lennon later recounted, their first experience with drugs.

'I wrote to Cliff saying I wanted to meet him and write about him,' says Ellis. 'I got a letter back from Ray Mackender, who was by now helping Cliff's mother deal with all the fan mail, inviting me to a broadcast that Cliff was doing with the Drifters at Radio Luxembourg.

'Cliff didn't really take me on at all because he didn't really relate to anyone in those days but Jet Harris did immediately and so my first friendship was with Jet. It was only after quite a while that Cliff decided I was harmless.'

Ellis and the Drifters worked together on some poetry and music projects, a Soho version of what America's beat poets had been doing for some years in the North Beach area of San Francisco. Ellis called it 'rocketry'.

'We did a television show and some gigs with him,' remembers Meehan. 'We didn't play our normal style of music though. It was more jazz-orientated as far as I can remember. It was different, it was interesting, and it was a bit of extra money.'

Driftin' With Cliff wasn't an in-depth account of life on the road but it did supply interesting snapshots: the communal singing of American rock 'n' roll songs on the coach, the cushion fights, the pit stops where they'd all have greasy fry-ups and Cliff would have his favourite drink of Tizer with a scoop of ice-cream.

Off stage Cliff was wearing 'a blue continental-style jacket, fawn tapered trousers and white calf-skin shoes which he had brought back from Italy'. At night he wore pink pyjamas. His favourite reading matter was science fiction and his favourite singers Connie Francis, Ricky Nelson and Elvis Presley.

Before the show the musicians would often go out to see a film.

After the show, they would play cards until the early hours of the next morning. Cliff stayed in a separate hotel to the Drifters.

'Cliff was always a mystery to me,' admits Ellis. 'He kept himself to himself. He wasn't a part of the gang. Often, when all the others were on the coach, Cliff would be in a car with his manager Tito Burns. It was very difficult to get close to him.'

One of the most noticeable differences between Cliff and the rest of the musicians was in his attitude to girls. Whereas he obviously enjoyed the mass hysteria he could provoke when on stage he never followed it through off stage. As Bruce Welch puts it, 'If there were women available we in the Drifters would be having them but Cliff wasn't interested.'

It wasn't just that he appeared to believe that sex was for marriage—at that time there were many other boys of his age who felt the same way—but that he didn't seem moved by sex at all. This was an observation made by almost all who knew him.

'From the moment I met him women were of no interest to Cliff,' says Tito Burns. 'I'm not by any means saying he's gay. Not at all. I just don't think sex meant anything to him. People find it hard to understand that there is such a thing as being completely sexless, totally unaffected by sex.'

Ronnie Ernstone thought he was 'undersexed—it just wasn't important to him,' and Maggie Streader says, 'I think there was so much going on in his life that sex played the smallest part. I think he had a very low sex drive.'

His friends didn't know what to make of this behaviour. Some thought it was naïvety. Some thought he'd grown up with an overly protective attitude to women as a result of having to look after his younger sisters. Others blamed his relationship with his mother which they felt was smothering.

When he moved back to Cheshunt from his London flat one national newspaper took the opportunity to say that Cliff was 'running back to Mummy'. The accusation stung him badly and it is one of the reasons why his mother has remained wary of the press.

Alluding to this incident, Royston Ellis (writing as Jet) defended Cliff against the charge of being a 'mummy's boy' by arguing that this couldn't be so because he spent so much time away from home.

'True, he is attached to his family, but then most normal sons are,' he said. 'Then there is the question most girls are wondering—why hasn't Cliff Richard got a girlfriend? The answer is simple—Cliff hasn't found the right girl, and he has no time.'

For *Expresso Bongo*, which he started filming at Shepperton Studios almost as soon as he came off the road, his role as a virginal young pop singer discovered in a Soho jazz cellar was remarkably close to reality although it had not been written with him in mind.

Created by Wolf Mankowitz as a satire on the Tommy Steele phenomenon, it had originally been a West End play starring Paul Scofield as the manager and James Kenny as the manipulated boy star.

Bongo Herbert is supposed to be an eighteen year old so madly devoted to his music that he has no time for anything else. 'For me, it's more like a drug,' he confesses. 'Takes my mind off a few things.'

His sharp-talking manager Johnny Jackson (Laurence Harvey) introduces him to the glamorous but fading American star Dixie Collins (Yolande Donlan) who agrees to have him as a guest on her London show and she is eventually eclipsed by him.

Dixie clearly wants to seduce Bongo but he is more interested in talking to her about his love for Lambrettas. She asks him what he'd like to have behind him on the pillion seat if he was to get his motor scooter and he tells her that he was thinking of having a box fitted for his sandwiches.

In one scene, set in her luxury apartment late at night, Dixie purringly asks him whether he has a steady girlfriend.

'Why's everyone always on with this girlfriend routine?' responds a defensive Bongo. 'It's not unnatural or illegal you know,' says Dixie.

'Girlfriends just pin you down,' says Bongo. 'They're always wanting things.' Dixie slowly sinks into a sofa and looks up at Bongo. 'Sometimes,' she says, 'the feeling is mutual, you know.'

In another prescient scene Johnny Jackson (whose character was modelled on that of Larry Parnes) tries to add a fresh dimension to Bongo's image. He suggests a song about mother love but the songwriter hired to supply the material can't come up with anything that gells.

'So far, what have we got?' asks Johnny. 'Sex. Beat. Violence . . . we've got it all. We've got it all except for one thing—religion! We've got to get religion!'

'I put that in because religion is always exploited in the common music hall reference out of which this type of music came,' says Mankowitz. 'Mothers and religion have always gone very well together. This suited Cliff too, I think.

'Cliff wasn't our ideal choice for the part because he didn't have the acting experience but he had the right sort of androgynous look. You could start him off quasi-innocent and have his lack of innocence as a singer come through.'

Although he had a clean-living image at the time (noted newspaper journalist Maureen Cleave had called him 'an abstemious paragon'), Cliff was not religious. He had abandoned confirmation classes because, he says, 'I couldn't understand what it was all about'. He didn't doubt the existence of a God and he would pray in times of difficulty but that was the extent of his belief. The crucifix he wore, which fans thought must have religious significance, had belonged to John Foster, who had promised to give it to him at the first sign of success.

His first public connection with a religious organization came when he opened the 59 Club in Hackney Wick and became the club President.

The 59 Club was a new kind of church youth club set up by John Oates, a 27-year-old motorcycling curate, who wanted to create a club which felt more like an espresso bar so that local teenagers could wander in and out without feeling conspicuous.

'I chose Cliff to open the club because I knew he was someone who would attract the young people,' says Oates. 'On the opening night we had 450 people turn up. The following week they all came back and brought their friends. It was chaotic!'

By the autumn of 1959 the effects of stardom were starting to tell on Cliff. The persistent clamour of fans and the lack of privacy brought him a sense of isolation.

'I honestly can't say I enjoy it much,' he grumbled when asked by *Melody Maker* to comment on his status as a 'teenage idol'. He said he worried about the 'innocent faithfulness' of the girls who screamed at him night by night and he couldn't understand why he'd lost all his friends from Cheshunt.

'When I was at school I had lots of pals. Now I've only got one real one from those days,' he said. 'Look, I'm no different. My house is still there and any of my old mates are welcome to come any time and my mother takes care of us all. But it isn't like that any more.

'Suddenly these old friends, my one-time gang, are all peculiar and stiff and strange. And they take the mickey too and try to impersonate me. Mickey-taking in any shape I can't stand—not by anybody or about anybody—but why should they? What bites them?'

The interview displayed what the fan magazines chose to ignore: his tetchiness about being criticized, his doubts about the rewards of stardom and his sense of having lost out on a normal experience of teenage life. It also revealed his competitive attitude towards the charts.

'I've just slipped from top spot in the Hit Parade,' he told the interviewer. 'Craig Douglas has taken over ... However I think I've got something in store for Craig to worry about. It's a new song called "Travellin' Light" that I've just recorded ... Simplicity is everything on this one and it's got a real smooth easy tempo. I think it's an even better song than "Living Doll" and I'm banking heavily on it.'

All Cliff's singles so far had been British-written but 'Travellin''

Light', a lazy country-flavoured number, was the work of Sid Tepper and Roy Bennett, two veteran New York songwriters who had been writing together for over twenty years. By 1959 they had contributed songs to two of Elvis' films, 'Loving You' and 'King Creole', writing them to order from early drafts of the scripts which would be handed out to a pool of songwriters.

'Travellin' Light' had been written in this way for a scene which was subsequently cut from 'King Creole'. It was put out on the market and picked up by Cliff who, until the writing of this book, hadn't realized that it had been written for Elvis.

The sparse, almost acoustic arrangement, with Jet's stalking bass line accentuated with Meehan's tambourine and Hank's whining guitar, acknowledged the country mood of 'Living Doll'. Like 'Living Doll' it reached number one.

To rock 'n' roll die-hards, like Jack Good, this change of pace was the beginning of the end. 'Living Doll', he claimed, was his least favourite song ever. Its lyrics were twee and its tune trite. Cliff had abandoned the true faith of rock 'n' roll.

'There was a period of cooling off between me and Cliff,' admits Good. 'I was moaning about these songs and Cliff abandoning rock 'n' roll. I think I moaned a bit in my *Disc* column. I got no direct feedback but I think he got a bit fed up with me.'

Speculation about rock 'n' roll's death had been rife since the first records were released but 1959 marked the start of a hiatus which would last until the coming of the Beatles. Elvis was in the army, Jerry Lee Lewis had been disgraced over his teenage bride, Little Richard had given up rock 'n' roll to study the Bible, Chuck Berry had been arrested on a sex charge and Buddy Holly was dead.

When Royston Ellis asked Cliff whether rock 'n' roll was dying out he had answered, 'No. It's not dying out at all. Just cleaning up.'

Asked what he thought would take its place he had said, 'I don't know, but rock is leading to a strong beat ballad style of singing,' a trailer perhaps for his second album, *Cliff Sings*, where Norrie Paramor split the repertoire between rock 'n' roll and orchestrated standards such as 'The Touch Of Your Lips' and 'As Time Goes By'.

No one expected to be singing rock 'n' roll into adulthood. In *Expresso Bongo* Bongo is asked by Dixie Collins whether his manager has made plans for his career when he's no longer a teenager. Bongo slowly shakes his head. He can't imagine what it must be like to be twenty.

Recording standard songs with an orchestra was thought to be the obvious way of extending stardom; of proving that you were a mature entertainer.

'He wants to cover everything in show business,' wrote Ellis. 'He would like to tackle every medium there is and make a success of it. This way, and this way only, will he be able to prove that he is a more talented youngster than people care to credit.'

The implication was that talent in rock 'n' roll alone was not real talent. The goal was to become an 'all-round entertainer', and Cliff was well on his way. Ballads suited his vocal style and, unlike a lot of rock 'n' roll singers, he had never abhorred the older songs.

'Although I was in at the beginning of rock 'n' roll I was also in at the end of the era that preceded it,' Cliff says. 'I knew all the songs of people such as Bing Crosby, Frank Sinatra, Teresa Brewer and Rosemary Clooney. When Norrie suggested recording with an orchestra I thought it was a wonderful idea.'

In November he made his debut on 'Sunday Night at the London Palladium', the biggest entertainment show on British television at the time, and Sir Winston Churchill appeared at the première of *Expresso Bongo* (which had been given an 'X' certificate because of its strip club scenes. Today it is rated PG).

Cliff started to dress more conservatively. In October 1959 he was wearing a black leather jacket and white buckskins but by 1960 they were hung up in favour of smart jackets, neckties and suede shoes.

'We used to talk about the teenagers and the mums and dads,' Cliff admits. 'We were very conscious that our careers depended on the mums and dads and that we needed to appeal to them to get going.'

His accent, which in *Serious Charge* sounded like a mid-Atlantic teenage drawl, was becoming more well-rounded. He was losing the Anglo-Indian lilt that he had brought to Britain and, remarkably, he hadn't inherited the North London tones of his schoolfriends.

'His most lasting influence... [has been] his speaking voice,' wrote rock critic Nick Cohn at the end of the sixties. 'Before him, all pop singers sounded what they were, solidly working class. Cliff introduced something new, a bland ramble, completely classless.

'It caught on—David Frost uses it. So do [disc jockey] Simon Dee, Sandie Shaw and Cathy McGowan... It has become the dominant success voice. I'm not suggesting anyone deliberately copied it from Cliff, but he was where it first broke through.'

The Drifters were by now known as the Shadows. They had recorded an instrumental, 'Jet Black', and it was when they tried for a release in America that they discovered the existence of the original Drifters, who threatened them with an injunction over the name. To avoid further problems they called themselves the Four Jets for this release.

It was Jet who came up with the name the Shadows one day while they were drinking at the Six Bells in Ruislip after a ride out on their Lambrettas. He'd thought of the idea because when the spotlight shone on Cliff, as it invariably did, they were performing in the shadows. Also that year a film was released, directed by Jon Cassavettes, called *Shadows*.

On 17 January Cliff and the Shadows topped 'Sunday Night at the London Palladium' and drew a television audience of nineteen million, the most that had ever watched a light entertainment show in Britain. Eddie Cochran, on tour in England at the time, saw the broadcast and thought Cliff was 'quite a good performer but I have seen a lot better in Britain.'

'Living Doll' was Cliff's third American single and had by now become a minor hit, reaching a high point of number thirty in the *Billboard* charts. This was a considerable breakthrough at a time when British artists rarely had trans-Atlantic success. His first two American singles, 'Move It' and 'Livin' Lovin' Doll' had flopped dismally.

Sensing an opportunity of reversing the fortunes of British pop in America, Tito Burns planned to tour Cliff and the Shadows, eventually signing a deal with Irving Feld of the General Artists Corporation, one of America's biggest booking agencies, who specialized in putting together top-rate rock 'n' roll package tours.

His 'Biggest Show of Stars 1957' had featured Fats Domino, Chuck Berry, Frankie Lymon and the Teenagers, the Everly Brothers, Paul Anka, Clyde McPhatter, the Drifters (the American group) and Buddy Holly. It was on his 1959 tour, 'The Winter Dance Party', that Buddy Holly had been killed.

For 'The Biggest Show of Stars 1960' Irving Feld planned to feature ten acts on thirty-three dates that would stretch from Montreal to Dallas and across to New Jersey and Philadelphia. His bill reflected the change that was happening to rock 'n' roll with good looks now taking precedence over great talent.

Before Elvis Presley, American pop had been dominated by Italian Americans—men such as Frank Sinatra, Perry Como, Tony Bennett, Al Martino and Dean Martin. Now that rock 'n' roll was apparently on the ropes it was time for the Italians to return.

Feld's billtopper was Frankie Avalon (age twenty, real name Francis Avallone), who sang anaemic high school rock and had become a star on 'Dick Clark's American Bandstand'. Symbolically, it had been Avalon who replaced Buddy Holly on tour the night after he died.

Supporting Avalon on the 1960 bill were Bobby Rydell (age seventeen, real name Robert Ridarelli) and Freddy Cannon (age nineteen, real name Frederick Picariello), both of whom sang the same bowdlerized rock 'n' roll.

Then there was Johnny and the Hurricanes who'd met at high school in Toledo, Ohio, and had had hits with instrumentals 'Reveille Rock' and 'Crossfire', Clyde McPhatter (who'd led the original Drifters), the Isley Brothers, Sammy Turner, the rhythm and blues group the Clovers, the Crests ('16 Candles') and Linda Laurie.

Cliff's name was added at the foot of the poster (mis-spelled Cliff Richards) as an 'Extra Added Attraction—England's No. 1 Singing Sensation'. No mention was made of the Shadows. Cliff had insisted they should back him despite pressure from the promoter to use the resident tour band.

America was a thrilling place for a group of teenagers to be going to in 1960 when few of their contemporaries in Britain ever left the country. It was the land where the future had already arrived; where there were highways instead of main roads, Cadillacs instead of Morris Minors and Hollywood instead of Borehamwood.

'It was a real eye-opener for us,' says Bruce Welch. 'It seemed so far away from home at the time and it was where rock 'n' roll had come from. Just to be flying on a plane was mind-boggling enough but we were going to be meeting all these American acts and playing in front of crowds of 10,000.'

Sammy Samwell, who had become the Shadows' unofficial manager, remembers the anticipation.

'I was already steeped in American culture because I had two uncles who worked on American air bases,' he says. 'They brought back magazines which had adverts for wonderful wide cars which did about six miles to the gallon and had four happy people driving in them. I had all these wonderful images in my mind as I set off!'

The tour was booked to start in Montreal, Canada, on 22 January and so Cliff and his father, the Shadows, Samwell and Burns flew from London to New York on 18 January and were met at Idlewild Airport (later renamed JFK) by two limousines, one black and one white.

Once in New York the Shadows bought themselves trendy 'pork pie' trilby hats and checked out legendary jazz clubs like Birdland and the Metropole. Cliff appeared on 'The Pat Boone Show', where he sang 'Living Doll' and 'Pretty Blue Eyes' and engaged in some tame scripted banter.

◀ July 1958: first publicity portrait taken at EMI Studios, Abbey Road

August 1958: (from left to right) Terry Smart, Cliff and Ian Samwell playing Butlins as the Drifters ▼

Cliff with 'Oh Boy!' producer
Jack Good in 1958 ▶

◀ Cliff puts Good's
'hypodermic syringe'
move into action

13 September, 1958:
Cliff's debut on
'Oh Boy!' ▶

February 1959: Cliff and Donna at the first 'Oh Boy!' party at Ray Mackender's Chelsea flat ▶

February 1959: (clockwise from centre) Cliff, Donna Webb, Tito Burns, Joe Lee (chauffeur), Hank Marvin, Tony Meehan, Bruce Welch, Jet Harris, Len Saxon (road manager), George Ganjou and Dorothy Webb ▼

May 1959: Cliff modelling
Ronnie Ernstone's sample
'Cliff Richard Shirt' ▼

▲ On the road, 1959: Royston Ellis (second
right) with Cliff, band members and friends

May 1959: The 'Oh Boy!' line-up. Among the
group, Cherry Wainer (front, standing), Dallas
Boys (left), Billy Fury (back, third from right),
Cliff (back, fifth from right) ▼

June 1959: Cliff enters the gate of Elvis Presley's home in Bad Nauheim, Germany (top left), knocks on the door (top right) and returns disappointed (bottom left)

▼ July 1959: filming Expresso Bongo

◀ 1960: Cliff with David Kossoff in 'Stars in Your Eyes'

◀ August 1959: (from left to right) Rodger Webb, Dorothy Webb, Cliff and Ray Mackender

1960: Cliff and Carol Costa (left) at a party during the time of their brief affair▶

▲ February 1960:
Cliff with fans in
America

(above right) On tour
in the US: (from left to
right) Freddy
Cannon, Jet Harris,
Hank Marvin and
Johnny Paris (of
Johnny and the
Hurricanes)

The Shadows—
Britain's first instantly
recognizable rock
group ▼

▲ Cliff with friend and confidante, Cherry Wainer,
at the Lotus House restaurant, Edgware Road

▲ Summer 1961: Cliff with girlfriend Delia Wicks in the garden of 2 Colne Road, Winchmore Hill

▲ June 1961: Filming The Young Ones—(from left to right) Cliff, Carole Gray, Melvyn Hayes, Annette Robertson, Richard O'Sullivan and Teddy Green

All the musicians on the tour met up on 21 January and left New York for Montreal on two Greyhound buses which, with their reclining seats and air conditioning, seemed like luxury to Cliff and the Shadows who'd spent the last year toiling around the B roads of Britain on a Bedford coach.

For the first show Cliff had worked out a set of five songs: '40 Days', 'My Babe', 'A Voice In The Wilderness' (from *Expresso Bongo*), 'Living Doll' and 'Whole Lotta Shakin' Goin' On'. The only change made before the end of the tour was that 'My Babe' was replaced by 'Dynamite'.

The reaction to Cliff's set was beyond all expectations. Every night the show-stopping acts were Cliff and the Shadows, Bobby Rydell and Clyde McPhatter.

'No one could follow after we had finished,' Cliff remembers. 'The crowd were still screaming for more. It was very difficult for the next act to go on. That happened right from the first show.

'I remember there was a big black tour manager and he would get on the coach and say, "Well, I think we should all give a big hand to our friends from England", and they would all applaud us. It was fantastic and I thought we were really going to make it.

'The trouble was that I never saw anyone from my record company [ABC/Paramount] in the whole six weeks. They should have been there. My career in America is littered with lost opportunities.'

From Montreal they drove down to shows in Rochester, New York, and then to Philadelphia before returning to Toronto and Kitchener. Most of the travelling was done at night to avoid traffic and as the winter weather set in and the air conditioning failed everyone would be forced to sleep in their overcoats.

After Canada they wound down through the Midwest to Kentucky, home of the Everly Brothers, and then on to the East Coast. After five dates in North and South Carolina they flew the longest leg of the tour on to Fort Worth, Texas.

'We ran into an electrical storm and everyone was terrified,' remembers Tony Meehan. 'The plane was an old Dakota and the fact that Buddy Holly had died in an air crash on the last tour was still pretty fresh in our minds. I went to sleep though. I was that young and that optimistic.'

In Texas they played Fort Worth, Houston, San Antonio and Dallas before coming to Buddy Holly's home town of Lubbock where they played the Coliseum. Holly's family came to the show and they were moved to tears by the sight of Hank Marvin on stage with his Fender Stratocaster and horn-rimmed spectacles. From the back of the auditorium it looked like a visit from beyond the grave.

The segregation in the Southern states bemused them. They could visit clubs and see black performers such as James Brown and Bo Diddley but they couldn't eat out with black musicians like Clyde McPhatter and Sammy Turner who were on the same tour. They even had to travel on separate buses for a while.

It was after the 19 February show in Wichita, Kansas, that Cliff flew back to London via New York to appear at the *NME* Poll Winners concert at Wembley Pool and then, later the same day, on 'Saturday Night at the London Palladium'.

It had been too expensive to bring the Shadows back as well so Tito Burns advised Cliff to surround himself with the best session musicians available. Cliff ignored this advice and instead hired Brian Parker's new group, the Parker Royal Five.

It was a mistake. Jet-lagged on arrival, he had to rehearse that night until half past four in the morning and didn't sleep until after the Wembley show that afternoon. When they tried to wake him in time for the Palladium he was in such a deep sleep that they had to throw cold water in his face to bring him to.

He sleepwalked his way through the performance and was roundly criticized for being lacklustre. He later apologized to his fans, admitting that 'I was just too tired to give you my best,' and then flew back to Milwaukee with his mother for the last night of the tour.

'I honestly was homesick by then,' he explained later that year, 'and I know it isn't just a place you get homesick for, it's the people.

And of all the people in the world I miss most, Mum tops the list.'

With the tour finally over he headed to New York with his parents for a series of press interviews to promote *Expresso Bongo*, which was opening at the Sutton Theatre in a fortnight.

They even managed a meeting with Colonel Tom Parker, Elvis' illustrious manager, at the Warwick Hotel where he was staying as he awaited Elvis' arrival from Germany. There was talk in the air of Colonel Parker being able to do something for Cliff in Hollywood.

The Colonel made an immediate impression on Cliff and his parents by asking them if they would like to join him for lunch. After they eagerly accepted the great man's offer he reached into an office drawer and pulled out three packets of sandwiches which he then handed around.

On 2 March Cliff flew back to London and was met at the airport by Ray Mackender. The next day, in Frankfurt, Elvis Presley boarded a plane for Fort Dix, New Jersey, where he was demobbed after two years as an army private.

Before he left Germany he had given an interview in which he said that he knew Cliff Richard's work and owned some of his records.

'Sure I'd love to have met him,' said Cliff later that year. 'But I wanted to get home even more. Some day we'll meet and I can think of nothing I'd like more than sharing a bill with him. That would really be something, wouldn't it?'

13

'With Carol it was the first full-blooded romance'

D espite the thousands of miles travelled and the great success of his act, Cliff hadn't made the slightest impression on the American market. You had to do much more than sound like an American to succeed there.

'I'm afraid they had about 4,000 Cliff Richards over there already,' says Tito Burns. 'They just didn't have the appetite for yet another one.'

Sammy Samwell says more or less the same thing. 'The timing was all wrong. He was a little too late and a little too generic. He was somewhere between Elvis Presley and Ricky Nelson and they already had both.'

In Britain he was rapidly becoming the country's highest-paid entertainer, commanding upwards of £1,000 a week for variety shows and £4,000 for a single television appearance. This was in addition to income from record sales, films and the granting of merchandising licenses to companies who were making everything from 2/6d photo books to 5/11d Cliff Richard pillowcases ('You can soon misplace lockets or bracelets, but you will never lose your own pillowcase. Will last for years, and will not fade in the wash').

All of this meant that at nineteen years of age Cliff Richard was rich by the standards of his contemporaries, who would have been lucky to have been going home on a Friday night with ten pounds.

One newspaper calculated that he was earning more than the entire government cabinet put together. True he was paying Burns ten per cent of his income, George Ganjou a further ten per cent and had four musicians each on twenty-five pounds a week, but it still left a sizeable amount.

Yet Cliff was not a conspicuous spender. He was happy to have been able to allow both his parents to relinquish their jobs and regain their dignity after years of hardship, but he was never tempted to live particularly ostentatiously.

His pocket money was rationed to ten pounds a week until September 1960 when it was raised to fifteen pounds. His one luxury was cars. Having had the Sunbeam Alpine for almost twelve months, he traded it in at Lex Garage in Brewer Street, Soho, and bought a red American Thunderbird with a white roof for £4,000.

His parents still didn't own their own home and so in May 1960 he bought them a corner house at 2 Colne Road in Winchmore Hill, North London, for £7,000. It was unexceptional by show business standards—a neat suburban semi with a front gate and slatted garden fence—but it was equipped with what were called 'luxuries' at the time: a telephone, a stereo record player, a 21-inch television set, a radiogram, a leather-topped bar and wall-to-wall carpeting.

For a family that hadn't so long ago been sitting on chairs made out of deal packing cases and squashing four children in one bedroom it was paradise. 'This house and everything in it is all paid for,' he proudly announced to visiting members of the press. 'It will last us a lifetime.'

He tried to live as normal a life as was possible, the only difference being that 2 Colne Road was often besieged by fans and so the front gate had to be padlocked and the garden fence had to be raised two feet to prevent intruders.

Dick Teague's sister Sheila was still close to Cliff's youngest sister Joan, and would spend weekends at Winchmore Hill. She remembers that Cliff's room was in the roof and was reached through a door on the landing which looked as if it was the airing cupboard.

'When you opened the door you went up this beautiful deep blue velvet carpet to Cliff's room,' she says. 'It was like a concealed room and I remember it being all green and yellow with sheepskin rugs.'

To a ten year old like Sheila, who was still living on a council estate in Cheshunt, the house at Winchmore Hill seemed like part of another world.

'We were all very poor and so seeing a taxi arrive for Cliff's mum to take her to the hairdresser was like watching royalty,' she says. 'Cliff wasn't big-headed though. He was very calm, very relaxed and very casual.

'He showed a lot of love to his sisters and he'd often spend time in the garden with his dog getting it to bite on the end of a rag and then swinging it around. He took us all out in his car sometimes but when he tried to park he would get recognized and he found he just couldn't go shopping.'

From the outset Tito Burns' plan had been to loosen the bond between Cliff and the Shadows. He wanted to establish the idea of Cliff Richard—solo artist, so that when the beat boom was over Cliff would be able to turn his hand to almost anything.

'The way I saw his career advancing was to turn him into Cliff Richard rather than "Cliff Richard and the...". The "and the" was alright, providing Cliff was right up front,' says Burns.

'I wanted him to be accepted in his own right even if he didn't sing "Move It" and have three guitarists backing him. When he reached that pinnacle it wouldn't matter whether he had seventy strings or the Shadows because you'd know they had come to see him.'

Says Hank Marvin, 'Tito probably hated the music anyway and he would much rather have seen Cliff with a group of professional musicians. I don't think he understood what we did or what was happening. He gave more than an impression that he was trying to drive a wedge between Cliff and ourselves.'

Cliff was as unhappy as they were. He'd fought hard to get them on the American tour and had persuaded Norrie Paramor to give them a recording deal in their own right. As far as he was concerned, they hung together like a five-piece band for which he was the singer.

The Shadows' contract with Columbia had so far produced three singles, but none of them had made an impact. Then, after a show in Cannock in April 1960, they were played an instrumental which had been written by Jerry Lordan, who was in a band backing the other singers on the tour.

'I'd written this tune called "Apache",' says Lordan. 'It had been recorded by the guitarist Bert Weedon but I hadn't liked the result so I played it on my ukulele to the Shadows who I knew were looking for new material.'

Bruce Welch and Hank both liked it and took it to Norrie Paramor for their next single but Norrie wanted them to do a version of the traditional tune, 'Quartermasters Stores'. A compromise was reached with 'Apache' on one side and 'Quartermasters Stores' on the other.

For British teenagers the Shadows were the first home-grown group where names could be put names to faces and characters to names. The simple Gretch drum kit, the solid-body guitars and the tremolo arms completed the image of the archetypal rock 'n' roll outfit.

When the Beatles were still wearing leather jackets and jeans on stage Brian Epstein took them to the Liverpool Empire to see a Cliff and the Shadows concert, pointing out their mohair suits, their choreographed footsteps and the way they bowed at the close of the show. Epstein told them that this was how big-time groups dressed and moved and the Beatles took his advice right down to the last bow of the head.

To maintain their separateness from Tito Burns, who never had any say in their career, the Shadows hired a young Irishman to be their tour manager. His name was Mike Conlin, and they had met him at the 2 I's. Within six months he found himself doing the same for Cliff and moved in to 2 Colne Road so that he could be on hand twenty-four hours a day.

When on tour Cliff would be eminently sociable during the daytime, eating with the group, going to the cinema and participating in crazes such as archery, pistol shooting and home movies.

'You have to remember that he was the idol of his day,' says Conlin. 'There had never been an English pop star of this magnitude and everwhere he went he was harassed. But when he wasn't constrained by the eyes of the world being on him he was one of the lads.

'If we went to a gig I would often drive him in my car and we would sing all the way down. It wasn't until we got within ten miles of where we were going that we'd have to pull our horns in and work out how to get in the theatre without being torn apart.'

It was at night that they tended to live separate lives. The Shadows' idea of a fun time was to surround themselves with drink and girls and to party into the night but Cliff—who didn't smoke or drink— would only make token appearances at these affairs before disappearing back to his room.

'The Shadows thought they had the world on a string and they really did give it some,' remembers Ronnie Ernstone who would often spend his weekends on the tours. 'Cliff was a bit removed. If he came to a party he wouldn't partake.

'He had great power at the time but he chose not to use it. In fact, rather than choosing not to use it I think he just didn't want the things that he could get with it.'

Sometimes he would take long drives in the night to clear his mind. He later told Royston Ellis, 'I just drive because it's rather a strain to be with people all the time. Even my mother doesn't know this. I'll just drive around for about an hour and a half and then I'll come back and I'll feel great. I go straight to sleep and wake up feeling great in the morning.'

It was around this time that he found himself being drawn into a relationship with Jet's wife, Carol, who was now the mother of baby Ricky B. Harris. She told Jet that their son was being named after Ricky Nelson but to her it was an abbreviation of Richard, as in Cliff, the man she still desperately wanted to have.

Although they had been married for less than a year, Jet and Carol were at break-up point. The explosive arguments which had seemed engagingly bohemian when they were young lovers were now becoming bitter and increasingly violent as Jet's drinking habit got worse.

One night Tony Meehan saw Jet attack Carol after returning drunk from a concert. He dragged her to the floor and knelt on her arms while punching her. Meehan had to dive in and knock Jet out by smashing his head against the wall before he could pull him away.

'It was awful stuff,' Meehan remembers. 'He was out for two or three minutes, enough time to stop him doing awful damage. That's the sort of relationship they had. It wasn't a happy marriage. They weren't suited.'

The more Jet deserted and abused Carol, the more Cliff found his sympathy aroused and he began to comfort and support her. When she was pregnant he'd bought oranges for her to satisfy a craving and when Ricky was born he was the first to visit Carol in hospital, bearing a giant bunch of flowers.

'It bothered me that Jet and Carol weren't very happy together,' says Cliff, 'and that played a part in drawing me back to her again. I never saw Jet hit her but he was obviously a bit of a rough dog. Some people can drink really well but he can't. His problems domestically and artistically were all to do with drink. His problems with Carol were due to the fact that he was drunk most of the time.'

In June Cliff began the most extended engagement of his career: a six-month stint at the London Palladium. This was Tito Burns' biggest coup so far and the show business magazines were buzzing with the story of the office clerk who was now topping the bill at the London Palladium and raking in an estimated £24,000.

Burns had managed it by striking deals with agent Leslie Grade who had exclusive booking rights for this period at the Palladium and who desperately wanted to be involved in Cliff's career. Knowing the extent of his enthusiasm, Burns used Cliff as a bargaining tool to get other artists of his on at theatres that Grade controlled.

'I wanted to establish Cliff not just as a rock 'n' roller with a few hits but as a personality, somebody who would mean something in years to come,' says Burns.

'I left the rock 'n' roll side to Cliff while I devoted my energies to getting the right things that would further him as a stayer—like the various television shows, like the Palladium over which I battled for a month.'

Leslie Grade was one of three brothers called Winogradsky who had emigrated to London's East End from Russia. Lew and Leslie Winogradsky changed their surname to Grade, Leslie becoming a top show business agent while Lew became managing director of ATV. Linking up with the Grade agency was a significant move for Cliff, for between them the Grades had enormous power to establish an act through film, television and theatre circuits.

The third brother, Bernard, changed his surname to Delfont and became a theatre impresario. 'Stars In Your Eyes', as the Palladium show was titled, was a variety performance which attempted to feature something for everyone. There was up-and-coming comedian Des O'Connor, television actor David Kossoff, pianist Russ Conway, Canadian singer Edmund Hockridge, a team of Palladium dancers, fall-about comedian Billy Dainty, and Joan Regan, a top recording star in the early fifties.

Cliff and the Shadows closed the show with a five-song set, which was interrupted every night by David Kossoff in character as the cockney Alf Larkin from the popular television series 'The Larkins', who would scream abuse from the royal box before making his way on stage and doing a soft-shoe routine with Cliff.

'Almost nothing I said could be heard because of the screaming,' says Kossoff. 'This was to me an entirely new and frightening experience in that I was working with someone who, every time he moved his body, had the audience screaming in orgasmic delight.'

Seven weeks into the 26-week run the Shadows' 'Apache' was released and went into the top twenty. The group pushed to include it in the show but Tito Burns refused them. From his point of view it would detract from Cliff.

The Shadows were understandably resentful. It seemed to them petty to exclude one of the summer's biggest hits from a show where they were part of the headline entertainment. On 20 August 'Apache' actually knocked Cliff off the top of the hit parade when it replaced 'Please Don't Tease'.

Hank and Bruce Welch were now writing together for Cliff. The album *Me And My Shadows* was released in October, and was a prototypical beat record with over half the songs written by them or Jet, Samwell and their friend Pete Chester. It was the first time a British group had recorded aso much self-written material and was an early indication of the changes that would occur in the record industry after the Beatles. Like *Cliff Sings*, it went to number two in the LP charts.

'I'm still really proud of that album,' says Cliff. 'A lot of people such as Eric Clapton and the guys in Fleetwood Mac were inspired by it because of Hank's guitar work. I think we invented our own English rock 'n' roll. It wasn't American, but neither was "Rock With The Caveman".'

Committed to the Palladium for six days a week, there were still concerts out of London on Sundays. On one of these dates Jet had a brief fling with a hairdresser and word got back to Carol who threatened to leave him.

When Jet returned a fight broke out which left Carol with a split lip. She called Cliff who came down to their Brixton flat and took her and Ricky to the safety of her parents' home in Hounslow. That night he consoled Carol and promised to stay in touch.

Over the next few weeks they met whenever they could and Cliff began to get more openly affectionate, telling her that he loved her.

The relationship had to be clandestine, not just because of Jet, but because of his career. They would meet up at the flats of trusted friends, in a central London car park close by the Palladium or they would drive out into the Essex countryside, always with Mike Conlin on hand as a lookout man.

Cliff had been drawn into the affair because he was flattered by the attention and he had responded to her hurt. If he had not been enticed the relationship would almost certainly have remained affectionate but unconsummated. But Carol was sexually experienced and very determined.

'She made a beeline for him in a very subtle way which, when you're young, you sometimes mistake for mutual attraction,' says Tony Meehan. 'You don't realize you are being pursued. She had all the allure of a woman and all the forcefulness of a man and she totally dominated him.'

After a Sunday night concert in Blackpool, Carol saw her opportunity to be alone with Cliff. They were travelling back on an overnight train and Meehan was booked to share a sleeper with Cliff but, just after boarding, Carol approached him to do a swap. During the night she tried to seduce Cliff but he seemed afraid of going all the way. He later explained to her that he was a virgin.

Soon after, they did make love twice at the Ealing home of Vicky Marshall, a dancer who had appeared with Cliff in *Expresso Bongo*. Cliff told his parents that he needed to stay in London overnight for business and instead slept with Carol in an attic room.

'It was one of those things,' he admits. 'I'm not going to deny it. It was part of my life and I look back on it with not much pride and a different set of values.'

Almost immediately he tried to end the affair but found he didn't have the courage. He poured his heart out to Cherry Wainer, telling her that he wanted to recapture the feeling that he had for Carol before she had met Jet but that now it seemed lost.

'Cliff was a very loyal person,' says Cherry. 'I think he felt sorry for Carol but he knew that feeling sorry doesn't make it. I think this was what he had come to realize. You couldn't go back into a relationship just because you felt sorry for somebody.'

The end was triggered by an intimate letter sent by Carol to Cliff. Cliff's mother opened it thinking it was fan mail.

'We got back from the Palladium late one night and Cliff's parents were waiting up for him,' remembers Mike Conlin. 'His mother had the letter in her hand. They asked me to go up to bed and then they talked to Cliff until the small hours.

'I never saw the letter but it more or less gave the game away. It was a hell of a lot more personal than a fan letter should have been and his mother and father talked to him all night about the evils of sin and I think that was what broke it off.'

His sister Jacqui was only twelve at the time but she can recall the night.

'I remember Cliff coming home and being yanked off to a room and I closed my bedroom door,' she says. 'I knew they were having a serious talk and I knew the subject was Carol. I don't know what was said but my dad would have been seeing it from a spiritual point of view.

'He wouldn't have been so concerned about the effect on Cliff's career or what the neighbours might think but the fact that what he'd done went against God's commandments. That's what would have been uppermost in his mind.

'I remember my mother telling me very bluntly that the Christian way was not to have sex before marriage. She said that sex was something given to married couples. That's all she said! I can remember being a bit taken aback because they didn't normally discuss things like that openly.'

Cliff couldn't bear to offend his mother and matters were made worse by the fact that his father had recently been taken ill. While playing a game of badminton at the club he had suddenly collapsed. The doctor diagnosed thrombosis. Cliff was worried that the news about Carol might kill him.

In desperation he asked Tony Meehan to make the call that would end the affair.

'He couldn't handle it so he asked me to do it and I said, yes, because someone had to do it,' says Meehan. 'The relationship was destroying him and it was likely to destroy the group. It was getting too close.

'The way I looked at it was that there was no future in it because he really wasn't prepared. I asked him whether he would be willing to give up his career for this because that's what it amounted to in those days. That she was a married woman was quite a scandal in itself. I said that he would have to jack it all in for her and go away somewhere because the fans wouldn't put up with it.

'When I called up she was quite furious. Understandably so. I think he may have said a few words to her but he was definitely crying. It was a very romantic, child-like affair and it had been making a lot of demands on him.'

The episode is surprising not because a pop star had an affair with a married woman, but because it was so out of character for Cliff, who seemed so uninterested in sex and had gone into print saying that girls who 'throw themselves at men . . . are making themselves cheap'.

'I suppose in my naïvety I thought no one would either know about it or believe it,' says Cliff. 'It didn't seem to matter at the time. It went against my principles but when you are experiencing these things your principles become unimportant.

'Looking back I can see that they weren't important to me because God wasn't important in my life. He was there, but what part did he really have to play? My parents instilled values into me but possibly if I hadn't have become a Christian they wouldn't have come into play any more.

'When you live a life outside of God you think, well, even if there is a God he's there and I'm here. So what if I steal or commit adultery? I guess that was what was in my mind because I didn't really feel a great deal of guilt. I feel more guilt now over it.

'With Carol it was like the first full-blooded romance, I suppose. It was a love affair. It was one of those things people go through.'

Carol seemed an unlikely girl to have broken down his fabled resistance. She was nothing like the 'slightly shy', demure, plain-looking girl who knew 'when it was time to say goodnight' that Cliff had always claimed to be his ideal.

She harked back to the large-bosomed, pouting-lipped fantasy of Brigitte Bardot but, more significantly, she happened to be around at a time when all the Shadows had married and he was beginning to feel lonely.

'Carol obviously got into the inner circle once she'd met Jet,' he says, 'and the next thing I realized was that she was there travelling around on tour. At the Palladium everyone would be there, Carol included, and we became a social unit. Brief encounter though it was, it was a growing-up experience for me.'

It didn't bring him the consolation he needed. Some of his friends felt that it pushed him further away from a fulfilling relationship.

'If you want to be blunt about it Carol had sex with Cliff rather than the other way round,' says Tony Meehan. 'She was tough and determined and Cliff had always been timid with women.

'I think he had a very romantic notion of romance and sex. It was like a schoolboy view. As soon as he was confronted with the reality of it, the forbidding was too strong. So, he was never able to make the jump from schoolboy to man.'

He continued to like female company but he would never again have sex even though, for the next four years at least, there was no religious reason to remain celibate. 'I never got round to it,' he explains. 'There was still a fairly old-fashioned bit left in me I suppose.'

To a lot of observers in show business such a muted interest in sex was interpreted as homosexuality.

'There was much more speculation in those days because it was illegal,' says Mike Conlin. 'If someone was in the theatre and not going out with a girl it was assumed that they were gay.

'Cliff was a target for homosexuals because he was a sex symbol and he didn't have a girlfriend. The fact is that at the time Cliff was terrified of homosexuals. He never wanted to be left alone with them.'

The only time an aggressive homosexual did get close to Cliff was after a concert in Portsmouth when a man managed to get into his hotel room late at night.

'I can remember being nervous because the guy wouldn't leave,' says Cliff. 'I kept saying, "Look, this is my private time and this is my room," but he just kept advancing.

'Mike Conlin always slept in an adjoining room and I called out for him and he came and got rid of the guy.'

'Funnily enough,' says Conlin, 'at the same time that all these rumours were going around I knew that Cliff was having this affair with Carol that no one else knew about.

'Also, I spent twenty-four hours a day for months on end with him, travelling the world and sharing hotel bedrooms, and there was never a sniff of anything that you could even begin to raise an eyebrow at.

'I think that if he got burned over the affair with Carol it may have left a scar and made him loathe to go into anything else.'

In November 1960 he was interviewed by Steve Race and Royston Ellis for the BBC Radio programme 'Frankly Speaking'. He emerged as an assured, if slightly naïve, young man who was much more in control of his career than his interviewers appeared to have given him credit for.

His image was already set. He spoke of his respect for his parents, his lack of interest in party politics and his belief that he needed to be single for the sake of his career.

'Because I am a male singer,' he confessed, 'my fans like to think that perhaps they have the chance of dating me. I have to stay this way as long as I possibly can. It's not always a good thing, because people then say, "Well, he's not really relying on his singing, he's relying on the fact that girls like him."'

Royston Ellis asked whether he'd ever felt like exploiting his position to go out with as many girls as he could.

'No, I haven't,' said Cliff. 'In fact I think I've only ever dated one fan. But I found the reaction from fans wasn't too good so I just gave up on it altogether.'

Steve Race then leapt in. 'Can I speak here as the elderly parent type?' he said. 'In this teenage world you have this image that regardless of the opposition you will marry the girl you love. "They try to tell us that we're too young, but we're not" and so on. Now you're saying that "love is all" but my teenage audience want me unmarried so I won't marry. Isn't that a betrayal of your attitude?'

'Oh sure, I'll marry her eventually,' Cliff answered. 'But I shan't make it public that I'm going out with a girl. It's a sly way of doing it but I haven't met the girl I love yet anyhow. I don't think I will because at the moment I've dated, perhaps four or five girls and none of them more than two or three times each.'

It was a fair point. There was an irony in the fact that the great icon of teenage romance had to deprive himself of romance to keep his position. But that's the way things were and Cliff would admit to no regrets.

'As far as I'm concerned, it [my career] may die out next week,' he said. 'Well, I've done everything I could possibly want to do and possibly everything anybody could want to do. I've got a gold disc, I've been to America, I've filmed, I've made records. So if it all ended for me, the one thing I could say is that I've lived a fuller life than most people will ever do.'

14

'He's the person to make a film with'

T
wo days after Christmas 1960, Cliff's father's health took a turn for the worse and he was rushed into hospital where he stayed until 28 January. Over the autumn months he had got weaker. He was having difficulty in breathing and spent most of the days lying on a settee. During this time his relationship with Cliff slowly changed.

'Dad became helpless and I had to do everything,' says Cliff. 'I hadn't done anything before because he wouldn't let me but suddenly I had become the head of the house. Not only was I the breadwinner but I had to change the plugs.'

No one who saw Cliff and his father together ever thought there was the normal bond of familial affection. Most would say that there was no real love. Some go as far as to say that they believed Cliff resented his father. As one friend put it, 'Cliff always showed respect to his father but I don't think he ever really had respect for him.'

Cliff admits that he was always frightened of his father but there was never any discussion of what might have gone wrong between them, even when his father was dying. 'We just didn't talk like that,' he says.

Because Cliff was still under the legal age of consent, all contracts, including those with EMI and his management, had to be approved and signed by his father, Rodger, who feared that his son could be exploited by those only interested in short-term gain. This fatherly concern naturally annoyed those who wanted a free hand in shaping Cliff's career.

Tito Burns gave him an office desk and a handsome salary of £100 a week. 'He felt that he had become beholden to his son,' says Cliff's aunt, Olive Queenie, 'and that was a terrible thing for him to feel. Instead of him supporting the family, his son was supporting the family. When Cliff gave him the job it made him feel he was doing something.'

Burns had to tolerate the arrangement because it had been he who had originally charmed Cliff's parents into giving him their boy, but privately he considered Rodger Webb the biggest drawback in Cliff's career and he resented his attempts to offer business advice.

'He was a very dogmatic man,' he says. 'He had his ideas but I thought they were all wrong. We ended up having arguments because he was quite ill and getting very edgy. He wanted my management contract with Cliff ended although he gave no specific reasons and, under the terms of the contract, there should have been.'

Burns suspected that the real reason was that agent Leslie Grade wanted more control over Cliff's career. Grade had just bought the option for his next film from Mickey Delamar for £7,500, and was courting Cliff's parents.

'I was involved in a dispute with Leslie Grade over what Cliff should be paid for the film,' says Burns, 'when in walks Cliff's father smoking a big cigar. I knew then that the only person who could have given him that was Grade.

'I think he was giving the old man money to make my severance pay. When it came within £1,000 of what I would have got if I had seen the three-year contract out, I said OK.'

When Burns' departure was announced in the press in February 1961 it was said to be 'amicable' and Rodger Webb claimed he was now 'looking after' his son. Neither of these statements was true.

Burns was furious to have been rowed out in such dubious circumstances and although Cliff's father may have momentarily held the reins that was only because he knew someone even more proficient was coming in to take over.

Peter Gormley was a 41-year-old Australian who had served in the war and then taken on various media jobs which had prepared him for his real role in life, that of being a personal manager to show business stars.

He had been a journalist, a literary agent, a film director's assistant, the manager of a circuit of cinemas and, most recently, the manager of an Australian singer called Frank Ifield. It meant he not only knew about publicity and journalism but about making and screening films. Most importantly, he knew how to get bottoms on seats.

He'd arrived in Britain in 1959 to prepare the way for Frank Ifield. Frank was a country-style singer with a trademark yodel and Gormley had a recording contract with Columbia waiting for him in England by early 1960.

Three top fifty hits followed that year and in the summer Norrie Paramor approached Gormley to look after the Shadows now that they were a pop act in their own right. He listened to 'Apache' and saw them in 'Stars In Your Eyes' at the Palladium before he agreed to become their manager.

Peter Gormley was as unlike Tito Burns as a manager could possibly be. Where Burns oozed showbiz patter and was still appearing on television as a performer while managing Cliff, Gormley was soft spoken, modest and eager to stay out of the limelight.

The Shadows were impressed with his quiet but thorough ways and it was natural that when Burns was dismissed by Rodger, Gormley would start to manage Cliff as well.

'The request came from Rodger and Cliff's lawyer,' says Gormley. 'I was already managing the Shadows so first of all I had to satisfy myself that it was all clean and clear between Cliff and the Shadows and then I had to meet with Rodger to make sure there was no conflict going on, no resentments or undertones.'

Most unusually for a show business manager, Peter Gormley didn't draw up a contract, preferring to do business on trust, and refusing to take anything for the first year because it wasn't work that he had negotiated.

Two months after Gormley had taken control, Rodger had a sudden relapse and was rushed into an intensive care unit at Highlands Hospital, Enfield, where he was immediately put into an oxygen tent.

'I don't know whether he knew he was dying but he was such a stubborn man,' says Cliff. 'They actually caught him once undoing the oxygen tent from the inside so that he could have a smoke. He managed to hide a safety pin so that he could pull the zip up from the inside. He was a dominant character right to the end.'

On 15 May, at the age of fifty-six, he died. It was a shock to Cliff because he was just beginning to get close to him and felt that if he'd had the right treatment earlier he could have lived longer.

'At the funeral I can remember not being able to control my tears and it didn't bother me,' says Cliff. 'It was one of the first times I had ever cried publicly.'

By now he was in rehearsals for the first film set up by the Grade Organization's film department after the Delamar buy-out. For months rumours had been circulating. It was suggested that Cliff would star in *Hide My Eyes*, a murder thriller written by Margery Allingham. Several actresses were mentioned as being under consideration as his co-star, Carol Lynley, Heidi Bruhl, Helen Shapiro and Diana Dors among them.

Then came the announcement that Cliff's debut as a leading man was to be in an original musical produced by Kenneth Harper. None of the stars whose names had been bandied about were mentioned.

Kenneth Harper was a tall, well-spoken man in his forties who had an apartment in Mayfair and offices in a Regency terrace off St Martin's Lane.

Since coming to London after the war he had worked for a theatrical agency and, for the past six years, as an independent film producer on films such as *For Better, For Worse* with Dirk Bogarde, *Yield To The Night* with Diana Dors and Sean Connery's debut film *Action Of The Tiger*.

Now, working from within the Grade Organization, Kenneth Harper was focusing his attention on Cliff Richard.

'I found that Cliff was filling cinemas on a Sunday when films were emptying them,' says Harper. 'I went to see him and he was knocking the audience out. I thought, if he can knock an audience out on a Sunday night in a cinema that is absolutely full, then he's the person to make a film with. We hadn't made proper musicals in the UK before and no one believed we could.'

Kenneth Harper and Leslie Grade took the idea of a Cliff Richard musical to Jimmy Wallis, Head of Production at ABC (Associated British Picture Corporation), who asked them to come up with a figure. Harper asked for £110,000 and got it. When Leslie Grade later asked him how he knew it would cost £110,000 he said, 'I haven't a clue. It'll probably cost more but let's just go for a nice round figure.' It was eventually to cost half as much again.

With the money in hand Harper set about gathering a creative team. To write the screenplay and the production numbers he called on lyricist Peter Myers and composer Ron Cass who had worked together on a number of popular West End revues including *Intimacy At Eight* (1952), *For Amusement Only* (1956) and *For Adults Only* (1958).

To direct it he chose Sid Furie, a 28-year-old Canadian who had made the well-received *A Dangerous Age* when he was only twenty-four and *A Cool Sound From Hell* before coming to Britain in 1959 to make *The Snake Woman, Doctor Blood's Coffin* and *During One Night*.

The initial problem was finding a story to turn into a musical. The most obvious device was to do *The Cliff Richard Story* in the way that Tommy Steele had done *The Tommy Steele Story* but Harper had found Cliff's 1960 autobiography *It's Great To Be Young* so devoid of drama that he'd abandoned reading it after ten pages. He then gave to it to songwriter Herbie Kretzmer who had scolded him by saying, 'I don't know how you could conceivably make a film with any attraction at all when the only thing that has ever happened to this boy was when a microphone broke down at the Elephant and Castle when he was eighteen!'

The idea that eventually became *The Young Ones* emerged from an evening session at Kenneth Harper's flat when Sid Furie, Peter Myers and Ron Cass met together to toss ideas around. None of them wanted to make a rock 'n' roll movie but they all had affection for the old MGM musicals.

They talked about *Babes in Arms*, the Rodgers and Hart musical that starred Mickey Rooney and Judy Garland as the teenage children of retired vaudevillians who put on a show to raise money. The idea developed of a group of young people getting together to save their youth club from being torn down by a rich property developer—youth clubs and property developers were of particular interest in 1961.

'We watched every old MGM film that Mickey Rooney ever made,' says Harper. 'I didn't see anything wrong in pinching from things that have already been a huge success. Most people had forgotten them anyway. There was nothing enormously original about the plot we used but I don't believe there is anything wrong with making something which is pure entertainment. We didn't want to send a message.'

Because Cliff was such an inexperienced film actor the plan was to conceal his inadequacies by surrounding him with talented actors and dancers. The property developer, Hamilton Black, was to be played by Robert Morley, Richard O'Sullivan, Teddy Green and Melvyn Hayes were to play the key members of the youth club gang and Cliff was to be Hamilton Black's son Nicky. The choreography would be by Herb Ross who had been working on Broadway.

Casting a female lead was difficult. If she was too beautiful the fans would resent her. If she was too ugly she would be unbelievable as

Cliff's love interest. While Kenneth Harper was in New York he had been taken by Herb Ross to see a show featuring a talented Jewish girl he thought would be right for the part. Harper wasn't as convinced and didn't invite her to an audition. Her name was Barbra Streisand.

The girl who eventually got the role was Carole Gray, a young dancer from Rhodesia who had come to London and had appeared in West End stage versions of *The Boyfriend* and *West Side Story*. She had fleshy lips, a long nose and narrow eyes and was almost totally unknown. After the attention surrounding the film had subsided she would return to her anonymity. She was the perfect girl for Cliff.

Much to the annoyance of Peter Myers and Ron Cass, who were writing the soundtrack, it was decided to import half a dozen pop songs to hook the teenage audience.

'Basically we weren't given a chance to write any of the alleged pop numbers,' says Ron Cass. 'We were just the work horses who did the vital and more difficult work.'

For the songs that would hopefully be hits, Norrie Paramor, musical director for the film, turned to Sid Tepper and Roy Bennett, the writers of 'Travellin' Light'. He sent music publisher Cyril Simons to New York with a script and a commission to write three numbers.

'I arrived in New York in the morning, left the scripts with Tepper and Bennett and told them I wanted a song called "The Young Ones",' says Simons. 'I then went on to LA and when I returned forty-eight hours later they had produced three songs, one of which was "The Young Ones", one was "Outsider" and the other was "When The Girl In Your Arms Is The Girl In Your Heart", which they had already written but which no one had recorded.

'I flew back to London that day and played them to Norrie and he loved them and Cliff had two number ones from them. They recorded "Outsider" but eventually decided not to use it because nobody was one hundred per cent sold on it.' (It was used on the album *21 Today*, along with another Tepper-Burnett song, 'Catch Me'.)

Most of the filming took place at the Elstree Studios during June and July 1961 except for the vaudeville finale which took place at the Finsbury Park Empire.

Although 'Stars In Your Eyes' at the Palladium had been blighted in Cliff's memory by the clandestine affair with Carol, it had also introduced him to the next girl in his life.

She was an attractive 22-year-old blonde called Delia Wicks, one of the dancers in the show, who had been selected from the line-up to play a special scene with Cliff where he sang a medley of songs about the moon and then kissed her. The girls in the audience would all shriek at this point and Delia was paid an extra four pounds a week for her hard work.

She had come to London from Leeds at the age of fifteen to learn dancing at the John Tiller School and had been a Tiller Girl for five years before joining Billy Petch's dancers at the Palladium.

They hadn't dated during the Palladium run and then, early in 1961, while making a promotional appearance at the Queen's Hotel in Leeds, he phoned her at her mother's and came to the family home in Dewsbury Road for tea. It was the start of a brief romance which no one but their families, Mike Conlin and Delia's friend Eve Sewell ever knew about.

'Our romance was very secret,' says Delia. 'He's never mentioned it before and so, out of respect for Cliff, I've never mentioned it either. It was a wonderful time in my life because, as you can imagine, I was absolutely overwhelmed by him.'

His arrival in Leeds was a bolt out of the blue for Delia who had assumed she would never see him again after the Palladium. 'He told me that he'd missed me,' she says. 'Then he started to call me up, often very late at night, while he was touring.'

Mike Conlin's memory is that during these early months 'he pursued her like a bat out of hell', driving back to her basement flat in Stockwell after one-night stands in the North of England and grabbing every available opportunity to be at her side.

'Once he drove all the way down from Newcastle after a show to see me and I remember he hadn't shaved and he was wearing a long leather coat,' says Delia. 'He parked his car outside and felt he couldn't stay too long because everyone would see his Thunderbird.

'Another day he came running to my flat, saying "I'm so lonely, Delia. I've got to see you." He fell though the door and gave me a big kiss and I was just standing there dripping wet because I'd been washing my feet when the doorbell rang.

'We used to go out for drives in the country and I would visit him at his home. On Sundays he'd sometimes hire the whole swimming pool at Dolphin Square [London's largest complex of serviced apartments] and Mike Conlin, Cliff's mum and his sisters would come.'

It was a busy year for Cliff. A typical week would consist of several one-night stands, a couple of press interviews, a late-night recording session at Abbey Road, a promotional appearance and a radio show like 'Saturday Club' or 'Parade Of The Pops'. Then there was the rehearsing and filming of *The Young Ones*.

In March he made his first tour of South Africa and encountered some of the most frenzied crowd scenes of his career. There were 3,000 fans at Salisbury airport when he flew in, and in Johannesburg a few days later 10,000 fans converged on the Carlton Hotel, where he was staying, bringing the city centre to a standstill. The police had to ask him to make an announcement from his balcony to pacify the crowds.

In Durban the local Indian population tried to claim him as one of their own, lining the route from the airport to the city and cheering him on. The Shadows noticed that he was disturbed by this response because it awakened the memories of the abuse he'd suffered over his racial identity when he first came to England.

Because of apartheid laws preventing mixed-race audiences Cliff agreed to do two shows—one in Harare and one in Cape Town—for an Africans-only audience, the profits being given to the Salisbury Society for Handicapped Africans.

Once back home his secret relationship with Delia continued. She had to promise not to mention it to anyone and when they went out they were not to be seen holding hands or kissing. At clubs and cinemas Delia had to make a separate entrance so that no one would connect them. In the street he would mask his face behind a handkerchief.

'I was prepared for the fact that these relationships would be difficult,' says Cliff. 'It was because of the kind of press I might get and what that might do. No one really knew whether it would damage your career, but I wasn't prepared to find out.

'It was hard to sustain anything that was going to have any meaning because we didn't see each other very often. I saw more of Delia during the Palladium run than I did when we later went out with each other.'

The impression Delia got was of a very harassed young man, denied a normal life, who just longed for some space in which to be himself.

'He hardly had any time to relax,' she says. 'He was always being pressured into doing things. He used to work so hard that sometimes when he came to see me he would just fall asleep in my arms.

'We were usually just so overwhelmed to see each other. You've no idea. It was such a relief for him. Everybody was always watching him and yet when he came to see me this was his big secret.'

He never mentioned his affair with Carol Costa to Delia and didn't seem about to repeat the experience. 'We kissed and cuddled but sleeping together was a bit taboo in those days,' she says. 'People didn't live together or anything like that.'

When his father died he seemed to change. Delia remembers him suddenly asking her out of the blue whether she was a Christian.

'He must have been thinking about it for a long time but it just came out like that,' she says. 'I don't think he would have carried on going out with me if I had said no.'

He also started to draw closer to his mother. Often when he came to Delia's flat he would call her to tell her where he was and he'd refuse to make decisions until she had been consulted.

'I used to ask him why he always had to ask his mother,' says Delia. 'He used to say he was very concerned about her. I suppose he felt he was looking after his family.'

One night, when Delia went to Winchmore Hill before going out with Cliff to see the American singer Peggy Lee at the Pigalle nightclub, Cliff's mother drew her aside as she was getting herself ready in one of the bedrooms.

'I can visualize it now,' says Delia. 'I was wearing a white strapless dress. She had said something before when we were downstairs but now she was saying it again. She was telling me not to get too fond of Cliff because his career was going ahead. I just shrugged it òff at the time. I thought Cliff could make his own mind up.'

In August he toured Scandinavia with the Shadows and sent Delia a series of postcards which indicated that all was still well. Some were written as soon as he settled in a new hotel and all of them started 'Hi Sweetie' and were signed 'Love, Cliff'. Then, on his twenty-first birthday, he left for his first tour of Australia, playing in Singapore and Kuala Lumpur on the way. After three sell-out concerts in Sydney he travelled to Melbourne where he sat in his hotel room and wrote a letter to Delia.

'Dear Delia

'I know I haven't written for a long time, but I've been confused in my mind about you and about myself.

'I have had to make, probably, one of the biggest decisions I'm ever going to make and I'm praying that I won't hurt you too much.

'Delia, I want you to try and understand the position I'm in. Being a singer I'm going to have to give up many things in life.

'But being a pop singer I have to give up one very priceless thing—the right to have any lasting relationship with any special girl.

'Delia, you must find someone who is free to love you as you deserve to be loved, and is able to marry you.

'I couldn't give up my career. Besides the fact that my mother and sisters, since my father's death, rely on me completely, I have show biz in my blood now and I would be lost without it.

'"D" all I can say now is, goodbye and don't think too badly of me. Love, Cliff.'

The letter arrived at the basement flat of 41 West Cromwell Road on the morning of 26 October.

'I remember that day so well,' says Delia. 'My whole world changed. I was heartbroken. I thought, gosh, I'll never see him again. I remember having to be at the Motor Show in Earls Court and I walked around not really seeing anything. I was absolutely dumbstruck about it because I knew he was terribly fond of me at the time.

'I never contacted him after that because I thought there was no point. I felt, "That's it". I went into mourning for about two weeks and didn't speak to anyone. I wanted to tell the whole world but I realized that I couldn't because our romance had still to be kept a secret.

'He had obviously wanted to get involved with me but then he got frightened and that was it. It was all so confusing. I've never got to the bottom of it.'

'I was a coward there,' admits Cliff. 'I didn't want to face her and tell her and I had been away a long time anyway and I thought that if I saw her again I could confirm it but I'd rather get it off my chest. I thought it was unfair, once I'd decided that it wasn't for me, to leave someone at home thinking that when I came back it was all going to be hunky dory.'

A brief study of postmarks and diary dates reveals that another reason for breaking off with Delia must have been the fact that he had met someone new.

At the end of August he had done his first season at Blackpool, a six-week run at the Opera House, and he had been enamoured by a nineteen-year-old dancer called Jackie Irving who appeared earlier in the show. Cliff would go out and watch her each night and remembers thinking to himself, 'Gosh. She's beautiful.'

It was an opinion shared by the rest of the Shadows. Jet Harris fancied her madly and Tony Meehan felt that she was one of the most beautiful women he had ever seen. 'After Jackie Irving was made,' he says, 'they threw away the mould.'

'Cliff was a bit timid and he asked me if I'd do him a favour,' remembers Jet. 'He asked me to introduce her to him. I thought, dammit! I want to introduce myself to her! So I got hold of her, took her to his dressing room, and I said, "Cliff, this is Jackie—Jackie, this is Cliff." And then I disappeared.'

Jackie was a local Blackpool girl whose mother ran a boarding house. She had large eyes, high cheek bones, long hair and a great sense of fun.

'We started going to all the after-show parties together and I found myself more attracted to her than anyone else and so I spent more time with her,' says Cliff.

'We went out dancing, we ate out and, of course, I went back and met her mum. It doesn't take that long to realize that something like that is happening.'

She soon moved down to London, taking a flat at 102 Hatherley Court in Hatherley Grove, Queensway, and Cliff and Jackie were seen as an inseparable couple. Everyone seemed to think they were perfect together and for the first time friends and family started whispering about marriage.

15

'My career had reached a plateau'

The Shadows' line-up had remained unchanged for almost three years, during which time they had enjoyed five top ten hits and had become the best-known beat group in Britain. Hank had become a guitar hero inspiring thousands of boys to strum their cricket bats in the mirror. It was the beginning of a lineage that would produce Eric Clapton, Peter Green, Pete Townshend, Jimmy Page, Jeff Beck, Mark Knopfler and Brian May.

Yet during 1961 frictions between the four members were coming to the surface. Hank was easy-going but Welch was an often tetchy perfectionist who prided himself on speaking his mind. One of the few occasions anyone can recall Cliff becoming violent was when he and Welch squared up at 100 Marylebone High Street after Welch returned one night to discover a dog sleeping in his bed.

'We always thought of Bruce as the moody guy,' says Cliff. 'If he couldn't tune his guitar he would sling it down and drive all the way back to London. He left the Shadows a number of times.'

In *The Shadows By Themselves* ('The Kings Of Beat Music Tell Their Own Fabulous Story') each Shadow was asked to comment on his colleagues and Tony Meehan had this to say about Welch:

'He is a great organizer and I often feel he would make a first-rate sergeant-major in the Guards.'

It was a thinly veiled insult which Welch was quick to recognize, mentioning in his own comment that Tony was 'quick tempered', a 'bit of a brain' who 'knows what he wants and he'll end up getting it.'

Meehan was a precocious teenager who despite his lack of schooling read voraciously, had a keen interest in psychology and was a great lover of jazz and blues. Whereas the rest of the Shadows confessed to liking Agatha Christie and Dennis Wheatley (if they had time to read at all), Meehan put under 'reading matter' in the group's biography: *Mr Jelly Roll* by Alan Lomax and *Civilisation and Its Discontents* by Sigmund Freud.

Other than drumming, his interests were philosophy and psychoanalysis. Says Royston Ellis, 'Tony was the most intelligent and analytical of the Shadows.'

But after three years of hard work he was starting to slack. 'He had no respect for time,' remembers Cliff. 'The coach would be leaving, we'd be telling him that he was five minutes late, and while you were telling him he would be sitting down and ordering fried eggs and bacon. There were many times when we just had to leave him behind.'

In October, shortly before the group was due to depart for Australia, Welch and Meehan got into a flaming row which ended with Meehan walking out and suggesting they look for another drummer. Welch took him at his word and Brian Bennett, ex Marty Wilde's Wildcats, was brought in.

'It was all getting too much for me,' says Meehan. 'We worked seven days a week, we never had any holidays and I had just started my first family. We had been worked into the ground because nobody thought it was going to last.

'When we were at the Palladium we used to work for six days a week, do three shows on a Saturday and were then put on a train to do a Sunday concert for which we would be paid five pounds extra.'

Jet was the next to go. The official leader of the Shadows, he had been causing concern for some time because of the effects of his drinking.

In *The Shadows By Themselves* he described his favourite drink as 'shandy' but the truth was that he loved whisky. 'He was a lush,' says Meehan. 'He drank himself stupid. He was a totally self-destructive creature.' None of this was known to the fans at the time who were told that Jet suffered from 'nerves' and was 'taking the plunge to go solo'.

He has since blamed his descent into alcoholism on Cliff's dalliance with Carol but those who were around at the time say that the pattern had been established long before. 'It wasn't so much that he drank a lot,' says Cliff, 'but that he couldn't drink well.'

He would be found in theatre bars when he was due to be on stage and sometimes had to be pulled out of fights that had started when someone had suggested he must be 'queer' because he dyed his hair and wore fancy clothes. On tour in New Zealand he woke up one morning to find himself on the floor of a hut next to a Maori woman in full tribal costume. He had no idea how he came to be there.

When Bruce Welch broke the news to Jet on 15 April 1962 that he was no longer a member of the Shadows a replacement had already been found. A month before, on 13 March, Peter Gormley had had his first meeting with Brian 'Licorice' Locking, an unassuming young bass player who had been recommended by Brian Bennett who had played with him backing both Vince Taylor and Tony Sheridan.

What no one except Bennett knew at the time was that Locking was an ardent Jehovah's Witness who, when he was on tour, would seek out local members and carry out door-to-door evangelism. Bennett knew because he had introduced Locking to the teachings in 1958, because, although not a member himself, he had been raised as a Witness by his mother. Locking studied the teachings for two years and then became a baptized member in 1961.

'He was just a nice guy,' says Bruce Welch. 'We were twenty or twenty-one years old and you don't ask a guy his religion when he plays bass guitar. The question was whether or not he was a good musician. And we liked him.'

Although his stay with the Shadows was brief his influence was profound because it was through Locking that Cliff was led back to studying the Bible for the first time since his teens.

The biographies and autobiographies all state that Locking got into conversation with Cliff about religion while on tour in Australia, a story which can't be true because Locking never toured Australia with the Shadows. It must have taken place in England and would almost certainly have been in 1962.

'I remember the conversation,' says Locking. 'I think it was in a hotel room and it wasn't with Cliff alone. There were one or two other people from another group that was on the same tour. We were having a bit of an argument and the subject of spiritualism came up and I just brought out what I believed. But my initial conversations on the subject had been with Hank who seemed to be the most interested.'

Cliff's only comments on religion in his early autobiography make interesting reading today.

'Whatever else becomes public,' he said, 'one's own beliefs should be private. Religion is something that is in one's heart. I don't go to church a lot. Leading my hectic sort of life it's often difficult.'

His change of heart began with his father's death which pushed him into a more questioning mode. The satisfaction that he'd once received from doing a successful concert began to diminish.

'I was quite enjoying myself in showbiz ... but there was this "something" missing,' he wrote in 1968. 'I'd go on stage for half an hour ... and I'd be quite excited and exhilarated. Then, after the show, we'd all sit about and "wind down", talking about the show, the audience and so on. Gradually, the excitement would wear off, and I'd find myself thinking, "What a drag this all is!" This was before I began even thinking about religion.'

During the Australian tour of 1961 he idly began to contemplate the possibility of contacting his father through a medium. Some of the girls in the Blackpool show had been playing with moving glasses and he told a *Melody Maker* journalist that this had prompted him to think of 'delving into spiritualism'.

'After enjoying this new closeness with my dad just before he died I was beginning to feel dissatisfied with my career,' he says.

'I thought that if it was possible I would get in touch to find out what was happening, to find out why I was feeling this way and to see what was ahead for me. My career was going well but it had reached a plateau. I wondered where I was going.'

It was when he talked openly about contacting a medium that Locking jumped in with what the Bible said about dabbling with the spirit world.

'He jolted back and said—you shouldn't do that. It's dangerous,' Cliff remembers. 'He said the Bible prohibited it. I told him to show me. I wasn't prepared to accept his word for it.'

Locking got his Bible and read from the Old Testament book of Deuteronomy: 'There should not be found in you anyone who makes his son or his daughter pass throught the fire, anyone who employs divination, a practitioner of magic or anyone who looks for omens or a sorcerer, or one who binds others with a spell or anyone who consults a spirit medium or a professional foreteller of events or anyone who inquires of the dead. For anybody doing these things is something detestable to Jehovah.'

Cliff was impressed with this seasoned musician who quoted the Bible with such assurance.

'I think it was a bit of a revelation to Cliff that this rocker should be involved with something so completely divorced from rock 'n' roll,' says Mike Conlin.

'I know that he used to talk to Licorice because he was trying to understand it. He was trying to put a finger on what it was that made this guy someone who one minute would be playing rock 'n' roll and the next would be putting pamphlets through people's doors.'

Although because of his background he respected the Bible it wasn't initially what Locking said that got through to him but the zeal with which he said it. He had arrived at a point in his life when he needed more than his career to be passionate about.

The Jehovah's Witnesses had started in America during the nineteenth century and came to be characterized by their vigorous proselytizing techniques, including 'doorstep evangelism'.

They used their translation of the Bible as a source book but diverged from historical Christian teaching on key doctrines such as the trinity (Father, Son and Holy Ghost), the eternal human soul and the incarnation (Jesus as God in the flesh).

'Christianity hadn't been relevant to me before,' says Cliff. 'I didn't even know that God had a name—Jehovah. I started to read more and more. I was impressed by the prophecies they mentioned and by the fact that God could be understood rationally.'

Locking's entry into the group coincided with *Summer Holiday*, the second film put together by Leslie Grade. It was to be set in Greece because Kenneth Harper wanted to make a film which would pick up on the increased interest among young Britons in travelling abroad. He had toyed with the idea of setting a story in Spain, then untouched by mass tourism, but decided that it was too near and that Greece had more romantic connotations.

He kept the core of Cliff's gang from *The Young Ones*, Peter Myers and Ron Cass as writers and Herb Ross as choreographer. He wanted to keep Sid Furie as director but he didn't want to make another musical so Furie hired 33-year-old Peter Yates.

The problem for the writers was to get the characters from London to Athens.

'If they were basically classless but without the money for expensive holidays we needed a reason to get them abroad without them losing their identity as the Young Ones,' says Ron Cass.

'One day while travelling on a London bus it suddenly occurred to me that if we couldn't get them to Greece by air why not get them there on a London bus which we could convert into living quarters?'

Once the red double-decker bus had been cast in the lead role the screenplay fell into place. Cliff would be the leader of a gang of London Transport mechanics who decide to turn a bus into a hotel and drive it across Europe to Greece.

Interiors were shot at Elstree Studios but all the exteriors (except for a brief longshot in Paris) were shot on location in and around Athens starting in May 1962. Two London buses were bought for the film but the reality of getting a double-decker from London to Athens was considerably more difficult than the fiction.

Kenneth Harper remembers, 'We needed two buses because we needed one as a back-up but when they were driven overland they came across so many bridges that they wouldn't fit under. One of them actually made it eventually by road but the other one had to turn back and be sent by sea.'

There were also problems getting in the guns needed for a scene where Yugoslavian border guards challenge the bus. 'There was a most almighty fuss,' says Harper. 'My assistant producer, Andy Mitchell, was almost put in jail because they thought he was starting a revolutionary cell.'

Cliff's leading lady was nineteen-year-old Lauri Peters, a classically trained dancer who had spent the past two years in the Broadway production of *The Sound Of Music*. She had made one previous film, *Mr Hobbs Takes A Train* with James Stewart, and was recommended by Herb Ross as someone who might appeal to potential American distributors.

As with Carole Gray in *The Young Ones* she was not the glamorous lead that might be expected, and looked unlikely as Cliff's romantic interest. Harper was furious that she had put on a lot of weight just prior to filming.

'The choice of Cliff's leading ladies was always strange,' says Tony Meehan. 'I think the notion was to pick girls who were quite plain and who wouldn't threaten the fans. I think the girls liked leading ladies who they could identify with.'

There was never any off-screen romance between the two leads. Three days after Cliff arrived in Athens he was joined by Jackie Irving and Lauri had just got married to a young American actor called Jon Voight, later to star in *Midnight Cowboy*.

Una Stubbs, who played one of the stranded singers, remembers,

'Like most people who have just fallen in love, Lauri was wrapped up in just one person. I think she was dreadfully homesick and pining for him. She couldn't wait for the film to finish.'

Although Jon Voight came out to Athens for one weekend he was mostly confined to New York where he was in a play. 'Lauri confided in me one day,' says Melvyn Hayes. 'She said, "Where do you think I go on a Saturday night? I must tell somebody." I told her I had no idea. She said, "I fly back to America and then come back on the Sunday night because it's costing me that much a week in phone calls home." '

She played the part of a genderless-looking stowaway who eventually melts Cliff's heart despite having been told by him, 'Girls are all very well but date them once and then run. Date them twice and they get serious ... Next thing you know, you're hooked and wondering what's hit you. No. No girl is going to own me.'

This was remarkably close to Cliff's code of caution, a code reinforced by a song which he had written with Bruce Welch which was added after the location filming had been completed. Just as Tepper and Bennett's song 'The Young Ones' forever associated Cliff with youth so 'Bachelor Boy' connected him with a permanent state of singleness.

'We started the song just with the title,' remembers Welch. 'I wrote it with Cliff because I thought it would be a great song for him. We both wrote words and music. It was an afterthought as far as *Summer Holiday* was concerned but it became a million-seller.'

Una Stubbs was the girl in the film who many thought should have taken the lead role. She was a vivacious young dancer with a flicked-up bob haircut whose innocent freshness matched Cliff's own uncomplicated image. When Cliff saw her being auditioned he singled her out, catching the eye of the casting director and making the sign of the haircut to indicate his preference.

'I definitely think they should have cast Una in the lead role,' says Melvyn Hayes. 'They never got Cliff the right leading ladies. In *The Young Ones* he had a girl who looked as if she could have been his mother and then in *Summer Holiday* they had Lauri Peters who was great and yet wrong.'

In preparation for the filming Cliff went on a crash diet and also had his pointed tooth capped (he'd worn a temporary cap for *The Young Ones*). He'd started putting on weight during the American tour in 1960 and by the time he arrived at the Palladium run he was up to twelve stone.

Comments about his weight had been cropping up in the press since 1959 when Donald Zec, in a *Daily Mirror* interview, described him as a 'well-set, meaty youth' and Maureen Cleave had referred to 'chubby Mr Richard's tautened muscles in bathing trunks' when she reviewed *It's Great To Be Young*.

In the BBC radio programme 'Frankly Speaking' Royston Ellis had asked, 'Does your weight worry you at all? People say that you're getting too plump. Does this worry you?'

Cliff had replied that it did. 'But I don't know what to do about it. It does worry me because I should keep up my appearance. But how does one get rid of fat except by starving oneself?'

It was a comment of Minnie Caldwell, one of the original characters in 'Coronation Street', which finally prompted him to do something about it.

Transmitted in April 1962 and scripted by Tony Warren, the episode featured Minnie sitting in a park with Ena Sharples and Martha Longhurst listening to a brass band playing.

Ena Sharples: 'I'll have you know, I've got perfect pitch. To hear folks talk now you'd think everything began and ended with "Annie Get Your Gun".

Martha Longhurst: 'You can't beat the old tunes though can you?'

Ena Sharples: 'Oh I don't know. Have you ever heard *West Side Story* on Sandy McPherson?'

Martha Longhurst: 'Aye. But it doesn't seem the same thing somehow.'

Minnie Caldwell: 'Isn't Cliff Richard a lovely chubby lad?'

'He used to go to a store just off Tottenham Court Road and buy Indian sweetmeats called Jelabis,' recalls Ray Mackender.

'They had more calories in them than you can possibly imagine and the result didn't exactly enhance his photographs. The comment about him being a "chubby lad" on "Coronation Street" hurt him and from then on Jelabis were out and he became an absolute addict at keeping fit.'

By the time he started shooting *Summer Holiday* on 25 May he was down to eleven stone, the same weight that he maintains today.

Already conscious of the value of the youthfulness which he had feared was skipping away the day he left his teens, he was now, at twenty-one, becoming aware that the lean physique and the wide smile had to be worked for.

In October 1962 Cliff and the restructured Shadows toured America for the second time, this time to promote *The Young Ones* (retitled *It's Wonderful To Be Young* by Paramount and disastrously re-edited). The idea was great. The first half of the evening would be a screening of the film and the second half would be a concert.

What no one could have imagined when planning the tour was that America and Russia were to teeter on the brink of nuclear warfare that month over the issue of Soviet missiles being set up in Cuba. It wasn't until 28 October that President Kennedy called the bluff of Russian premier Khrushchev, and Khrushchev promised to remove the weapons.

The Cuban Missile Crisis was the closest that the superpowers came to conflict during the Cold War years and it meant that during Cliff's tour America was in a state of panic, with few people venturing out. As a result the concerts were poorly attended, sometimes only half full.

While in Memphis another attempt was made to meet Elvis but again it didn't work out. 'It was arranged that we should go to his home, Graceland,' remembers Locking.

'When we got there we realized he was out of town and so his father, Vernon, met us and took us on a guided tour of the mansion.

He didn't say much to us and all I can remember was seeing piles of teddy bears in his bedroom upstairs.'

It may seem surprising today that Britain's biggest act was met with a lack of interest but it has to be remembered that the American fascination with British groups only built up after the Beatles. In 1962 the idea of a group of Englishmen playing rock 'n' roll appeared to have as much potential as Americans playing cricket.

The only real success to date had been Lonnie Donegan's version of 'Rock Island Line', which had reached number eight in the charts during 1956 and had been backed up with a four-month tour. Marty Wilde reached number forty-five with 'Bad Boy' in March 1960, but wasn't able to follow it up.

Although other acts, such as Billy Fury, had released singles in America, nothing had come of them. The only British acts to reach the number one slot at the time were Acker Bilk with 'Stranger On The Shore' in 1961, and Vera Lynn with 'Auf Wiedersehen' in 1952. (The Tornadoes were to have a surprise number one with their instrumental, 'Telstar', in December 1962.)

When Cliff arrived back in London on 13 November he told *Melody Maker* that despite the month-long tour and appearances on the 'Ed Sullivan Show' and 'Dick Clark's Bandstand' he was still very much an unknown in America. 'You've got to fight to make yourself known there,' he said. 'You're up against so much.'

But the tour was significant in that Cliff was able to ask more questions of Locking, and went to his first meeting of the Jehovah's Witnesses in Miami.

'We were swimming in the hotel pool one day and someone came through and asked for me,' says Locking. 'I wondered who it could be because I knew no one in Miami.

'Apparently a room maid had seen my JW Bible, which in those days had a green coloured cover, and she'd taken a look inside to see who it belonged to because she was a Witness. She then invited me to a local meeting and Cliff and Hank joined me.'

For Cliff again it was the enthusiasm that communicated to him. 'I was just so overwhelmed,' he says. 'Everyone was just so friendly. We got big hugs and everything. It was incredible. It was the feeling of being in a charismatic [Pentecostal-style] meeting long before I knew the word charismatic. When I came back to England I introduced it to all the family.'

What Cliff didn't know was that his mother was already considering the claims of the Jehovah's Witnesses because her Uncle Vincent (Vincent Bridgwater) and his wife May, who had come to England in the early fifties, had been converted by doorstep evangelists and she had seen a lot of them after Rodger's death. One day May noticed a Bible by Dorothy Marie's bedside and talk turned to religion, beginning a conversation that went on until four o' clock the next morning.

'She then gave me a couple of magazines and asked me to read them,' says Dorothy Marie. 'She told me that she had been a very strong Roman Catholic and that nothing would move her. But she had decided that the church was doing nothing for her and she became a Witness.

'So I had the magazines, Cliff was on tour in America and when he came back he had got copies of the same magazines. He said he was interested in the Jehovah's Witnesses. So we all started studying together.'

Studying was necessarily spasmodic for Cliff, who was hardly ever in the same town two nights running. In January 1963 he returned to South Africa with Jackie Irving and Carole Gray appearing in the shows as dancers.

In Salisbury, Rhodesia, Cliff and Jackie went along with Licorice Locking to a local meeting house. That June they were back in Blackpool for a long summer season at the ABC with Dailey and Wayne and Arthur Worsley and Cliff attended JW meetings in nearby Thornton Clevely as well as meeting twice a week with Locking and a local JW to discuss Witnesses' view of the Bible.

Locking was never sure what was motivating Cliff to study in such depth without ever committing himself, or describing himself as a

Jehovah's Witness. 'I just got the impression that he was interested,' says Locking. 'He was looking for something to commit himself to.'

When *Summer Holiday* was released at the close of 1962 it broke all previous box office records for a British film. Kenneth Harper had deliberately scheduled a winter première to increase the impact of the film.

'I had told Leslie Grade to pray for snow the week the film came out,' he says. 'We were lucky. It did snow. Everybody was frozen and they went into the cinema and it was like having a summer holiday.'

By this time Cliff had been a major star for four years in a business where runs of success were typically counted in months if not weeks.

His original opposition had by now disappeared. Tommy Steele, Marty Wilde and Terry Dene were never again to appear in the charts. Vince Eager, Duffy Power and Johnny Gentle, the great hopes of manager Larry Parnes, never had a hit single between them.

The only serious competition was from Adam Faith and Billy Fury, who had both started in the business around the same time as Cliff but whose chart careers hadn't started until 1959. By 1962 they'd both had over a dozen hits but neither of them had developed the family appeal that helped Cliff reach out beyond the original teenage audience.

Fury had a great voice—perhaps the best rock 'n' roll voice of his generation—but he was painfully shy and compensated for this by developing a writhing stage act which newspapers reported as 'suggestive'. The management of Dublin's Theatre Royal once dropped the curtain on the act because it was considered too 'offensive'.

Faith was a less threatening proposition but he also suffered from stage nerves and didn't have the voice to sustain a long career. He sang in the wavering tones of Buddy Holly, and his vocal deficiencies were expertly covered up by John Barry's string arrangements.

'I suppose I felt a certain amount of competition from Cliff,' says Faith, 'but, amazingly enough, we never got to know each other well in those days because we were both so busy. The only times we would meet would be at a transport café and he'd say, "I've just been to Grantham. Where are you going?" and I'd say, "Well, I'm off to Southampton." Then we'd meet at the *New Musical Express* Poll Winners concerts at Wembley Pool and we'd sit and chat. He was a nice lad but there was a big enough audience for all of us.'

The real threat to Cliff's standing as Britain's number one pop idol was to come from the Beatles, who had their first hit single in October 1962. Appearing, with their floppy haircuts and collarless jackets, to be the challenge of the next generation, they were contemporaries of Cliff's who had started playing skiffle at exactly the same time. John Lennon was five days older than Cliff.

The Beatles first met Cliff at a party thrown by Bruce Welch after they had played the Lewisham Odeon on 29 March 1963. Although they had never bought Cliff's records there was awe involved in meeting the man they had to topple to be Britain's best.

They gathered in Welch's kitchen and John Lennon made jokes about Cliff holding off his next release so that the Beatles could stand a chance of getting to number one with their follow-up to 'Please Please Me'.

Then they got out their guitars. Cliff and the Shadows played 'Lucky Lips' while the Beatles sang 'From Me To You', which they had recorded three weeks previously.

The one exchange of the evening that Cliff still remembers came when he expressed an interest in Ray Charles and Lennon said, 'I used to like him until everybody else started to like him.' The elitism of the comment perplexed Cliff.

'The Beatles were fairly small at the time but I remember we spent the whole night talking,' says Mike Conlin. 'They were very worried about the effect of Cliff's next release.

'We all got on very well and when we played the Blackpool season later that year I would meet up with Paul when they were doing Sunday concerts up there and he always made me feel welcome. He never made any snide remarks about Cliff.'

In April 1963, shortly after the birth of Julian Lennon, John took off to Spain for a private holiday with manager Brian Epstein. They booked into a hotel in Sitges where Cliff and the Shadows were staying while recording the album *When In Spain* in Barcelona. Mike Conlin remembers Lennon being a bit distant, as though he wanted to get into a conversation but felt it was a bit beneath him.

'It was winter time and there were no other English people around,' says Conlin. 'We used to see Brian and John every day in the street and you could see John half thinking that he'd spend some time with us but then sniffing and turning away. I never knew what effect that had but it was after that that Lennon began sounding off about Cliff.'

In a conversation which took place the following month, recorded in Michael Braun's book *Love Me Do*, Lennon said, 'We've always hated Cliff. He was everything we hated in pop. But when we met him we didn't mind him at all. He was very nice. Now when people ask us if he's a bit soft we say no. We still hate his records but he's really very nice.'

What they hated was his 'niceness' when singing rock 'n' roll. They had spent years in sweaty cellars learning how to rock audiences until they dropped from exhaustion. To the boys from Liverpool, Cliff was a British Frankie Avalon, a house-trained rock star for the family audience.

'From Me To You' went to number one, and 1963 belonged to the Beatles who had three number ones in a row. It wasn't as if Cliff had a bad year. His next three singles were all top five but it was enough to suggest that his reign as the undisputed king of British pop might be coming to an end.

It unnerved him that 'Lucky Lips' was not only beaten by 'From Me To You' but by 'Scarlett O'Hara', the second single by Jet Harris and Tony Meehan who'd teamed up after leaving the Shadows. For someone who has always been concerned with his showing in the singles charts this was a public humiliation.

He told *Melody Maker* that he became quite agitated when 'Lucky

Lips' stalled at number four.

'I went home and poured my heart out to Mum and shouted, " 'Lucky Lips' isn't getting to the top." You need someone to talk to. People think the showbiz life is cushy. But Jet's right in saying that you need nerves of steel. You go to bed at night wondering if things will still be the same tomorrow, if you'll still be at the top.'

In another interview he was asked whether he was buckling under the challenge of the new groups from Liverpool. 'I don't think it's that that has stopped me,' said Cliff.

'The record of mine just wasn't strong enough. Perhaps we have slipped into a rut, but it's not just a sound that sells records. They have to be good. We will just have to be more selective in choosing material. I'm certainly not going to be "Beatled" into making a disc for the sake of it.'

Getting in the lower half of the top five was hardly a disaster and the song became his bestselling single ever in Germany. But it was the start of press speculation about his future, particularly as the beat group boom was throwing up new acts every week.

After years of 'Cliff Is Tops Again' headlines, they were writing 'Is Cliff Slipping?', 'Cliff At The Crossroads' and 'We're Not Has Beens Says Cliff'.

'These are dangerous days for Cliff Richard and he is facing them with zest, honesty and fervour,' wrote Ray Coleman in *Melody Maker*.

'After five years of glory during which he has established himself as Britain's top solo pop idol, it has been said that the route from now on can only be downhill.'

16

'I'm thinking about God'

In October 1963 Licorice Locking made the surprise announcement that he would be leaving the Shadows in order to devote more time to his religious activities.

'I love being with the group,' he told the *Daily Mail*, 'but the constant touring doesn't allow me to fulfil my promise to life. I have thought about this step for a long time. It has become a strain dividing myself into two—being loyal to the show and being loyal to my beliefs. I feel I must stay in one place and do my work there.'

Locking completed his recording commitments and was then replaced by John Rostill, a handsome young bass player the Shadows had met in Blackpool.

On 2 December, with the Beatles at the top of the hit parade with 'She Loves You', Cliff left for the Canary Islands and *Wonderful Life*, the third of his films with the Harper, Cass and Myers team and the second to be directed by Sid Furie.

Just as *Summer Holiday* had been the best received and most lucrative of Cliff's films, *Wonderful Life* was to be the worst received and least lucrative.

There were problems right from the start. To sustain the rhythm started with *The Young Ones*, filming should have been the previous summer with a release date in early 1964 but because of the Blackpool summer season the momentum was lost.

Then there was a problem with the story that Ron Cass and Peter Myers had written. Originally Cliff was to have played the role of a dashing guardsman mysteriously called out to Mexico on the death of an uncle. While travelling through the dry Mexican countryside his train is ambushed and he is taken prisoner by a gang of bandits who blindfold him and take him to the uncle's village. When the blindfold is taken off it is revealed that the uncle was the leader of the bandits and that as his only living relative the guardsman must now adopt the mantle of The Shadow.

The rest of the film was to have shown him desperately assuming the bandit leadership while simultanously trying to ensure that those under his control committed no real crimes. 'It would have been a very different film for Cliff,' argues Ron Cass, 'and very, very funny.'

After a costing of the film based on this script Kenneth Harper broke the news that it would be impossible to do something set in Mexico.

'Andy Mitchell went out to research the possibility and found that it was absolutely out of court,' says Harper. 'So we went out looking for islands that were closer at hand and finally decided on the Canary Islands. That's when we realized we were going to have to change the story.'

Through changing the screenplay to fit a new location the heart was taken out of the film. Much of the final script was written on location with scenes changing day by day as weather conditions affected the shape and colour of the sand and made continuity a nightmare.

'I can't really take the same pride in the result as I did in *The Young Ones* and *Summer Holiday* because it was all over the place,' admits Ron Cass.

'I've always said that a musical should be fanciful but the idea we used of a group of young kids making a film was too fanciful. There comes a certain point where people reject "fanciful" and say "impossible". The screenplay grew rather than arrived.'

The problems didn't end when they reached the Canary Islands.

The filming was held up by rainstorms, Melvyn Hayes broke his leg falling down a flight of steps and one of the leading actors, Dennis Price, had to be replaced mid-way through shooting.

'There was no excitement at all on that set,' remembers Royston Ellis, who was flown out to research a book of the film that was never written. 'There was this scandal because Dennis Price was totally drunk and incapable of filming. Cliff asked me to try and straighten him out so they could get the film done but it didn't work out. He had to be flown home and his part was taken over by Derek Bond.

'By that time Cliff was keeping very much to himself and was very into discussing religion with Una Stubbs and Hank Marvin. That was when a lot of us became aware that Cliff had got religion and word got out.'

The lack of excitement is confirmed by Melvyn Hayes, reckoned by most to be the liveliest of the cast.

He remembers a journalist from a national paper flying in to write a story along the lines of 'High Jinks On Cliff Film' and asking him what really went on. Hayes turned to him conspiratorily and said, 'I'll tell you what really happens. We have a wake-up call at 6.30. We do make-up. We then get into a terrible jeep which takes us forty miles to Las Palmas which is like an oven. Then we work until lunch time.

'The sun is so hot we don't enjoy our food. Then we film all afternoon until the winds start getting up at four o'clock and it starts turning cold. The sand whips into our faces and cuts us like sandpaper. But we haven't finished yet.

'We go on until the light drops and then we get back into the bus and feel sick and rough from the heat. We eventually get back to the hotel, have a bath, go to the restaurant and fall asleep.

'This wasn't good enough for the journalist so he found Richard O'Sullivan and pushed him into the swimming pool. Richard pulled the journalist in with him and when the story came out it was all about the things we all got up to at night, like throwing each other into the swimming pool.'

It was during the making of *Wonderful Life* that Cliff's relationship with Jackie Irving reached crunch point. He had now been seeing her for almost two and a half years but whereas he seemed content to have her as his high school date Jackie wanted the relationship to mature.

'I think that for Cliff it was a very platonic relationship,' says one friend of the period. 'I don't know what Jackie would have called it. It wasn't physical. She was just the girl that he would take to things.'

His physical caution was matched with a refusal to discuss where they were headed. Newspapers had been speculating on their likely marriage since September 1963 but Cliff never mentioned the subject to Jackie.

'All this week, since these rumours that we were getting married started, people have tried to ask me about it,' Jackie told the *Daily Mirror*. 'I have just kept away from them. That kind of thing is embarrassing for both Cliff and myself.

'Obviously I like him a lot. So does my mother ... but neither of us is planning to get married. There's nothing like that.'

Cliff's response was to say, 'Jackie is my only girlfriend.'

But although they never spoke of marriage to each other they contemplated the possibility when alone. Jackie assumed that Cliff's reluctance to put the relationship into a higher gear was because his mother was restraining him. One evening, while on tour in Birmingham, she came to Dorothy Marie's hotel room and tried to sort the matter out.

'She thought I was putting a spoke in his wheel,' says Dorothy Marie. 'I said, "My dear girl, I'm nothing to do with him. Cliff is grown up. He's a man. If he wants to get married he'll get married. If he doesn't, he won't. There's nothing that you and I can do that will change him."'

The 'forbidding' that Tony Meehan had talked about was again in evidence. He was comfortable with a schoolboyish friendship but balked at the idea of what an adult relationship might entail.

'Jackie Irving was the first girl that I thought I might marry,' Cliff says. 'I thought that if I was going to get married at all it would be to Jackie.

'I went to Peter Gormley and said, supposing I wanted to get married . . . and Peter said, "Well, you might lose ten per cent of your fans but that doesn't mean too much." He was saying that if I got married I'd still keep ninety per cent of my fans.

'That's when I decided not to get married because as soon as the cards were dealt out and I had the OK I went, ooh, I don't know if I want this anyway.'

The bottom line was that he loved being Cliff Richard so much that commitment to anyone else would be second best. There was no room in his life for a Mrs Cliff Richard. The fires of sex, which could have driven him into marriage, were never as fierce as his determination to enjoy his career.

'I don't think I'm cut out for marriage. Even though I have enjoyed the relationships I've had I have always felt fairly dispassionate afterwards and able to say I'm glad I didn't get married,' he admits. 'I obviously haven't been hit by the same bug that has hit others.'

Jackie had joined Cliff in the Canaries and it was here that he broke the news that he had decided not to see her any more.

'Obviously it takes one person to bring up the subject and I was the one to bring it up,' says Cliff. 'I said, look, I don't want to get married. So we called it off.

'What she felt like when I told her I don't know. I can't speak for her. I don't think she was hysterically happy but I've always felt it's best to get things said. I've never wanted to live a lie. At least I have been upfront with everybody and told them I couldn't do it.'

A brief flirtation with Una Stubbs followed but Cliff felt inhibited by the fact that although her relationship with actor Peter Gilmore was breaking up she was still married to him.

'We had been keen on each other for quite a while,' says Una. 'Then, during *Wonderful Life*, it turned into a romance although I always kept very quiet about it. Even my closest friends didn't know.'

Cliff was still in Las Palmas when the news came that the Beatles had arrived in America to be greeted by 4,000 screaming fans in an unprecedented display of pop devotion. Like Cliff they had then appeared live on the 'Ed Sullivan Show', the difference being that they had drawn the largest audience in the history of entertainment television. To cap it all, 'I Want To Hold Your Hand' had gone to number one in the US charts.

All this must have been galling to someone who had spent five years struggling for American recognition. *It's Wonderful To Be Young* hadn't done great business, none of his ten singles since 'Living Doll' had made a mark ('Lucky Lips' had rolled around the bottom end of the top one hundred) and his new American label, Epic, were just starting to have some success with 'It's All In The Game' after having launched what it called 'one of the greatest introductory campaigns in our history'.

Now the Beatles, with a recording career of just over twelve months, were causing a sensation on their very first trip. In fact it had been the failure of Cliff's career in America that had determined the nature of the Beatles' conquest.

'Cliff went there and he died,' John Lennon told author Michael Braun on the eve of their visit. 'He was fourteenth on a bill with Frankie Avalon and George [Harrison] said that *Summer Holiday* was second feature at a drive-in in St Louis.'

To avoid such indignities the Beatles waited to take America until they could be guaranteed top billing and maximum exposure. The airport welcome was part of a well-orchestrated campaign by Capitol Records.

There were major features in the trade press, DJs were primed to announce the arrival time of the plane, Beatle souvenirs were being mass marketed and five million posters saying 'The Beatles Are Coming' were posted all over America in December 1963.

But success on such a grand scale cannot be explained by marketing techniques alone. The Beatles captured the mood of international cultural change in a way in which Cliff never had and never would.

They were the first of a better-educated, more sophisticated generation of rock musicians who wrote their own songs and guided their own careers.

Cliff took the news philosophically. He was still Britain's most popular male singer even though, in the *New Musical Express* annual points survey, which reflected the number of weeks an act was in the charts, he was now eleventh in a list that he had topped the year before.

'We're not going to contest the beat groups,' he said. 'We won't follow trends. We will continue doing what we do until the public stops buying our records.'

There was premature talk of him retiring. At the end of 1963 he had bought Rookswood, a six-bedroom Tudor-style mansion in Upper Nazeing, Essex, where he would live with his mother and sisters. He also bought a holiday home in Portugal.

At that time the Algarve coast was completely undeveloped. There was no airport at Faro and the only way to travel there was to fly to Lisbon and drive the rest of the way. Peter Gormley heard of it through Muriel Young, then a disc jockey on Radio Luxemburg, who had built a house in Albufeira at a time when only two other British people had homes in the region.

'It was completely undiscovered,' she says. 'Peter came down initially because he was a deep-sea fisherman and he ended up buying six houses—two for Leslie Grade and one each for himself, Cliff, Frank Ifield and Bruce Welch.

'It was because these people were all so famous that the place got written about. The Algarve burst wide open six or seven years before it might have done because of the attention it got through stars such as Cliff.'

Mike Conlin remembers him being at his happiest when he was able to disappear to Portugal.

'He liked being able to get away completely from the show business scene,' says Conlin. 'We used to go down for a month at a time. There was a fellow we knew who was at university near Lisbon and he used to take us to restaurants and introduce us to the local fishermen.

'We used to go out on the boats all night sardine fishing, things like that, and Cliff would sometimes come back and sing to the fishermen in their homes. None of them had any idea who he was and that's what he liked about it. He could go anywhere and not be recognized.'

The retirement talk had started when he had casually remarked that Portugal seemed to be the ideal place to retire. It took on added significance because Cliff was known to be deeply involved in the teaching of The Jehovah's Witnesses and some thought he might eventually follow Licorice Locking's example and quit the business.

One of those disturbed by his new obsession was Jay Norris, his old form mistress from Cheshunt, with whom he had stayed in touch over the years. Educated in a convent school, she knew enough of the Bible to know he was flirting with a quasi-Christian group, but not enough to correct him.

For help she turned to the school's religious education master, Bill Latham, a 26-year-old evangelical Christian who had an easy-going manner and an exceptional gift for communicating his beliefs. She also entertained the idea that Bill would make an ideal friend for Cliff.

'I'm a natural organizer of other people's lives and I thought they would have a lot to offer each other,' she explains.

'Cliff had no nice ordinary friends. He was stuck in the pop world where the people were often second-rate and Bill had a lot of Christian friends. Actually I thought that Bill had much more to offer Cliff than Cliff had to offer Bill. Being a pop star could be lonely and dull.'

On the surface of things Bill Latham was an unusual match for anyone to make for Cliff. The only things they appeared to have in common were a lower middle-class background (Latham was born and raised in Finchley), a father who worked in the catering business

(Latham's father had worked in a Camden bakery) and an interest in religion.

Latham was not a rock 'n' roll fan, dressed comfortably rather than fashionably and spent a lot of his evenings and weekends as a leader in an interdenominational Christian youth organization called Crusaders which arranged Bible studies and outdoor activities for teenage boys.

His own conversion, in 1952, had been through this group which happened to hold their weekend meetings in a room of the school he attended. He went with them to a summer camp in Norfolk where he understood the Christian message for the first time.

'Crusaders influenced my life very significantly, both directly and indirectly, after that,' Latham says. 'I began to be trained as a leader and that had one of the most profound shaping effects I have ever known. At the age of seventeen I was being put into positions of authority and the experience got me out of a fairly introverted life.'

Each July Jay Norris celebrated her birthday with a car rally which met at her house and then dispersed into the Hertfordshire countryside with sheets of clues imaginatively written out in rhyming couplets. In July 1964 her plan was to assign Cliff to Bill Latham's car.

'I wasn't intimidated when I met him that day at Jay's house but I was certainly curious,' remembers Latham. 'I was slightly apprehensive as to how we would get on because it was an interesting set-up. I was almost working to a brief. I was under strict instructions to get him into a spiritual discussion and this was a tall order in the context of a car rally.'

Cliff's recollection is that they 'spent the whole time arguing'. Latham thinks they didn't have the time. 'The car was full of people so there wasn't really a chance,' he says.

'I talked to him more when we got back to Jay's house but I don't think the JW thing came up but something must have been sown because sometime later there came an invitation to go to Rookswood to talk about JWs with him and his family.'

Remembers Jay, 'I had to do it all again after the car rally because they didn't see each other. The next thing was that Cliff came to supper with me alone and talked about the JWs and I said, "I can't answer these questions but Bill can." So he asked me to bring Bill along to his home.'

After this meeting Latham felt he needed theological support as the questions were now quite specialized, focusing on differences between the teachings of Jehovah's Witnesses and those of historical Christianity. Having a fastidious mind, Cliff wanted to be absolutely sure of all the possible interpretations of the key passages in the Bible.

'None of the family were actually paid-up members at the time but they were all quite in favour and arguing from a Jehovah's Witness position,' remembers Latham.

'The discussions were very high-powered right from the word go and with my somewhat limited Crusader theology I found myself on pretty thin ice. I thought I was floundering and was aware that I needed to bring in people who had more authority than I had.'

Graham Disbrey, a friend from Finchley who was also involved with the Crusaders, was recruited for the next meeting. It took place in December 1964, while Cliff was appearing at the Palladium in the pantomime *Aladdin and His Wonderful Lamp* (for which the Shadows had written the entire score). They arrived at around eleven o'clock at night and Cliff's mother served them coffee as they waited for Cliff to return.

'It must have been after midnight when he finally got back,' says Disbrey. 'I remember him saying—right, where are your Bibles? Let's get down to it! He wanted to get on with things straight away. He went out of the room, came back armed with a Bible and we started discussing.

'I can't remember exactly what we talked about. Bill and I were very young, very naïve and terribly conservative in our views and we just fired everything we had at him and he fired everything he had at us.

'It was a heavy time and I think we were basically trying to score points off each other. The core of the discussion was about whether Jesus was alive today, whether you could enjoy a personal relationship with a loving God, and how it affected our daily lives.

'This went on for most of the night. When Bill and I got back to Finchley the dawn was breaking.'

The next person brought in to bolster the cause was David Winter, a lay-reader at Latham's local church, St Paul's in Finchley, and editor of the magazine *Crusade*. Winter had a keen intellect, a good grasp of theology and an ability to discuss it in non-specialist language.

The surprise for Winter was to find that Cliff's questions weren't those typical of an unbeliever but of someone who respected the Bible but was unsure of the correct interpretation.

'Most people searching for Christianity have moral objections and questions,' says Winter. 'They want to know whether their lives will have to change. They don't want to be seen as nuts or religious maniacs. They can't stand church. They think Christians are weirdos. But with Cliff there was none of that.

'He would say, "I can't see how you can believe that Christ is the Son of God. The Bible doesn't teach that." What his experience with the Jehovah's Witnesses had done for him was to convince him of the authority of the Bible. He didn't want any other arguments. Arguing with him like this drove me back to the Bible and I know it drove Bill and a few others back to the same place to find the answers.'

Graham Disbrey was Latham's closest friend at the time. They had known each other since they were boys, had been Crusaders together and were now both teaching at the same school. But, following the meeting at Rookswood, Disbrey noticed that Cliff was taking his place in Latham's life.

'It was actually quite difficult for me,' he admits. 'Bill and I used to do things together and suddenly his time was taken up and he couldn't exactly say why. He was very discreet and wouldn't tell me what was happening but I would know that the big car was outside his house which meant that Cliff was there.

'I suppose I was a little envious. My nose was put out of joint. Bill used to collect me in the morning to take me to work and it was a bit difficult to know how to start a conversation at the beginning of the day. Bill wouldn't always say whether Cliff had been around the previous evening or exactly what was going on.'

Clearly Latham was becoming more than a religious adviser. Despite the gulf in their interests and in their experiences of adulthood the friendship was obviously fulfilling a deep emotional need in Cliff's life.

It wasn't as though Latham was replacing any close friends in Cliff's life. All his friends since leaving school had been business associates of one sort or another. There were no ties to cut because no ties had been made.

'I think Cliff desperately needed somebody who was wholly trustworthy and that he could look up to because everyone was looking up to him,' says Disbrey. 'He needed somebody to spend time with who was utterly reliable, absolutely confidential and I think he found that in Bill.'

It was this friendship and the wider circle of Latham's friends as much as the theological arguments that attracted Cliff to Christianity.

'I was so much into my Christian circle of church fellowship, youth fellowship and Crusader classes,' says Latham, 'that I thought the best exposure I could give Cliff was to meet Christians and introduce him to a Christian lifestyle.'

When Bill taught his Crusader class in Finchley, Cliff would sit quietly at the back listening. At first the young people were impressed to be joined by a pop singer but after a few weeks they just accepted him as one of them. He even attended church services at St Paul's, finding himself attracted to the sheer ordinariness of the people.

He was now arguing far less from the Jehovah's Witness viewpoint and was beginning to absorb the outlook of those around him. David Winter remembers that the most significant change came when he shifted to arguing from an evangelical Christian point of view.

Wonderful Life was premièred in July, the same month that the Beatles made their film debut in *A Hard Day's Night*. Whereas *Wonderful Life* had a contrived madness about it, *A Hard Day's Night* managed to communicate a refreshing irreverence, and whereas Cliff had adopted a middle-class accent and had middle-class values, the Beatles rejoiced in their working-class roots.

Cliff was beginning to look dated. Almost all the new groups had long hair brushed over their foreheads. They dressed in Cuban-heeled boots, leather waistcoats and high-collared shirts. Cliff was still neat and Brylcreemed with well-polished shoes and mohair suits.

The music too was changing. The Shadows sounded clean and clinical in contrast with the raunchy, often distorted, sounds of those who had schooled themselves in primitive rock 'n' roll and the electric blues of Chicago.

Cliff was sometimes heard commenting on the 'noise' of the Rolling Stones, or saying that the Beatles played out of tune. He failed to realize that part of the appeal of the new music was its uninhibited nature. The point wasn't to play and dress with precision, but with feeling.

The subject matter of pop was also becoming more adult. Sparkling innocence was giving way to expressions of anger, boredom and restlessness and a desire for social change. It was also no longer taken for granted that teenagers were sexually inexperienced.

A twenty-year-old 'beat fan' interviewed by *Melody Maker* in a feature which looked at shifting tastes said, 'I grew out of my Cliff Richard days a couple of years ago. When I look back I think how soppy I must have been. Groups now like the Beatles and the Stones have really got something and I can't see me getting tired of them. Not until I'm old anyway.'

It was just before Christmas 1964 that the press finally caught on to the fact that Cliff was becoming increasingly serious about religion. A *Daily Express* reporter approached him outside Rookswood and asked him about the rumours that he was a Jehovah's Witness.

'I am thinking about God,' he admitted. 'This is a very personal thing. It was Licorice Locking who set me thinking. I am not considering joining the Jehovah's Witnesses... I'm just thinking a lot about God. That's all. It's very important to me.'

17

'The closing of one door and the opening of another'

T o his colleagues in the music business it seemed quite bizarre that Cliff's social life was now centred on a group of young North London schoolteachers. Who else, given unprecedented fame, money and female attention would eschew it all for teenage Bible classes in the leafy suburbs and the occasional drink in a Hertfordshire pub?

'What on earth do they find to talk about?' asked an incredulous Bruce Welch at the time.

Yet it was in the company of these Crusaders, none of whom knew much about pop music, that Cliff was to negotiate his re-entry into normal life.

For six years he had been living in a world where he was over-protected, over-praised and over-paid. In Finchley he could almost be Harry Webb again. No one wanted anything from him and no one appeared to be over-awed by his status.

'He gave the impression of being very happy to join in my lifestyle,' says Bill Latham. 'He seemed to be glad to be doing ordinary things again. He'd had all those years of a pop star's lifestyle and now he was mixing with people who had nothing to do with show business.'

Because of the Christian ethos it was also a sexually unthreatening environment. There was no pressure to couple up because singleness didn't have the stigma it had elsewhere, and none of the group believed that masculinity was proven by sexual conquest.

Peter Graves met Cliff in September 1965 while waiting to take a diploma in education at Oxford.

'I think that one of the things that attracted him to our group was the fact that there were no girls to bother him,' says Graves. 'We were an all-male group. If girls did join us they were always on the fringe.'

During Easter of that year he joined twenty-four young Crusaders for an eight-day boat trip on the Norfolk Broads and was relieved to find himself treated as just another crew member. He played guitar for their sing-songs, cooked shepherd's pies and was subjected to pillow fights before lights-out.

The interviews he gave around this time show that these simple activities were making an impression. He wistfully envied the less-pressured lives of his new friends and could see that a great schoolteacher probably did more for the world than a celebrated pop star.

'Records don't mean all that much any more,' he told the music weekly *Disc*. 'Sometimes I'd love to have a job where I could work regular office hours and have weekends off.'

To the *Daily Express* he admitted that he was catching up with the life he had missed out on as a teenager.

'I feel I could do a lot more with my life. If this feeling continues for another year I will make a decision about my future. I could probably work in show business for the next twenty years. But if the day comes when I don't feel satisfied, I'll get out.'

For the first time in his career, Cliff was clearly out of sync with the times and apparently unconcerned. While he played cabaret at the London Palladium and put out singles like 'Wind Me Up' and 'The Time In Between', the sounds that would eventually define the decade were being produced: songs like 'Help' by the Beatles, 'Satisfaction' by the Rolling Stones and 'My Generation' by The Who.

'Christianity had become pre-eminent in everything I did,' says

Cliff. 'It changed my priorities. I had been rejuvenated and my career seemed uninteresting. At the same time the success of the Beatles and the Stones had shelved me and the Shadows. We were now the oldsters.'

He was also spending a lot less time with his mother, a situation which profoundly affected the still-young widow.

After Rodger had died in 1961 Dorothy Marie had seemed to blossom. No longer burdened with the problems of financing a home or being under the rule of a much older man she was enjoying the perks of being a pop star's mum.

'She was a totally different person after Cliff's father died,' remembers Pete Bush. 'She seemed to come out of her shell and want to be with Cliff. I don't know if it was out of wanting to be protected because of the loss of a husband but she seemed to be with him a lot more.'

Olive Queenie remembers it as a time of high excitement, 'All of these things were happening to Cliff and she was enjoying life for the first time. Instead of having to slave away to get things for people it was all coming to her easily and she was going overboard with it.

'She married her first boyfriend more or less straight from school and never knew what it was like to be adventurous and flirt and do all the things that girls do.'

She had become Cliff's constant companion as he attended film premières and ate out at fashionable restaurants. But with Cliff's involvement with the Crusaders, that began to change. Cliff no longer required her company as much as before and he was frequently absent from Rookswood for days while he stayed with Bill Latham and his mother Mamie.

'It was difficult for Cliff's mum to see him leave her and join another family,' Latham admits. 'It was compounded by the Christian dimension because she was getting more involved with the Jehovah's Witnesses. In the early days I think she thought that I had poached him and I know that she voiced this apprehension to other people.'

She began to feel lonely and it was in this state that she drew close to Derek Bodkin, a chauffeur hired for her by Cliff as she didn't drive and felt cut off living in a country house. Bodkin would take her shopping in London and to visit relatives. He would play badminton with her at a local club and later moved into a lodge at the entrance to Rookswood.

Out of this close association developed an unlikely romance between a 45-year-old mother of four children and a 23-year-old driver. At first, no one suspected anything because the two had so little in common. He wasn't a Jehovah's Witness, didn't have an interest in pop music, and admitted to being clumsy around women. Their continuing closeness was excused on the grounds that it was Bodkin's job to be at her beck and call.

'She came to see me when I was living in Manchester,' remembers Olive Queenie. 'Derek had driven her up. He was introduced to me as the chauffeur. I had never met him before. I was a little bit worried because by certain things that were said you could tell something was going on. I was thinking—surely not! He's younger than her son!'

By February 1965 Cliff had become so integrated into the Crusaders set that he considered himself a Christian. When Ray Coleman of *Melody Maker* asked him what he thought of John Lennon's stinging comment that he found his singing voice 'too Christian' he responded, 'I'm glad it shows because I am a Christian and I don't want anyone to get any other idea. That's the way I am and I have no intention of covering up the fact.'

Yet his Crusader friends felt that even though he was becoming more 'Christian' by imitation he had not yet become a Christian by conviction. He appeared to regard Christianity as the highest level of decent living rather than as a change of heart.

'He was doing all the right things with all the right people in all the right places but I think that in his inner self he knew he hadn't reached the point of commitment,' says John Davey, a Crusader leader in Sussex.

▲ July 1962: Cliff with his leading lady, Lauri Peters (far right), and other members of the cast of Summer Holiday

Cliff with the Shadows in their new line-up which included bass player Licorice Locking (rear) and drummer Brian Bennett (centre) ▶

Cliff with girlfriend Jackie Irving. Taken while on tour in South Africa ▼

▲ 1962: Listening to a playback of the sound track for Summer Holiday—(from left to right) producer Norrie Paramor, engineer Malcolm Addey, Licorice Locking, Cliff, Hank Marvin, manager Peter Gormley

▲ October 1963: Rehearsing with Susan Hampshire for dance scenes in Wonderful Life

Mobbed by British fans ▶

◀ July 1964: Hunting for clues during a car rally— Bill Latham and Cliff on the day of their first meeting

April 1965: Graham Disbrey (third from left) with Cliff on his first Crusader holiday on the Norfolk Broads ▶

◀ Bill Latham (left) and Cliff on board one of the Crusader holiday boats

▲ 16 June, 1966: Cliff addresses the crowd of 5,000 which couldn't get into Billy Graham's Earls Court rally. This was the day Cliff's Christian faith became public

▲ Cliff with Norrie Paramor—producer, arranger and father figure

◄ California, July 1968: (from left to right) John Davey, Graham Disbrey, Cliff, Bill Latham, Peter Graves and Peter Hutt

April 1968: Cliff with the Settlers—(from left to right) John Fyffe, Cindy Kent, Mike Jones, Cliff and Geoff Srodzinski ▼

1968: Cliff and the Settlers returning to Britain after playing a groundbreaking gospel concert tour in Croatia (then Yugoslavia) ▶

▲ Cliff sings 'Congratulations', Britain's entry in the 1968 Eurovision Song Contest

▲ April 1970: Cliff speaks and sings at Kingsway Hall, London, as part of his Christian work

▲ May 1970: Cliff plays student Clive Harrington alongside actress Pamela Denton in Peter Schaffer's stage play Five Finger Exercise

◄ Cliff and Una Stubbs in his early seventies BBC TV series 'It's Cliff Richard'

Cliff with the beard he grew for the part of James Callifer in Graham Greene's The Potting Shed ▼

October 1971: Cliff with his long-standing friend Olivia Newton-John ▶

▲ On stage in the mid seventies: (from left to right) Terry Britten, Cliff, Alan Tarney, Olivia Newton-John and Trevor Spencer

'I think we all sensed that he was very close and there was a great deal of speculation between us about what would happen if he did make a public announcement.'

During a Crusader camp at Lewes, Graham Disbrey posed him the simple question: 'How can you be sure that you are a Christian?' Cliff later confessed that this was the provocation he had needed on the final stretch of his spiritual search. It bothered him that he had no answer other than to say he was British, he didn't think himself particularly evil and he believed in the existence of God.

Neither Cliff nor Bill Latham is now sure exactly when he made the decision that removed all doubt. In interviews of the period he refers back to 1965 and on 20 March 1966 he gave a talk on 'Christian Maturity' at Lewes YMCA, yet in his biography *Which One's Cliff?* he pinpoints May 1966 when he was making *Finders Keepers*, the last of his youth-orientated films.

What isn't disputed is the fact that it was in his bedroom at the Lathams' at 124 Etchingham Park Road, Finchley, that he prayed the prayer that ended the search.

A Crusader friend, Roger Stacey, had recommended that he check out the third verse of Revelation chapter twenty, the last book in the New Testament. He told him that there he would find the key to his questions.

Before going to sleep that night Cliff opened his Bible and read the words of Jesus: 'Here I am! I stand at the door and knock. If anyone hears my voice and opens the door, I will go in and eat with him, and he with me.'

'I thought that this was it,' he remembers. 'I thought that if this was true I wanted to become a Christian. I didn't know how to do it though. I knew that the door was, figuratively speaking, the door of my life but I thought—how do you open it?

'I just remember saying the words, "Come on in. I want you in my life." Then I went to sleep. I didn't feel very religious the next day but, when I look back, that's when things started to change.'

June 1966 was an important month for British evangelical

Christians. Billy Graham, the best-known preacher of his generation, was coming to London for a four-week crusade at Earls Court,
his first in Britain since 1954.

There had been no public announcement but word of Cliff's
conversion had spread and an invitation came from the Greater
London Crusade asking him to appear as a guest on the night of 16
June, a youth evening at which England cricketer Colin Cowdrey
would be reading the lesson.

His career, he knew, would be on the line. If it was seen as a
gimmick, it would backfire, and even if he was believed to be sincere
there was no guarantee that his fans would continue to support him.
In the era of drugs and mysticism Christianity was not a cool religion
for a pop star to embrace.

His management were naturally concerned that Cliff could be
exploited by the American evangelist, whom they knew little about,
or that he could become so absorbed by religion that he would let his
career slide.

'They were worried about it,' admits Mike Conlin. 'They had
already had the trouble with Licorice Locking. But it was a vague
worry rather than a fretful worry. They thought that if he gets into
that kind of rubbish we'll have to watch him like a hawk otherwise
he'll be knocking on doors.'

The night of the appearance there were 25,000 people packed
into the Earls Court arena with an additional 5,000 outside listening
to the service on a sound-only relay. Cliff, who had been seated on
the platform along with churchmen and dignitaries, made his way
forward to the lectern, dressed in a corduroy jacket and horn-
rimmed spectacles.

In a brief statement he credited his parents for rearing him on the
Bible and ended by saying, 'I can only say to people who are not
Christians that until you have taken the step of asking Christ into
your life, your life is not worthwhile. It works. It works for me.'

He then sang 'It Is No Secret', a gospel song which Elvis had
recorded, and when he walked away from the lectern he found he

was so nervous that his arms remained in their outstretched position. When the meeting ended, Cliff went outside and addressed the crowd of five thousand who hadn't been able to get into the arena.

Two days after Earls Court his mother married Derek Bodkin at Epping Register Office. The first Cliff knew of the impending wedding was a call from someone in a public phone inviting him to the reception at Rookswood. He went and filmed the couple as they were showered with rose petals from a balcony over the front door and then they drove off for their honeymoom in an E-type Jaguar.

Confronted by the press at Pinewood Film Studios where he was shooting *Finders Keepers*, Cliff kept up his usual jaunty exterior, admitting that he hadn't known of the wedding until that morning but saying that he hoped his mother and Derek would be very happy. 'I'll be buying them a house as a wedding present and they'll be going to my place in Portugal.'

The pleasant chatter concealed his real feelings. He was disturbed by the relationship, not because he disliked Bodkin, but because he thought that the age-difference problem would be insurmountable.

Having lost Cliff to Bill Latham had she, in effect, married on the rebound? Bodkin himself may have unwittingly put his finger on the problem when he later said in an interview with the *Sunday Express*: 'I suppose I have taken over Cliff's place in Dorothy's life.'

Cliff's old way of life was fast disappearing. His mother was gone, Jackie Irving was dating his old rival Adam Faith and for the first time in six years (since 1960) he didn't appear in *NME*'s annual points list of best-selling singles.

Whatever was left standing he dismantled himself. His highly successful official fan club which Jan Vane had been running since 1958 was wound down, Rookswood was put on the market and in November 1966 he announced that he would be making no personal appearances during 1967.

'It was the closing of one door and the opening of another,' says Cliff. 'Up until that time I had felt responsible for my family. When my mother married I knew I could do what I wanted—which I did. I moved in with Bill and his mother. I wanted a different scene.'

For his fans the most staggering news was that Cliff was considering becoming a schoolteacher. The notion had been floated a few times before, usually out of admiration for friends such as Bill Latham and Graham Disbrey, but now he appeared to be serious.

Through John Davey, a teacher at Lewes County Grammar School in Sussex, he arranged to take an O level in Religious Education and by sitting in on lessons at the school he was able to test the response of ordinary pupils to his presence in the classroom.

He also spent two months at Oak Hill, an Anglican theological college, where he studied the Bible and learned how to articulate his faith.

'I was the one who tried to get him to be a teacher,' admits Jay Norris. 'I believed that he would make a good teacher. I took him to meet the principal of Trent Park Training College in Cockfosters who said that if he got a couple of O levels they would take him.'

He was now so surrounded by schoolteachers and lecturers that it wasn't surprising that education should become his chosen alternative profession. Of his Crusader circle of friends Graham Disbrey taught art and design, Bill Latham taught religious education, John Davey taught chemistry, Peter Graves became a professor of German and John Harvey was a lecturer in aeronautics.

At the same time he was questioning whether show business was a worthy occupation for a Christian. Could he be guilty of setting himself up as a 'false idol' for teenagers? A recurring theme in interviews of the time was his desire to 'do something' with his life.

These misgivings, which had been building up long before his conversion, were confirmed by those Christians who thought that the entertainment industry was ungodly anyway. Some of them didn't own televisions on principle, never went to the cinema and maintained a Puritan attitude towards the theatre.

Coupled with a disapproval of smoking, drinking, dancing,

swearing and make-up, it meant that a life on the stage was unthinkable for the thoroughly evangelical Christian because even if you weren't doing bad things you would surely be rubbing up against those who were.

The prohibition was rarely spelt out but anyone new to church circles would be quick to notice that there were no role models for committed Christians in show business. There had been actresses and pop singers who had converted but the happy ending was almost always that they abandoned their worldly trappings and were now happier than they had ever been in what was known as 'full-time Christian work'. When Terry Dene had become a Christian, in September '64, he got rid of his guitar and his records, and changed his name back to Terry Williams.

The implication was that show business, like sin itself, was something to be spurned and that anyone who secretly enjoyed the goings on at the London Palladium more than chorus singing at the church hall was spiritually suspect.

'The evangelical world had its own pressures which operated without a word ever being said,' says Cliff. 'I felt that I ought to leave show business. The majority of my friends hadn't actually said anything to that effect. They hadn't said, "Get thee out", but the pressures were vaguely there. I thought I'd move before it got any hotter and so I made my plans to leave.'

He talked it over with Peter Gormley who agreed to support him whatever decision he came to.

'I thought that was up to him,' says Gormley. 'It was his life. At one stage he asked me how much notice he would have to give to fulfil all his commitments and I can remember telling him that it would probably take twelve months.'

John Davey admits that initially his circle of friends did little to persuade him otherwise. They argued he could probably live comfortably on his earnings to date and could devote the rest of his life to worthier causes.

'He was at my parents' home in Lewes one day when the issue of him going to teacher training college came up,' Davey recalls. He actually rang his accountant up right there and then to find out what would happen if he didn't do any more show business work.

'He came off the phone looking quite shaken because he'd been given the news that even if he didn't do another day's work in his life he would be happily secure. He couldn't believe that he could safely sit back.'

The eventual decision to stick with pop was helped by a shift in attitude among some younger Christians who argued that evangelicals had been misguided in their rejection of the arts, media and entertainment. Even his normally conservative Crusader friends conceded that no area of culture was beyond redemption.

'I think we came to see that it would be a loss to show business if he stopped and a loss to Christianity if he didn't take advantage of the opportunities,' says John Davey. 'We realized that there was a definite job for him to do as a Christian believer within show business.'

The most encouraging discovery was a group who were meeting informally to discuss how Christians could become more actively involved in the arts. One of the group was actor Nigel Goodwin.

'We were discussing how it was possible to be a Christian and also to earn our wages as artists,' says Goodwin. 'I had this vision of a centre being created in London where Christian artists could meet and debate with their peers. Cliff started to come along to these meetings.'

David Winter was another group member, and in his role as editor of *Crusade* he chided those who withdrew from the arts and then became dismayed when other world-views came to predominate. He encouraged his readers to listen to what non-Christian artists had to say about the human condition.

Winter helped to persuade Cliff that he had two valuable assets which he shouldn't waste: his performing talent and his audience.

Independent of these discussions Winter was involved with American film director Jim Collier in developing the story for a Billy

Graham movie which would be set in contemporary London. Although Cliff wasn't under consideration at the beginning, this was to be the project which confirmed him in his growing belief that he could marry his faith to his work.

The result, *Two A Penny*, with a screenplay by Stella Linden, would not have merited much attention outside the Christian community had it not been for Cliff's involvement. The brief review in *Halliwell's Film Guide* called it 'Naive religious propaganda sponsored by the Billy Graham movement and featuring the evangelist in a cameo. A curiosity.'

Yet for the Billy Graham Organization it was a departure from the conversion stories disguised as dramas which it had been making since the 1950s. The main differences were that *Two A Penny* was marginally more realistic and the hero of the film, played by Cliff, didn't get 'saved' on camera. The puzzle was left with the audience rather than solved by the film maker.

Cast as a drug-dealing art student called Jamie, Cliff at least tackled the role of someone less virtuous than the squeaky-clean hero of *The Young Ones* and *Wonderful Life*. He got to fight, swear, shout and wear stubble on his chin.

'Among Cliff's Christian friends there were people who were quite pleased that he was thinking of giving it all up,' says Winter. 'But Jim Collier was the person who tipped the balance. He said, "Look what you can do! You can't throw all this away."'

Because Cliff had never been someone to whom people looked for guidance on daily living it was harder for him to find a natural way of expressing his new-found beliefs through his work. His songs didn't articulate his inner anxieties.

Show business, to be successful, had to reassure rather than disturb, to sweep people off to a fantasy world of sweetness and light rather than plunge them into debates about the security of their souls.

It was easier for novelists or those in the fine arts to incorporate spiritual discovery into their creations than it was for a man who performed other people's songs. During 1967 Cliff struggled with the issue of whether it was possible to Christianize his brand of entertainment.

His first steps towards working out an answer were necessarily faltering. There were no examples to follow. Norrie Paramor suggested that he might like to do a gospel album. After all, Elvis had recorded gospel material and it hadn't adversely affected his career.

Cliff acted on the suggestion and in February 1967 he went into Abbey Road Studios to begin recording *Good News*, a collection of spirituals, hymns and gospel songs, while the Beatles recorded their 'Magical Mystery Tour' EP in the studio next door.

Yet while the Beatles' lyrics were dissected by those keen to understand the group's shifting point of view, and only rarely were the group interviewed in depth, Cliff was increasingly being drawn into debate and argument about his faith. For producers of religious radio and television programmes he was a welcome alternative from the parade of vicars and bishops which dominated the 'God slots'. For Cliff it was an opportunity to say what he could never say in his singles.

In the 'love and peace' summer of 1967 Cliff was to be found on British television discussing his faith with Billy Graham and 'Ready Steady Go' presenter Cathy McGowan. In July he was brought into ABC's studios to face a roasting by ex-Manfred Mann singer Paul Jones, who had just starred in *Privilege*, Peter Watkins' futuristic film of a pop singer who is tamed by the church and then used to curb teenage behaviour by making young rebels subservient to the state.

The programme, 'Looking For An Answer', began by showing a clip from the film contrasted with shots of Cliff at Earls Court with Billy Graham. Jones, then an outspoken atheist, accused Cliff of being an instrument of the established church.

Cliff denied that he was being used in this way. 'I put myself in God's hands and say, "Look, if this is the thing I ought to do I shall do it," he said. 'The Church is just, I think, a front. You know, it's a name. We are always fooled by words and names and things.'

Jones: 'Well, one of the bishops in *Privilege* says, when he is accused of using the pop singer to further the ends of the Church: "Once they used a Spanish Inquisition and this is less painful." You know, it's exactly what you have just said, really.'

Cliff: 'Before I came on the scene Graham packed out places like Earls Court. He doesn't need me.'

Jones: 'But people don't know what they're coming for. Billy Graham knows why people go to his meetings is the same reason people in American spent $125 million in one year going to fortune tellers. They are insecure; they're unsure. They don't know what they're going for. Right, so you say: "We are giving them Christ." I say you're not. You're giving them a show . . .'

What Cliff offered was not a dazzling display of Christian apologetics—in fact his statements were often extremely unsophisticated—but a simple admission that he had 'accepted a thing called salvation which means that if I die I can look forward to an eternal life of peace and joy and no pain'. (Interestingly, Jones went on to become a Christian himself.)

Within the next few years Cliff was to become one of the most visible defenders of the Christian faith. Just when the trend among rock musicians was to 'let the music do the talking' Cliff was pouring out the first of millions of words which would attempt to answer the public's questions on everything from Bible reading to nuclear warfare. Never before had a pop star committed so many opinions to print on behalf of something other than his own career.

With David Winter he collaborated on Christian books. The first of these was *New Singer, New Song*, a biography which had his conversion as a convenient last chapter and his confirmation by Graham Leonard (later to be Bishop of London) in December 1967 as the final page: 'It was another great turning point, in its way: like Hoddesdon, and Butlin's, and "Oh Boy!" and Earls Court; and yet so natural, so easy, that it seemed that all his life up to this moment had merely been a preparation for it. It was—and no simile could possibly please Cliff more—just like coming home.'

The next, *The Way I See It*, was a collection of answers to the sort of questions he had been bombarded with since becoming a Christian.

'We sat down with the questions and Cliff just spoke his answers into a tape recorder,' says David Winter. 'I often didn't agree with what he said but it all went in the way that he said it.'

It was a hard time to be saying the things that Cliff was saying. Although the sixties' search for alternative lifestyles was a rejection of materialistic culture, Christianity was too closely associated with the old order to merit much serious consideration.

At a time when, in the wake of the more widely available contraceptive pill for women, 'free love' was being advocated, Cliff was having to say, 'Sex outside marriage, for instance, is always wrong.' At a time when recreational drugs were all the rage Cliff was saying, 'Drugs ruin your health, turn you into a sort of zombie and, in many cases, finally cause death.'

To the hippie generation, listening to Cliff was like listening to their parents who were always advising moderation or abstention and who always seemed to think that the government knew best.

One of the questions asked in *The Way I See It* was 'Do you see yourself as a conformist?', to which Cliff answered that he was not a conformist because conformism is a result of peer pressure and he has never altered his views in order to gain the approval of his peers.

This is one of the paradoxes of Cliff's life, that while he always seems eager to please and his show business career is built on giving people what they want, he is determined to do things his way and never acts against his conscience.

His decision to go public as a Christian was an example of this. Faced with the option of staying quiet and continuing to fulfil audience expectations or speaking out and risking rejection he hadn't hesitated to take the more dangerous route.

'I don't think I've ever met anybody who is as sure of himself as Cliff is,' observes Tony Meehan. 'I don't think I've met anyone who was integrated in the sense that he believes he's right and that's it. He was always like that.

'The public often think of him as being soft. He's a very charming and personable man but beneath that I think it's sheer metal and that doesn't come across to the public.'

18

Dropping back into suburbia

pproaching the end of his first decade in show business Cliff was virtually unscathed while many of those who had shared in his success had already buckled under the pressure.

Jet Harris was an alcoholic and had suffered a nervous breakdown, Bruce Welch was on the brink of a divorce and, during a run at the Talk Of The Town in January 1968, bass player John Rostill collapsed with mental exhaustion and had to be temporarily replaced by Licorice Locking.

Yet while Cliff's level of personal contentment had risen, his creative stock had fallen. No longer 'too sexy for TV', he was beginning to dress like his schoolteacher friends, suppressing the instinct he'd once had to be beautiful and exciting.

While the younger generation indulged in a riot of kaftans and afro hairstyles Cliff was sporting a Beatles (circa 1962) fringe, tortoiseshell-framed spectacles and elephant-cord slacks. In a perverse way he seemed to be toying with the power of his fame; seeing how far from the sex idol he could move without losing the bulk of his fans.

The middle years of the sixties were a golden age for the pop single. You could take the top thirty for almost any week during 1966 and find it cluttered with songs now regarded as classics.

In June, for example, as Cliff was performing for Billy Graham, the following singles were in the top thirty: 'Strangers In The Night', 'Wild Thing', 'Sorrow', 'Monday, Monday', 'Sloop John B.', 'When A Man Loves A Woman', 'Pretty Flamingo', 'You Don't Have To Say You Love Me', 'Paperback Writer', 'River Deep, Mountain High', and 'Sunny Afternoon'.

Cliff, however, wasn't carried along on this wave of creativity. He was too busy developing his spiritual life and dropping back into suburbia.

In the years before his interest in religion he had enjoyed phenomenal chart success. Between 'Living Doll' in 1959 and 'Don't Talk To Him' at the end of 1963 he had had an unbroken run of twenty hit singles each of which sold over one million copies. Yet of the seventeen singles released between then and the end of 1967 only three had topped a million.

His domination of British pop was over. Cliff's high point had come in that dull period between Elvis' induction into the army and the Beatles' conquest of America when he pretty much had the show to himself in Britain. Now he was facing massive competition in a proliferating music market.

But the relative decline in his fortunes was also partly self-inflicted. His career had been his religion. He had worshipped it and forsaken all else for it. Now it had been toppled from this pre-eminent position in his life. 'God became more important than his career,' says Bruce Welch.

In 1966 he told journalist George Tremlett, 'I could leave show business tomorrow. It wouldn't bother me one bit. I'm sure of that. I know now that if someone was to tell me that I couldn't sing any more it wouldn't worry me at all. It's just the way I've changed. If someone had told me that four years ago I would probably have hanged myself. But I've changed a lot.'

It was a confused signal to send out to his fans. It suggested that he was half-hearted about recording and performing. Why should the public respond with passion to material that was no longer created with passion?

'That's what he wanted to do at the time and there was nothing wrong with that,' says Hank Marvin. 'The problem that resulted though was that he still wanted a career and still expected the same results while he wasn't putting the same sort of effort in. It was as though he expected things to happen by accident.'

Tony Meehan was hired to try to give him direction by introducing him to contemporary songs. Cliff had already hooked up with country producer Billy Sherrill who had taken him to Nashville and produced 'The Minute You're Gone' and 'Wind Me Up', both of which became big hits. Cliff then recorded 'Blue Turns To Grey', a song written by Mick Jagger and Keith Richards, which reached number fifteen.

'Norrie Paramor seemed to have lost direction completely at that point,' says Tony. 'I was brought in to try and bring Cliff up to date. Norrie was very threatened by it. I was supposed to carve myself a place in the office but I didn't fit in. It was hard having been one thing in an organization and then coming back as something else.'

At the age of fifty-four Paramor, who had overseen Cliff's recording career brilliantly from teenage rock 'n' roll star to show business legend, seemed to be losing touch with a market that was being flooded with new musical influences and new technology. While bands like Cream and the Jimi Hendrix Experience spent days over one song, experimented with new instruments and stretched recording techniques as far as they would go, Cliff was still only turning up for vocal sessions and expected to get at least five numbers recorded in a session.

After the watershed year of 1966 the only million-seller Norrie was to enjoy with Cliff was 'Congratulations' written by Bill Martin and Phil Coulter. It was a massive hit, selling over two and a quarter million copies, but it nailed Cliff to a jaunty Eurovision sound at a time when rock was actually returning to its roots with the re-release of Bill Haley's 'Rock Around The Clock', 'Lady Madonna' from the Beatles and the Rolling Stones' 'Jumping Jack Flash'.

Phil Coulter had sketched out a song called 'I Think I Love You' with a lyric that went: 'I think I love you/ I think I love you/ I think the world is fine/ When you say that you're mine'. He played it to his songwriting partner in their small Denmark Street office but Bill Martin found the sentiment risible.

'It was terrible,' he says. 'You don't say to anyone, "I think I love you." You either say "I love you" or "I don't love you", it's either a negative or a positive. It can't be a nebulous thing. It's got five syllables, why don't we try "congratulations and celebrations"?'

Martin had nursed the idea of writing a song around the word 'congratulations', thinking it might be possible to write another 'Happy Birthday' or 'White Christmas': a jingle for any cork-popping celebration.

'Congratulations' is now one of the most recorded songs in Britain with over one thousand versions. It was played outside Buckingham Palace after the wedding of Charles and Diana, and on the dockside at Southampton when British troop ships returned from the Falklands War.

However, in 1968 when it was Britain's Eurovision entry it lost by one vote to Spain's long-forgotten 'La La La'. It was a bemusing decision which came about in the final seconds of voting when Germany awarded Spain six points, bringing its total up to twenty-nine against Britain's twenty-eight.

'I remember that we were taken back stage to get ready to receive the award and then we were given the news that it had lost,' says Bill Martin. 'We were sure that Cliff had walked it and of course after that it became number one in all the main markets outside of America.'

Under Norrie Paramor's direction Cliff had moved away from the rock 'n' roll group sound and was now almost always backed by an orchestra. By 1967 less than a fifth of all Cliff's sessions were recorded with the Shadows and in the summer of 1968 he went in the studio with the Shadows for the last time. The title of the track was 'Not The Way It Should Be'.

On 19 December 1968 Hank Marvin, Bruce Welch, John Rostill

and Brian Bennett broke up and went their separate ways. The Shadows did not come into existence again until 1974 when the line-up was Hank, Bruce, Brian and John Farrar.

In ten years the Shadows had come from being Cliff's backing group to an internationally recognized group in their own right. They had had thirteen top ten hits but there had been a gap of almost three years since 'Don't Make My Baby Blue' reached number ten.

Like any band that had been together for so long and toured so hard they were beginning to irritate each other. John Rostill and Hank Marvin were constantly arguing, Bruce Welch had met Olivia Newton-John whom he wanted to spend more time with and Brian Bennett had recorded a solo album titled, tellingly, 'Change Of Direction'.

'We worked too hard and we saw each other too often,' says Bennett. 'If we weren't touring we were recording and if we weren't recording we were doing a film, a pantomime or television.

'In your late teens and early twenties you accept all those things as new experiences, but as you start to mature you realize that there are things that you are not going to put up with about each other.'

Cliff by now had bought a house with Bill Latham in Northcliffe Drive, Totteridge, where they lived with Mamie who looked after them as if they were both her sons.

For someone of his status, his lifestyle wasn't extravagant. His biggest luxuries were the houses, a six-berth boat on the Norfolk Broads and his two cars—an MG and an E-type Jaguar. He followed the Christian practice of tithing, which meant giving ten per cent of his income to charity, and continued to take only fifteen pounds spending money in cash each week from the office.

His holidays were now taken in August with his Crusader friends. The group was always exclusively male and bachelor, and became known as the 'holiday gang'. If any of them married—as John Davey and Peter Graves subsequently did—they inevitably dropped out, though they remained close friends.

For the first two years they went to Portugal, driving down

through France in 1966 in Cliff's E-type Jaguar and John Davey's Vauxhall Victor Estate.

'Cliff identified very much with the style in which we did things, which was very much on the cheap,' remembers Peter Graves.

'On the way down through France we camped and this was an entirely new experience for him. To him we were all extremely normal and he found that he wasn't put on a pedestal. There are a lot of insults flying between us, a lot of banter, and he soon got caught up in it. Once we'd all got over the initial excitement of meeting him he became an ordinary friend and that appealed to him.'

In 1968 the holiday gang—Bill, Cliff, Graham, Peter and John— met up in Los Angeles where World Wide Films had given Cliff the use of a plush apartment in Burbank and a large estate car in lieu of his fee for *Two A Penny*.

For a month they became tourists, taking VIP trips of Universal Studios and Disneyland, going to an Animals' concert at the Hollywood Bowl, seeing Tony Bennett play in San Francisco and staying at the Dunes Hotel in Las Vegas.

Neither Cliff nor Bill Latham had much time for the more traditional sightseeing. When John Davey arranged a trip to the Grand Canyon neither of them were interested in going. Similarly, a few years later, when they were all in Israel, Latham preferred to spend his time poolside at Jerusalem's Diplomat Hotel rather than visit the sites.

The Shadows couldn't wholeheartedly get behind the Christian side of Cliff's career, and he didn't expect them to feel as much a part of this work.

Bruce Welch in particular had no time for his religious beliefs and hot-footed it out of the dressing room whenever Bible studies were mentioned. This lack of empathy, plus the fact that the Shadows were suffering internal strife, gave Cliff the freedom to work with other musicians.

The first of these were the folk-rock group the Settlers. Early in

1968 he met the group's singer Cindy Kent, one of the few
evangelical Christians in the business. Feeling isolated from the
church after six years on the road, a friend had suggested that she
turn up at one of Cliff's meetings at a church in Barnet. Afterwards, in
the vestry, they were introduced.

'It was then that I mentioned to him that I was looking for a
church,' remembers Cindy. 'I wanted to find somewhere where they
would understand my lifestyle and the fact that I couldn't be there
every week. He immediately understood my problem and suggested
his church. I started going and we became good friends.'

A group from St Paul's, including Cliff and Bill Latham, later saw
the Settlers at the Festival Hall. Cliff was impressed enough to ask
them to be part of a special gospel tour he was planning to do on
behalf of Eurovangelism, a Christian charity which sent aid to
European nationals.

The international director of Eurovangelism was Dave Foster who
had met Cliff for the first time on location during the filming of *Two A
Penny*. The two men had sat in the back of a van in Shepherd's Bush
eating lunch and Cliff had again talked about the possibility of
leaving music.

'Cliff said, "Well, what on earth can you do in the business I'm
in?",' says Dave Foster. 'So off the top of my head I said—"Why not
gospel concerts?" He went away and thought about it and at first he
couldn't find any good Christian musicians to work with him
because there was virtually no gospel scene at the time. Then one
day he called and said he thought he'd found them. I hadn't heard of
them but they were called the Settlers.'

Cliff hadn't done a gospel tour before but was intrigued with the
possibility of creating a show that would promote his beliefs. With
David Winter he discussed whether it should be a programme of
hymns or whether new material should be commissioned. David
suggested a concert arranged in three sections on the theme of 'Help,
Hope and Hallelujah' which would involve gospel songs, spirituals
and hymns alongside some thought-provoking secular material.

'The Help section consisted of songs like "Nowhere Man" which were about the longings that people have,' says Dave Foster. 'The Hope section began with "In The Bleak Mid-Winter" and concentrated on the life of Christ through to the crucifixion and resurrection. Hallelujah was a rip-roaring gospel celebration at the end.'

Peter Gormley was uncertain about this new direction and didn't want the show launched in Britain in case it failed and damaged Cliff's primary market. As a result of this Dave Foster set up the first mini-tour with dates in Stockholm, The Hague and Zagreb.

'Cliff very much became a part of us on that tour,' says Cindy Kent. 'There was no feeling of him being the star and us the humble group of backing musicians. Looking back, I can see that it was a time when he was sorting himself out, trying to discover what it was he should be doing with his music and his life.'

Even though 'Congratulations' was the biggest hit in Europe that month, Cliff had decided that this was to be his first show without hits.

'I have sung pop songs in Stockholm before,' he told the crowd of 3,000 on his opening night. 'But this evening we want to sing only gospel songs because of the special purpose of this concert.'

No one complained in Sweden but the next day in Holland they found the venue half empty despite the success of 'Congratulations' and prominent national publicity. In a confidential Eurovangelism report after the tour it was noted that this could have been because: 'Some Christians steered clear of what they expected to be an irreverent fiasco and some secular fans shunned what they thought would be a sort of staid hymn singing session.'

Says Dave Foster: 'It was an unusual experience for Cliff to see a half-empty hall. I think the analysis we came up with at the time was probably true. Something like this may have been what Peter Gormley foresaw when he was less than enthusiastic at the beginning.'

The show in Croatia, then Yugoslavia with Tito as president, was a boost for local Christians who were harassed at every turn and refused access to the media. Cliff not only used a secular venue to tell the Christian story but was also allowed to appear live on national television for three minutes before their ten o'clock news.

'We were backstage synchronizing our watches and even changed the running order that night so that when we went live Cliff would be speaking about his faith and how he became a Christian,' remembers Dave Foster.

'At about a minute before ten he launched into "What A Friend We Have In Jesus" which then faded into the news. Yugoslav Christians, some of whom were really suffering for sharing their faith, were ecstatic that someone had got away with it on national television!'

The head of the country's Baptist Union, Dr Horak, was later called in by the head of Zagreb's secret police. Expecting a reprimand he was surprised to be offered a coffee and some mild appreciation about the concert. It turned out that the police chief's teenage daughters had been there and had loved it.

'That was really a turning point for the church in Yugoslavia,' says Dave Foster. 'The money raised was given to local Christians to help with a home for destitute children. This action helped raise their image.

'Two weeks later Dr Horak was asked to meet President Tito which was really something. Then, in 1970, Billy Graham was allowed to do his first visual relays by land line to Zagreb. I don't think any of that would have happened without Cliff.'

While his secular career entered a period of stasis, allowing challengers such as Tom Jones and Engelbert Humperdinck to snatch his crown as Britain's most popular male vocalist, Cliff was learning how to craft a show with a message, not such an easy task for someone whose success had been built on orchestrating female frenzy.

Although he had toyed with songwriting over the years, usually with Hank or Bruce Welch, it was only on becoming a Christian that he had taken it seriously, providing the title track of *Two A Penny* and, late in 1968, writing songs with David Winter for a Tyne Tees television series, 'Life With Johnny'.

Based on the parables of Jesus but set in the contemporary world, the half-hour mini-musicals were the idea of religious television adviser Maxwell Dees and David Winter, and just as 'Help, Hope and Hallelujah' was an innovation for Christian music in Britain so 'Life With Johnny' was a breakthrough for God-slot television.

Cliff was Johnny while Cindy Kent, Una Stubbs and Lynda Marchal (now known as the television writer and novelist Lynda La Plante) played his girlfriends. Twenty songs, some written by Cliff, others by David Winter and Mike Jones of the Settlers, were recorded at Abbey Road for the soundtrack.

'It was recommended at the time by the ITV Yearbook as one of the most imaginative bits of religious broadcasting,' says David Winter.

'There were very strong character actors in it and Tyne Tees spent a lot of money on it. Every company showed it except the four majors—Granada, Yorkshire, LWT and Anglia—who were upset that a small company had muscled in and made a programme for the main evening show.'

It was rumoured around this time that Cliff was dating Cindy Kent. After all, she did seem to fit the bill: she was wholesome, she had long hair, she liked music, she didn't wear too much make-up and she shared his Christian faith.

The *TV Times* approached her, ostensibly to write a profile, and during the interview asked what sort of man she would like to marry. She outlined her preferences and the interviewer casually suggested that it sounded as though she was describing someone like Cliff Richard. 'I suppose so,' said Cindy, and that was that.

'When the story came out it was run as part of a series titled "The Men In My Life",' says Cindy. 'They had rung Cliff's mum up to see what she thought of me.

'It was absolutely awful. Girls turned up at Cliff's house weeping, saying "It's not true, is it? He's not planning to marry Cindy, is he?" I rang him up straight away. I was so upset. He just told me not to worry.'

At the end of the sixties Cliff's secular career had settled into a dull and unadventurous rut. The only thing the singles had going for them was that they were 'catchy', in the sense that your postman could probably whistle them.

They certainly didn't have soul or musical innovation. Was it really possible to be moved by 'Good Times'? Did anyone care who played guitar on 'Big Ship' or what the lyric of 'Goodbye Sam, Hello Samantha' was attempting to describe?

A similar emptiness could be experienced by watching his television series 'It's Cliff Richard' in 1970 and 1971 where he played some of the same songs and indulged in safe humour with Una Stubbs, Olivia Newton-John and Hank Marvin (who was now one third of the group Marvin, Welch and Farrar).

Olivia seemed wonderfully suited to Cliff. With her attractive white smile and innocent beauty she looked like his female counterpart. The image of togetherness was enhanced by the duets they sang together during the series and a sketch in which they played bride and bridegroom. The public wished them on each other.

Cliff helped launch her career in Britain and Peter Gormley became her manager. After the debut on television he introduced her into his concerts and she and her friend Pat Farrar began singing backing vocals.

There was never any romance. From the time of her arrival in England in 1967 she was involved with Bruce Welch, eventually setting up home with him and getting engaged. When they split up in 1972 she had a relationship with her manager Lee Kramer before meeting dancer Matt Lattanzi on the set of *Xanadu* in 1980 and marrying him five years later.

But they were extremely close. Cliff kept framed photos of her at home and at the office and whenever she was in town they would end up going out together. Once they even called a radio station late at night from a hotel room and requested a song.

'I think it was Capital Radio in London,' says Olivia. 'Cliff called up and said, "Hello, this is Cliff Richard." The DJ said, "Yes, and I'm Elvis Presley." He didn't believe Cliff! Then I called up and said, "Hello, this is Olivia Newton-John." From then on it became a running gag.

'Every DJ that took over would say, "Cliff and Olivia, are you still there? Are you having your breakfast yet?" It was all quite innocent, but that's how rumours start!'

'There was only one girl we thought had a chance with Cliff,' his mother admits. 'That was Olivia. Knowing all the girls he's been out with and knowing him I think that was his chance. If he was going to marry, she would have been the girl.'

Yet, according to Cliff, it wasn't just the fact of her boyfriends that kept them apart.

'I don't think we would have got involved anyway,' he says. 'I'm very fond of her and I guess it's because we never got involved that we can remain such good friends. I feel totally comfortable with her and would like to think she feels comfortable with me. When we see each other we hug each other to death for about ten minutes.

'We feel that close and yet I know there was no romantic thing from my point of view and I never got the romantic vibe from her. Yet, having said that, I never felt put down by it.'

In 1971 Cliff was drawn into the then-lively pornography debate which saw him on the side of Mary Whitehouse, Malcolm Muggeridge and Lord Longford against the massed ranks of the various liberation 'fronts' and Marxist-Leninist splinter groups which had emerged from Britain's alternative culture.

The Nationwide Festival of Light had been founded by Peter Hill, a young missionary who had returned home to England and been shocked by what he saw as a sharp moral decline. In a very short time he motivated thousands of Christians to register their protest in marches and rallies throughout the country. It was to be a display of solidarity and a reassertion of Christian values.

Cliff was invited to perform at the opening rally on 9 September at Westminster Central Hall in London. The Gay Liberation Front, who saw the Festival of Light as an Establishment plan to curb the freedoms they had gained in the sixties, planned to disrupt the event.

Operation Rupert Bear, as it was code-named, was organized by Dennis Lemon (later to be taken to court by Mary Whitehouse in a well-known blasphemy case when he became editor of *Gay News*) and financed by Graham Chapman of Monty Python. It involved a group of GLF members who infiltrated the crowd dressed as nuns and then, as things got going, began shouting 'Glory Hallelujah' and 'Praise the Lord' while releasing bagfuls of white mice.

From that point on Cliff became a particular target of left-wing groups, anarchist groups and gay liberation organizations. The homosexual activists suspected that Cliff was a repressed homosexual dealing with his repression by attacking those who had 'come out'.

When he played a thirty-minute set at the Festival of Light's final rally in Hyde Park on 25 September he was jeered and pelted with eggs.

'It was early days for Cliff as a Christian and here he was being pitched into public opposition that most of us never have to confront in a lifetime,' says Bill Latham. 'But he took it all without flinching. There was never any question of him retreating.'

19

'A time of growth'

B etween 1972 and 1975 Cliff's career slumped to an all-time low. He was out of fashion, out of touch and, for long periods, out of the charts. He was a figure of ridicule to the new rock aristocracy who derided his music as too bland and innocuous.

Just as he had grown his hair, worn chunky crucifixes and started singing songs of love, peace and freedom, the rock culture he must have hoped to appear relevant to had abandoned the good vibes of the sixties for a taste of decadence.

David Bowie, who had appeared on one album cover in a full-length dress, had become the first rock singer to confess to homosexual experience. The American rock star Alice Cooper was grabbing headlines by attacking blood-filled baby dolls on stage with a sharpened axe, and Marc Bolan was draping himself with feather boas and liberally applying mascara.

With hippie culture Cliff had been able to take the buzzwords of love, peace, freedom and harmony and invest them with Christian meaning. The new darker mood of hard drugs, violence and sexual perversion couldn't be given the same sort of spin. You could possibly interest a hippy in discovering 'real peace' or 'real freedom' but you couldn't honestly claim that Jesus offered the tops in decadence.

Cliff was disturbed by Bowie's use of bisexual imagery and by the mock horror of Alice Cooper. It not only offended his Christian sensitivity but it went against his natural conservativism. His acid test was always whether it would embarrass or shock his mother. If he thought it would then, in his opinion, it had gone too far. It was indecent.

He spoke out against homosexual practice and began to identify himself more with Mary Whitehouse who, as President of the Viewers and Listeners Association, had been fighting a long battle against what she saw as declining moral standards in the media. She vigilantly monitored radio and television output and encouraged her followers to complain about obscene language or scenes of violence and nudity.

'What is this Bowie man/woman image on the stage doing to young people?' Cliff asked at the time. 'He upsets me as a man. There's a great responsibility all of us singers have to the ten year olds and some of us aren't living up to it.'

New Musical Express, which in 1958 had questioned his own suitability for television, was by now on the side of those who offended respectable opinion. It gloried in tales of sleaze, debauchery and drug-taking and saw in Cliff an appropriate figure of hate.

The paper repeatedly pilloried him for his celibacy, his Christian faith and his consummate 'cleanness'. Nick Kent, whose hero of the moment was Rolling Stone Keith Richards, was sent to report on Cliff's appearance at Spre-e'73, a Christian event at Wembley Stadium at which Billy Graham was preaching. There was no mention of the music. Cliff, he said, 'bounced around flashing his teeth' and looked as though 'he'd just come out of rigorous training for the John Denver "Wimp of the Week" sweepstakes'.

There were feeble attempts to be 'relevant' but they only served to show how out of tune he was. 'Power To All Our Friends' sounded like a belated response to 'Power To The People', but whereas John Lennon sang left-wing orthodoxy with passion and soul, Cliff sang candy-floss lyrics to a Eurovision beat.

'Take Me High' nodded in the direction of the coded drugs songs of the mid sixties, 'Honky Tonk Angel' mined the same territory as the Rolling Stones' 1969 song 'Honky Tonk Woman' and Sing A Song Of Freedom' was an all-purpose anthem with no real message which drew on the popular banner-waving slogans of campus politics.

What was more worrying, for Cliff and his management, was that the fans were no longer buying the singles in such huge volumes. His entire sales between 1970 and 1975 were easily beaten by the combined sales of 'Living Doll' and 'Travellin' Light' back in the early days of his career.

His first attempt to put out a religious song as a single was a resounding flop. 'Jesus' was his worst-selling record to date and didn't even make the top thirty. Later the same year (1972) he lost Norrie Paramor, who retired from EMI and moved to Birmingham to conduct the Midland Light Orchestra.

Norrie might have lost his magic touch but he'd been in the studio with Cliff for almost every session since 1958 and had become an important father figure. The first single he recorded without Norrie, 'A Brand New Song', was also the first of his career not to enter the top fifty. It seemed like a bad omen.

The challenge apparently gone from his music, his desire to act was rekindled. He was approached in 1970 by the New Theatre in Bromley to take on the part of Clive Harrington in *Five Finger Exercise*, Peter Shaffer's play about the 'deep friendship' between an artistic student and a tutor.

Controversial when first produced in 1958 because of its veiled treatment of homosexual affection, it was a strange choice of subject matter for Cliff's stage debut in a dramatic role.

'It was about a young fellow discovering his sexual identity,' explains William Gaunt, who played the part of the tutor.

'We discussed the play as a cast but Cliff never related any of the emotions to himself. It was all very much, "Yes, that's interesting—

let's get on with it". He didn't flinch from the subject, and he acted very capably, but at the same time I don't think he really put himself into it.

'When I visited his dressing room during the interval on the opening night I found him sitting there signing a pile of photographs. That was indicative of his attitude. It was a job he wanted to do in order to prove that he could do it.'

The local newspaper, the *Kentish Times*, felt that he couldn't ultimately master the role because of his natural niceness and his inexperience. The years hoofing it around in pantomimes and doing cute television sketches for tea-time audiences weren't an adequate training ground for serious acting.

'But within those limitations,' the theatre critic conceded, 'Cliff Richard's straight acting debut at the New Theatre Bromley was a success and a triumph for his determination to make his way in the theatre.'

Emboldened by the experience he returned a year later with his first beard to rehearse for a part in Graham Greene's 1958 play *The Potting Shed* but two days before opening night the theatre burned down and the production had to be transferred to Sadler's Wells Theatre in North London.

This time the *Kentish Times* saw an improvement: 'As the obsessed James Callifer he gives a nicely restrained performance that nevertheless has the undercurrent of poignancy and despairing drive.' Cliff has since said that this remains one of his proudest achievements.

The next year he took a part in a television drama, 'The Case', and then in 1974 he renewed his relationship with Kenneth Harper to star in *Take Me High* with Anthony Andrews and Deborah Watling.

The story of a young merchant banker who goes to Birmingham and revives a restaurant's flagging trade by inventing the Brumburger, *Take Me High* was an artistic and commercial flop.

'We all wanted to prove that we could do a musical film without dances and the answer is that you can't,' says Kenneth Harper.

'It was rushed into scripting and then rushed into filming. When you get to a point in the script and you think you're up a gum tree a great director can generally invent something but it just didn't happen this time. It didn't make its money back.'

Kenneth Harper and his director David Askey had made the film as if nothing had changed in the world since *Wonderful Life*. There was the same attempt at innocent joviality and coy flirtatiousness but cinema audiences no longer found the immaturity believable.

'As soon as I saw it I realized how old-fashioned it was,' says Anthony Andrews, who was then at the beginning of his film career. 'It was a hangover from a previous era. That was a slightly disappointing realization because during the making of it we'd had such fun. It was like being in *The Young Ones*.'

That year, 1974, Cliff released only one single, '(You Keep Me) Hanging On', and 1975 was his first year without a hit single. 'Honky Tonk Angel' was withdrawn after only a thousand copies had been pressed because it was brought to Cliff's attention that a honky tonk angel is not an attractive piano player but an American prostitute.

'I was at a Christian conference centre with Bill and I was taking questions from the audience when a girl asked me why my new record was about a prostitute,' says Cliff. 'It shook me rigid. I said, "You're joking, aren't you?" I promised to check it out and when I got back home I called Peter Gormley.'

Gormley wasn't sure but called friends in Los Angeles and confirmed that a honky tonk angel was at least a 'loose woman' who frequented honky tonk bars if not a whore. Cliff ordered the record to be stopped and even went on a pre-booked 'Russell Harty Show' to explain why he wouldn't be performing his latest single.

'I had already sent copies out to the DJs on Radio 1,' says Eric Hall, then Head of Promotion for EMI. 'To make sure the record was completely withdrawn I had to go round personally and take them back because I knew that if I just told them not to play it the records would end up as collectors' items.'

Yet while the first half of the seventies was an artistic and commercial failure it was a time of great spiritual growth. The let-up of pressure gave him the time to work out how the demands of his faith should affect his work.

'It was my growth time as a Christian,' he admits. 'It wasn't planned that way but it gave me time to get my Christian life to a point where I was totally comfortable with it.'

Having moved from Totteridge into a £70,000 house in the exclusive St George's Hill estate in Weybridge, he and Bill Latham regularly began to attend Sunday evening services at Guildford Baptist Church. David Pawson, a noted Bible teacher, would preach fifty-minute sermons to a congregation that was over seven hundred strong. Often the church was so packed that the service had to be relayed to ante-rooms on closed circuit television.

Although Cliff never became a member of the church he went as often as his job would allow and a small group was organized to pray with him when he was around and for him when he wasn't.

'When Cliff came to our church I made him a two-fold promise,' says David Pawson. 'One part of it was that I would never ask him to do anything unless he wanted to do it and the other was that I would never pass on any requests I got for his services.

'I wanted him to have one place where he could come and be himself and not be bothered by anyone else. He usually came in at the last minute and because there were no seats left he would sit on the floor with most of the young people. He was accepted as one of the congregation and the lack of special attention was quite noticeable.'

The move to Weybridge in 1973 had been made possible when Bill Latham gave up his job as a teacher to work with a fledgling relief agency attached to the Evangelical Alliance, an umbrella organization which looked after the concerns of evangelical Christians in all denominations.

A dynamic young vicar in his thirties, George Hoffman, had been hired by them to organize a series of social action projects, one of which was a fund for overseas aid which had been started in 1968 from money sent in by Christians who wanted to see something done in the world's disaster areas. It became known as The Evangelical Alliance Relief Fund, Tear Fund for short.

'The work grew rapidly,' says Hoffman. 'David Winter, who was editing *Crusade* magazine in the same building, said he knew the right person to help me. That was how Bill Latham came to be my assistant. He did what I didn't do and I did what he didn't do.'

Tear Fund bought food and equipment and also sponsored workers to help on existing relief projects. Cliff had made his first donation in 1968 when the £2,000 profit from his first British gospel concert bought a Land Rover for a group in Northern Argentina.

'It was very much a venture of faith on Cliff's part,' says Hoffman, 'because there was no way that he was identifying with an established or a prestigious organization. There was only me, Bill Latham, a secretary and a lot of enthusiasm.'

In 1973, more than a decade before Bob Geldof's celebrated visit to the refugee camps of Ethiopia, Cliff became the first major British pop star to visit the sick and dying in the Third World.

He had wanted to experience Tear Fund's work first hand and in November he set off for Bangladesh, the independent republic created in the aftermath of the Indo-Pakistan War, where refugees were flooding in from North India to avoid persecution. The camps were overcrowded and filthy, the refugees sick and undernourished.

He arrived in Dacca with Bill Latham, George Hoffman and photographer Clifford Shirley and was introduced to the local team supported by Tear Fund. On the first day he was escorted by Liz Huchison, a young nurse from Devon, who was working with children in a cluster of bombed-out buildings and makeshift shacks that was known as Mirpur Camp.

She picked him up in a Volkswagen minibus which then collected a group of severely malnourished children who needed to be bathed, fed and given medicine at a compound run by the Southern Baptist Mission.

'I don't think he'd ever seen anything like it before,' remembers Liz. 'It's very difficult to explain. You can see pictures but to physically touch and smell . . . it's very different.

'The children he saw were terribly underweight. Their emotional development was stunted. Some were very sick. I can remember going back with him that afternoon in the van and he couldn't say a thing. He was just staring out of the window and you knew it wasn't appropriate to talk. He was obviously trying to cope with all the impressions and emotions.'

During the rest of the stay he visited other camps dealing with similar problems. He saw adults with bullet wounds and burns and saw children dying of starvation. He began to feel a sense of shame about his own life of riches and glamour. What benefit was he to a sick and starving world? Wouldn't one month spent as a relief worker be better than all his years at the top of the charts?

At the end of each day workers and vistors met at the nurses' quarters for prayer and a Bible study led by George Hoffman. In one of the discussions that followed, Cliff expressed his longing to be of more practical use.

'He said, "You know what I've seen today makes me feel as though I want to give it all up and come out here and work",' remembers Hoffman. 'Liz Huchison turned to him very quietly and said, "Can you give an injection or put a person on a drip?" He said, "No, I'd be horrified." She said, "Well you go back home and raise money for us to do it. That's what you can do and this is what we do. That's what it's all about." '

This comment, made without reflection, was to mark a turning point in his life. His songs might not be the sort to change the world but the money they earned could be used to bring about change.

20

'The best thing I've done for years'

Cliff was still approaching his career with the attitudes of the fifties when singles mattered and albums didn't; when singers weren't expected to write or even choose their own material and when concerts involved singing a string of hits for twenty minutes.

He had always relied on Norrie Paramor to organize his recordings. After choosing the songs with Norrie and discussing possible musical arrangements, Cliff's only task was to drop by the studio and add his vocals—sometimes five or six in a day. Bruce Welch once said that if Cliff didn't have three hits completed by 10.30 p.m. he would think it had been a bad night.

The practice harked back to the days when record companies and music publishers controlled the business and used singers to promote their product. But all this had been broken down in the era ushered in by the Beatles. Power began to return to the artists.

After Paramor's fourteen-year reign Peter Gormley wanted to try different producers; to shift the work around much more. His first choice was Dave Mackay, a former house producer for EMI Australia, who had come to London to work with the New Seekers.

Mackay knew that Cliff's recording career needed turning round. It had lost momentum. He sat down and talked to him about contemporary music, played him tracks he liked and listened to some of the gospel material that Cliff found interesting.

One of the artists Cliff told Mackay about was Larry Norman, a Californian with shoulder-length blond hair and an acoustic guitar who was writing what the media called 'Jesus Rock'. This was a new type of Christian music that owed more to Bob Dylan and the Rolling Stones than it did to the sort of gospel music that Elvis Presley used to record.

Norman was a mesmerizing stage performer who planned every gesture for maximum effect. He often chided audiences for clapping during his concerts and developed the 'one way sign' (an index finger pointing heavenwards) to indicate where the appreciation should be directed.

Cliff went to see Larry Norman in concert at the Albert Hall and later they met up to talk.

'As soon as we met we started talking about the songs and the reasons I had for writing them,' says Norman. 'He explained the dilemma he was in having to sing music from his past, music for the future and also gospel music.

'He wasn't sure what was the most dignified or credible way to present the songs he really cared about. He seemed very wise and thoughtful about it all.'

Dave Mackay encouraged Cliff to write more of his own material and to work on his playing technique as a way of getting back in touch with the music.

'We had to break down the old routine,' says Mackay. 'I had to tell him that things had changed and that he needed to come in and work with the band. We needed to listen to songs, to work them out and to discuss the strengths and weaknesses. In the past he had only needed to decide what key to sing it in and the next time he heard the song it was already out as a record.'

Through Mackay he met a rhythm section known as Quartet, two of whose members were later to play a major part in reshaping his career.

Guitarist Terry Britten had come to England in 1969 when his band the Twilights, which had been one of Australia's top acts, broke up. Here Britten had joined up again with Alan Tarney (bass), Kevin Peek (guitar) and Trevor Spencer (drums) who had played in the James Taylor Move (nothing to do with the American singer of the same name), an Adelaide band which rivalled the Twilights.

'In those days you had to sing cover versions of pop hits in order to make a living,' says Trevor Spencer. 'But the cover bands in Australia were very good, a bit like the Irish cover bands but not as cabaret-orientated. The James Taylor Move—the singer's name was James and Kevin Peek's middle name was Taylor—played Jimi Hendrix and the Cream. The Twilights played the Hollies and the Beatles.'

Living in flats in West Kensington they had formed Quartet and signed to Decca Records. Fame though was not to come under this name but through working with Dave Mackay as session musicians and later as a working band with Cliff.

'Kevin Peek was the first to play on a Cliff session,' Trevor Spencer recalls. 'He replaced an Australian called Tweed Harris on a tour. When that tour finished they wanted Alan Tarney to join. Then Brian Bennett, who'd been playing drums, left to concentrate on the Shadows and I was brought in.'

Touring with Cliff at this point was a mixed blessing. The up-side was getting well paid for playing some of the chart hits of their youth. The down-side was the brain-deadening experience of playing songs like 'Goodbye Sam, Hello Samantha' and 'Flying Machine' in Northern night clubs where they often had to enter the stage from kitchens slippery with cooking oil.

Tales abound of musicians falling asleep on stage and losing their places in the music. There were times during runs at the Palladium when they would forget whether they were playing the matinée or the evening show. They called themselves the 'scumbags', a derogatory term for pick-up musicians, and planned to turn up wearing T-shirts reading 'Scumbag World Tour'.

'A lot of the musicians just didn't feel involved in what Cliff was doing,' says Trevor Spencer. 'They were more interested in getting drunk than playing. These were tours where we had to dress completely in black and there would be a black backdrop so that we would all merge into the background. They just about nailed the backing singers' feet to the floor so that they wouldn't distract from Cliff.'

'I found this period quite depressing,' agrees Terry Britten. 'I remember Batley Variety Club and these bleak Yorkshire days. You'd go to do the show and there'd be "Congratulations", "Living Doll" and all this stuff and you'd be sitting on a chair stuck behind a music stand, and it had the feeling of being a hired help.

'You'd do the show and there would be the clanging of knives and forks and the smell of scampi and chips everywhere. My heart wasn't in it. It was just a job. But Cliff always gave his best wherever he was.'

Some of his musicians hated the club work so much that they welcomed the annual gospel tours where, with songs like those of Larry Norman's, there would at least be a bit of speed and aggression.

Dave Mackay came into Cliff's career at its most crucial juncture. Without any more hits, Cliff was obviously destined to become a Tommy Steele or Frankie Vaughan type of entertainer who could always sell out a show but who no longer belonged on the top table.

It wasn't only Cliff who had lost his way. Rock music was suffering fatigue after the great party of the sixties. The Beatles, who had led so many of the changes, had broken up acrimoniously. Both Brian Jones of the Rolling Stones and Jim Morrison of the Doors were now dead. The British charts, which had such a short time ago been full of classics, were now laden with acts such as Chicory Tip, Donny Osmond, Lieutenant Pigeon and Terry Dactyl and the Dinosaurs.

Acts which had survived the sixties were no longer sure where they belonged. There wasn't a movement to be part of, and none of them were willing to compete with the likes of Slade, Mud and Sweet by becoming 'glam rockers'—it seemed like such a retrogressive step.

Mackay could see clearly the changes that would need to be made, but initially he wasn't in a position to make them. He had inherited the responsibility of producing a soundtrack to *Take Me High*. The songs, written by Australian Tony Cole, were vacuous and instantly forgettable. Mackay then produced the gospel album *Help It Along*.

Other than the Eurovision entry, 'Power To All Our Friends', which sold over one million worldwide, Mackay's singles were a commercial disappointment with one complete failure and three low-ranking hits.

The project which introduced the changes he had talked about was *31st Of February Street*, Cliff's first proper album since 1970. Released in November 1974 it didn't get great reviews, didn't produce any singles and wasn't a best-seller but, with its softer, more introspective mood it at least helped drag Cliff into the seventies and almost half the songs were self-written.

'The recording coincided with my renewed interest in my own career,' says Cliff. 'I suddenly started getting involved in the production side. I started writing.

'Dave would sit down with me and I would play him bits that I had written and he'd tell me what he thought was good and what he thought I should finish. Other than Bill and Tear Fund he was the only person ever to encourage me to write.

'That album was, to me, the turning point of my career.'

But it was Bruce Welch who was to take full advantage of Cliff's new attitude towards his music by laying the groundwork for one of the most durable comebacks in show business history. In one forty-eight-hour period in September 1975, Welch produced 'Devil Woman' and 'Miss You Nights'. These two records, more than any others, were to set the tone for the rest of his career.

There was some irony in that it was Welch who was to help re-launch Cliff's career because the two men had never been close. Privately Welch scoffed at Cliff's religious views and considered himself too down to earth and plain speaking for Cliff's liking.

'Cliff doesn't like my lifestyle and I can't believe his' was how he once put it. 'We don't have anything in common but our love of music.'

He'd come back into the picture through an off-hand remark made by Peter Gormley who was by now quite worried about the state of Cliff's record sales.

'Cliff was putting out records and they weren't becoming hits,' says Welch. 'He was making boring, bland records and he didn't seem to care. The only thing in his life was religion. Peter Gormley, who was still managing me as a member of the Shadows, happened to mention that whoever found the right songs for Cliff would have a strong chance of producing him.'

Since his successes with Olivia Newton-John (he had co-written and co-produced three of her American top ten hits) Welch was keen to do more production. He had good contacts among music publishers and songwriters and began to trawl for new songs, putting the word out that Cliff Richard was ready to shed his middle-of-the-road image. The 'Congratulations' era was over.

On a material-gathering trip to Los Angeles he met Lionel Conway, British-born head of Island Music in Los Angeles, who played him songs by his writers.

'I wasn't really struck by any of them but I said I'd take the tapes away and listen to them again,' says Welch. 'I came back to London and I was in my music room when I played them through again. I still didn't like them but I turned one of the cassettes over and there on the other side was "Miss You Nights"—a song Lionel hadn't even bothered to play me. I knew instantly that it was a smash hit.'

What he was hearing was the work of Dave Townsend, a 26-year-old writer from England, who'd recorded the song not as a publisher's demo but as a track for an Island Records album. Produced at a cost of £20,000, the album had been shelved as uncommercial. The only chance of recouping the production cost was through cover versions of the songs.

Dave Townsend had written 'Miss You Nights' while living in Somerset the year before. His girlfriend, Sally, had taken off for a solo holiday in Majorca and he had turned his feelings of longing and loneliness into a beautiful ballad with hauntingly fresh images. A swelling string arrangement by Andrew Powell on the recording had endowed it with an ethereal quality.

It was this version of the song that Welch took down to Cliff's home in Weybridge one summer evening along with 'Devil Woman' written by Terry Britten and 'I Can't Ask For Any More Than You' by Ken Gold and Michael Denne.

'Cliff put the cassette of "Miss You Nights" on in his music room and the hairs stood up on his arms,' remembers Welch. 'He'd already been given "Devil Woman" some months before but he hadn't done anything with it. I pushed him. I said, why on earth haven't you recorded this song?'

'Devil Woman' had started off as a riff which Terry Britten couldn't find words for and then he linked up with Christine Holmes, a singer and children's television presenter who had been produced by Dave Mackay, and she gave it a title and wrote the story of a seductive fortune teller.

'I had my ideas about this fortune teller song in my notebook and Terry had this guitar riff and we just put them together,' says Christine. 'We wrote it together at my flat.

'I knew it had to be a rock number. Helen Reddy had done a song called "Angie Baby" which was a really spooky song and used sounds in the mix that hadn't been used too much in pop music. I had it in my mind that I wanted "Devil Woman" to sound similarly spooky. We both very much knew what we wanted and Cliff copied the demo exactly.'

When Cliff went into Abbey Road to record the three songs, Welch, as producer, retained Alan Tarney and Terry Britten from Dave Mackay's rhythm section but added Graham Todd on keyboards and Tony Rivers, John Perry and Ken Gold on backing vocals.

'It was a great session the day we did "Devil Woman",' remembers Terry Britten. 'The engineer Tony Clark was standing in front of the speakers as it was played back and as quick as a flash he said, "America! This is gonna be a smash in America!" '

Tony Clark remembers the emotion of the session. 'You could feel something was happening,' he says. 'The actual groove of the track was something instant. When I said it was made for America I was probably more excited than anyone else. In those days it wasn't normal to stand up in the control room and shout out loud.'

Three months later, with 'Devil Woman' and 'Miss You Nights' still unreleased as singles, the same team returned to the studio to complete an album of the songs that Welch had gathered.

'I knew what I was capable of but I'd happily got into doing family shows,' says Cliff. 'For this album I was getting songs that publishers would never normally give me because they would insist on sending me material that sounded like "Congratulations". So it was the first time in years that I'd had the chance to stretch my voice and do some rock.'

It now sounded as though Cliff was working with a band rather than dubbing his vocals over a band. Although there were still ballads there was a looser, funkier feel to the tracks and a spirit of exploration that had long been missing in his music.

'I had told him that he needed to change the way he recorded,' says Welch. 'I told him I wanted rehearsals, that I wanted to make sure we got the right keys on every song. I changed the way he sang. He had never sung falsetto. He said he couldn't sing like that. I told him he could. He had just never tried it. Now he does it all the time.'

'Miss You Nights' was the first single to be released, in February 1976, because there was some concern that 'Devil Woman' might get confused with the Electric Light Orchestra's 'Evil Woman' which had entered the charts in January. It sold impressively and returned Cliff to the top twenty for the first time in two years, but it was 'Devil Woman', released two months later, which re-established him as a chart force.

'I was sitting in my kitchen in Epsom and the DJ said he was going to play a record and we should try and guess who it was,' remembers

Terry Britten of the first radio play he heard. 'He played this record and my ears went up when I heard the first couple of bars.

'Then everyone started ringing in and getting it wrong and he played it again and there was this tremendous excitement that this was Cliff Richard. No one could believe that Cliff could make a record like this.'

'Devil Woman' sounded like something that the Rolling Stones or at least Elton John would record. The voice was as clean as ever but the sound of the track was dirty and swampy. Cliff had never worked around a riff like this before and the story of being seduced by a fortune teller conjured up images of dark backstreets in New Orleans; of a world a million miles away from 'Take Me High'.

The writer, Christine Holmes, says that the song is about a man who is seduced by a fortune teller.

'It's a very rude song actually,' admits Holmes. 'But I'm not sure that Cliff was aware how rude it was. My whole thing was to convey that women can be very spooky and clever when they try to snare a guy. They can force a guy into doing things he wouldn't normally do. They can be witches when they want to be.'

Cliff has indeed interpreted the lyric in a different way, believing it to be a warning against dabbling in the occult. This view was endorsed for him when a young woman from Australia wrote to him to say that the song had been instrumental in her Christian conversion. 'I heeded the warning,' she told him.

The music press was enthusiastic about the single, seeing it as a definite return to form. There was talk of the Cliff Richard Renaissance. The record climbed into the top ten, eventually becoming his biggest international seller since 'The Young Ones'.

The album, *I'm Nearly Famous*, released a month later, featured Cliff on the cover lying on a single bed with a notepad and pen transcribing the lyrics of Eddie Cochran's 'C'Mon Everybody' which is spinning on an old fashioned monophonic turntable beside him.

On the walls were photographs of Elvis Presley, Little Richard, Chuck Berry and Ricky Nelson. Although it was hardly a return to fifties rock 'n' roll it was a return to his own roots as a working musician with band members who could write.

EMI was excited by the album and promoted it heavily, printing up 'I'm Nearly Famous' T-shirts and badges which began to be sported by celebrities such as Elton John, Jeff Beck, Pete Townshend and Elizabeth Taylor. Although he would never be taken up by the emerging punk generation, it was suddenly OK to admit to liking Cliff.

Bruce Welch says that *I'm Nearly Famous* was the album which gave Cliff his credibility back. 'He got great reviews and he had big hits. Since that moment he's just developed and developed. His concerts have got bigger and his money has got bigger.'

Reviewing the album in *Melody Maker*, Geoff Brown wrote, 'Cliff Richard has at last made the sort of album he could, and should, have been making for years. It is with some incredulity I have to say that for the past ten days I've been playing two albums consistently. One is Marvin Gaye's *I Want You*. The other is *I'm Nearly Famous*. The renaissance of Richard, for that is what I believe this album heralds, is long overdue . . .

'I doubt whether *I'm Nearly Famous* will rid Cliff at a stroke of his straitlaced image as Mary Whitehouse's favourite son, nor, I suspect, would he want it to; for that is what he most likely is. Neither will it win him a whole new concert audience overnight.

'However, it is the best album of new songs ever and, if there are enough unprejudiced ears around, could well mark the start of a fresh Cliff Richard record-buying public. Closet Cliff Richard rock fans? Why not? *I'm Nearly Famous* is, in its way, the most surprising album for many years. Hear it.'

Brown interviewed Cliff in the next issue for a major feature which struck a similarly positive note. Cliff spoke of the forty songs that Bruce Welch had collected and how they whittled the list down to the fourteen or fifteen that were recorded.

'I think it's the best thing I've done for years,' Cliff said. 'It may be the only hit album I'll have had in years. I had more to say about how

I would sing, and vocal harmonies and all that. We didn't go into the studio and say we're going to do a certain thing. What we did say was that we weren't going to record anything that sounded like "Congratulations".'

Elton John's manager, John Reid, heard 'Miss You Nights' and wanted to release it in America on his three-year-old record label, Rocket. Elton had long been a fan (he could remember seeing him in pantomime at the Palladium) and it was thought that maybe Rocket could launch Cliff in America in the way that it had recently reversed the fortunes of Neil Sedaka in his home country.

Rocket's Executive Vice President in America was Tony King, a flamboyant English bachelor who had once worked for the Beatles' Apple label, and was closely acquainted with almost everyone who mattered in the rock industry.

He listened to the album and concluded that although 'Miss You Nights' was a good song, it was 'Devil Woman' that stood the better chance of becoming a hit. He had the track remastered to match the sound quality of American radio and it was released in June.

'We cut it really hot,' says King. 'Then I brought in a publicist called Sharon Lawrence who said that if we really wanted to crack America Cliff would have to be brought over for a month to do press and radio. Peter Gormley agreed and so I went on the road with Cliff.

'Whenever I had met him before I had been in awe of him and very much on my best behaviour. The thought of spending four weeks with him made me feel a bit nervous.'

The tour party, which consisted of Tony King, Cliff, Sharon Lawrence and Peter Hebbes from Gormley Management, flew from coast to coast taking in major cities such as New York, Chicago, Boston, Memphis, Detroit, San Francisco and Los Angeles. In each city there would be a party for the media and then Cliff would spend hours being interviewed.

For Tony King it was a revelation. He had expected to wilt under withering Puritan scrutiny but instead found himself totally accepted by Cliff. The two became firm friends.

'I was pleased to find that he wasn't quite as abstemious as I had thought,' King says. 'He never got drunk but he liked a glass of wine and enjoyed getting jolly. In fact we ended up calling it the White Wine Tour of America because there would always be white wine at these receptions and by the end of the tour Cliff was getting to the wine waiter before me.

'I had always thought he might be offended if I swore and yet he just shrugged it off. I don't think he minded bad language or a clever double-entendre. If it was clever then he was one to laugh but what he didn't like was coarseness.

'People imagine he looks down his nose at everyone because of his Christian faith but I found him a really relaxing person to be with. He wasn't at all judgmental. We had a lot of personal talks about our lives and about religion.'

In Atlanta they caught up with Elton John and went to his show at the Omni auditorium. In Los Angeles Olivia Newton-John threw a party for them at her new home. In New York, King, who was a close friend of John Lennon and had been responsible for bringing him together with Elton John, almost managed to arrange a reunion between Cliff and the former Beatle.

'Cliff was fascinated by the fact that I was close to John,' says Tony. 'He would ask me lots of questions because he always wanted to know what other people were like. I think the John Lennon of that period would have got on very well with Cliff. He was a much softer character and I had told him that I thought he would find Cliff quite interesting. John was up for it.'

He was even given his third and final opportunity to fulfil his earliest rock 'n' roll ambition—meeting Elvis. A magazine journalist, who said he was a personal friend, was ready to bring them together but when he then suggested bringing a photographer along Cliff changed his mind.

'The Elvis I wanted to remember was the one whose door I knocked on in 1959,' Cliff says. 'I didn't want to meet the big fat Elvis. I thought I'd wait until he got himself together.'

Cliff's career in America up to this point had been undistinguished. He'd scored a hit with 'Living Doll' and had twice been on tour but the films had flopped and Rocket was the ninth label to try to do something for him.

It was a source of frustration to him that while he'd conquered Europe, the Far East and all other English-speaking countries he had never become a household name in the country which had given rock 'n' roll to the world.

In America it was possible to have a regional hit but never to be known nationwide. The only realistic way to become a household name was to tour extensively and repeatedly and to spend at least half of each year there.

'I don't think Cliff was willing to give up his life here in England in order to make it in America,' says Peter Gormley.

'We had offers in television that would have meant staying there for up to a year compèring shows and being a part of other shows. He was offered a six-month contract with "Solid Gold" which Dionne Warwick was presenting. We toyed with the idea of flying over every week but then threw it out.'

Sharon Lawrence's game plan in 1976 was not to concentrate on Cliff's past achievements, great though they had been in Britain, nor his standing as a Christian spokesman, but to launch him as if he was a new artist. To have harped on about his string of British hits would have been to have projected him as a failure.

'We had to promote him as someone fresh,' says Tony King. ' "Devil Woman" started picking up interest and getting added to secondary stations in each area but we still needed to crack a primary station. Within a month it began to edge in at the lower end of the charts and then we knew there was a chance it could make it.

'The most important radio stations to get on were those controlled by RKO. If you got on an RKO station it looked as though you were going to make it. The chain was run by a man called Paul Drew who was a friend of mine and of Elton John's and of John Lennon's but he was a tough guy and he wouldn't do anything to give me a break.

'However, because he was a friend, if he saw that I had something that looked as if it had "legs" he would maybe tip it a little in my direction. But only if the evidence was that he couldn't be accused of helping out a friend.

'When "Devil Woman" looked as though it was really happening he gave us the break that really cracked it. He gave us the number one station in Boston and that gave us a good chart position the next week. Once it performed well on that station the rest fell like dominoes.'

The record entered the US charts at number eighty-eight at the end of June and slowly began to climb through July and August. When it finally broke into the top ten Cliff was playing in Leningrad and Moscow on a ground-breaking Russian visit—the first by a Western rock artist. It was a strange experience of playing to a mixture of sober-suited party officials and excited teenagers, with security guards leaping into action every time anyone showed any visible signs of appreciation.

'We were calling back home to get the *Billboard* chart positions all the time,' remembers Terry Britten. 'The news that it was going up really kept us going out there.'

'Devil Woman' went on to reach number five in the *Billboard* charts and to become an American million-seller. *I'm Nearly Famous* became his first album to make the British charts in a decade.

21

'Age has nothing to do with it'

I n September 1976 Cliff went back into the studios with Bruce Welch to record a follow-up to *I'm Nearly Famous* that would build on its success. This time there were over fifty songs to choose from because publishers no longer had him pegged as a Eurovision singer.

'I think this album is much better,' he said as he recorded what would later be called *Every Face Tells A Story*. 'I think it's more positive. With *I'm Nearly Famous* we accidentally found a new way of doing things. This one says—now we know what to do, let's do it! Everything seems more confident, there's a greater sense of continuity and it's just better.'

It's part of Cliff's upbeat personality to feel that his current project is the best thing he has ever done. In the case of *Every Face* the truth was that there had been little advance. He had hits with 'My Kinda Life' and 'When Two Worlds Drift Apart' but nothing that reached the top ten. The initial American success was never built on.

'It offers no radical departure or development from *I'm Nearly Famous*,' commented *Melody Maker*. 'Bruce Welch's production is clean and powerful, the songs are, once again, attractive and the musicianship is precise if occasionally verging on the coldly clinical.'

Despite the change in the fortunes of his career Cliff stuck resolutely to the mix of charity work and show business that had been his lifestyle since 1966—over a decade. For his first British tour since the comeback he went out for a twenty-concert gospel tour, often staying in the homes of local Tear Fund supporters rather than hotels. He even played to an audience of 1,200 in the centre of Belfast at a time when almost no English acts would take the risk.

His Christian vision remained undimmed. He told concert audiences that his Christian faith was by far the most important factor in his life and that everything else had to take second place. Quizzed by a reporter one evening as to why he divided his career into 'pop' and 'gospel', he answered that it was out of fairness to people who didn't want to sit through an evening of gospel songs. He wanted to be fair in letting the public know what they were getting.

'I'm not misusing my platform. I still have a responsibility to those who don't want to come to a gospel concert so I do a secular tour. I still do a smattering of gospel in that, but I choose music that I think is valid musically, so nobody minds that. There's no other real reason for separating them because I think that musically all of it stands up.'

Coming off this gospel tour (which raised £37,000 for Tear Fund) he went straight into his first secular tour of Britain in two years and then in 1976 paid a return visit to Bangladesh and India.

'We thought it would be a good idea to go back and see how things had changed in three years,' Cliff said. 'And the thing was, it had changed. Things were so much better than they were. We made a film strip to encourage Christians in the West and to show them what can be done in three years.

'There weren't as many beggars in Dacca. Twenty thousand of them had been given housing in this great encampment with thatched huts and gardens. They've had a couple of good harvests as well.'

In India he performed gospel concerts in Delhi, Bombay and Calcutta, seeing the city of his childhood for the first time since his family boarded a train at Howrah station in August 1948.

It was a very different Calcutta that he returned to. He recognized the old landmarks such as Howrah Station, Chowringhee Road and the Victoria monument but was shocked at the sight of people sleeping in the street. With George Hoffman and Bill Latham he visited Mother Teresa at her hospice and spent a day watching her care for the sick and dying, later praying with her and reading from the Bible.

Because he was performing a gospel concert in Calcutta his visit was well publicized and the Bengali community welcomed him like a local boy who'd done well in the world and was on a quick visit home. George Hoffman had notified the British Embassy in Calcutta of Cliff's visit and the party was assigned a security guard.

'He was mobbed everywhere he went,' says Hoffman. 'We could never leave the watch of the security. The crowds were just flocking around and Cliff was signing autographs all the time.'

Once back in England he set about recording his third gospel album, *Small Corners*. It had been natural to offer the project to Bruce Welch after the success of *I'm Nearly Famous* and *Every Face Tells A Story*, but Welch wasn't interested in being involved in this side of Cliff's life.

Remembers Tony Clark: 'He was asked but said he didn't have anything to offer a spiritual album with God lyrics. Cliff was obviously determined to do it and so he chose to produce it himself using me as his engineer because by then our working relationship was very strong.'

It was harder for him to come up with good material for his gospel albums because the pool of writers available to draw on was necessarily smaller. Most of the songs on *Small Corners* were written by American writers of what was becoming known as Contemporary Christian Music, which was really Jesus Rock under a different name.

'The problem is that I don't write,' said Cliff during the recording sessions. 'If I was a writer I would probably have done more gospel albums. So I rely on the fact that I listen to a whole lot of albums and then use the best songs in my stage act. This album is full of stuff I've sung in concert for a long time but never recorded.'

While he was preparing to record *Small Corners* the Sex Pistols had become one of the better-known groups in Britain, mostly through swearing on live early evening television and getting thrown off the EMI record label for courting too much controversy. If there were two polar opposites in the music business it would have to be Cliff Richard and Johnny Rotten, who projected an arrogant petulance on stage and professed not to care about anything.

Cliff was bemused and angry about punk. It broke all the cardinal rules of show business. It was too loud, it was out of tune, it was irresponsible, it appeared to glory in images of destruction and its proponents showed neither love nor respect for their audience.

'The Sex Pistols are probably the worst band ever,' he said. 'Johnny Rotten can't sing and the band can't play. The fact that they can have any sort of a career is an indictment on the record-buying public. I know that I was criticized for being wild when I launched my career but that was by people who were relating what I did to a previous form of music. The Sex Pistols are trying to play rock 'n' roll and they're doing it badly.'

Not that the notoriety of the Sex Pistols had the remotest effect on Cliff's new rise. He was now committing himself to bigger and better tours and had left behind the club and cabaret scene.

In 1977 he went to South Africa, Australia, New Zealand and Europe. The day he returned from his summer holidays in Portugal he saw a television news flash that Elvis had been taken to hospital. He went to bed thinking it was a hoax, but at three o'clock in the morning he was woken by a call from LBC Radio asking him to comment on Elvis' death.

'I couldn't think straight,' he remembers. 'I started arguing with the guy and telling him not to be ridiculous because they had said he was alright on the television news. He then said, "I hate to tell you this but it's true."'

At the age of forty-two the one-time king of rock 'n' roll was dead from a heart attack, a bloated victim of self-indulgence. Although Cliff had never met Elvis the loss he felt was deeply personal because he knew that if it hadn't been for Elvis he would still be Harry Webb.

In January 1978 Cliff went back into the studios to record *Green Light*, his third album with Bruce Welch. By now Terry Britten was becoming Cliff's major songwriter. On *Green Light* he was involved as writer on half the album's songs.

One day during the recording, when Peter Gormley was discussing with Cliff the need to penetrate the American market, Bruce Welch suggested that the next album should have a consistent style of music.

'I had said that America was much different to Britain and Europe in that they tend to pigeon-hole you,' says Bruce. 'The songs in the album have to be in a similar vein. You can't do "Miss You Nights" and then "Devil Woman", because it's wrong for America. I suggested that what we should do is to get the same writer—perhaps someone like Terry Britten—to write the whole album. Now this was said to my manager, Peter Gormley, and to Cliff. I didn't hear any more about it.'

Assuming that he would be producing the next album, Welch spent the following months collecting new songs. Then, in July 1978, just as he was leaving Abbey Road Studios Welch bumped into engineer Tony Clark who supposed he would be seeing him next week in Paris. 'What do you mean, Paris?' asked Welch. 'For the new Cliff album,' said Clark.

Welch had not been told that Cliff's new album, *Rock 'n' Roll Juvenile*, was scheduled to start recording at Pathé Marconi Studios in Paris on 18 July and that not only had his advice been heeded in that Terry Britten had authored almost all the songs but that Britten had also been made co-producer with Cliff.

Welch fumed at the news. It wasn't the fact that he'd been replaced as producer after playing a key role in the launch of Cliff's recording career but that he hadn't been told, even though Peter Gormley was his manager. It opened up a rift between Welch, Gormley and Cliff that has never healed.

'Our relationship ever since then could be described as strained,' says Welch. 'No one could call us close and I still think that someone like myself, who has been with him through thick and thin, deserves better than that.'

'I can understand him being disappointed, but not angry,' says Cliff in response. 'I'm not tied to anybody anymore. Bruce may have assumed he was doing my next album, but I didn't.'

The words to half the songs on *Rock 'n' Roll Juvenile* were written by B.A. Robertson, a tall lantern-jawed Scot who was to enjoy his own pop career the following year beginning with the hit singles 'Bang Bang' and 'Knocked It Off'.

He'd been introduced to Terry Britten by bass guitarist Herbie Flowers who had played on Robertson's debut album *Shadow Of A Thin Man* in 1976 and the two had started writing songs together.

The most successful song from the partnership was 'Carrie', which was to make number four in the charts. The riff and the title came from Terry Britten. The story was told by Robertson.

'The strength of the song comes from the fact that you're never quite sure what it's about,' says Robertson. 'You don't know whether Carrie is homeless or whether she's squatting or what.

'You don't know whether Cliff, as the narrator, is the husband, boyfriend, lover, brother or father. Nowhere in the song does it say what his relationship with Carrie is. It's a very mysterious song and musically it falls in the same groove as "I Heard It Through The Grapevine".'

Rock 'n' Roll Juvenile was an attempt to explore fresh subject matter but Terry Britten doesn't believe it worked.

'I think his fans want to hear him sing love songs,' he says. 'We did a lot of songs on that album that had very little to do with love and I honestly don't think they're liked by his fans.'

Much to Cliff and Terry Britten's chagrin the album's hit song was the one track that they hadn't produced. 'We Don't Talk Any More' was a last-minute addition, produced by Bruce Welch and surrounded in controversy.

In May 1979 Welch and Alan Tarney were producing an album for Island Records artist Charlie Dore and during a recording break Tarney referenced a cassette of 'We Don't Talk Any More' which he had written for his next album with Trevor Spencer. (The duo were signed to A&M as Tarney-Spencer.) When Welch heard it he immediately wanted to play it to Peter Gormley.

'I wasn't keen to lose the song but he pleaded and pleaded,' says Tarney. 'When he came in the next day he had played it to Peter and Cliff and they said they wanted to record it as soon as possible. We finished up the Charlie Dore album on the Friday and on the Saturday, which was Cup Final day, we recorded it with Cliff.'

Trevor Spencer remembers the session at R.G. Jones Studios: 'I don't think Cliff was all that keen on recording it at the time. He was so locked in to the *Rock 'n' Roll Juvenile* album. But all that was needed really was for us to remake the demo. Bruce then took the tapes to Abbey Road and popped Cliff's vocal on it.

'Alan felt sure that Cliff didn't want to do the song as he started it but then the vocal got better and better as it went on. There were only three or four takes. You can still hear him come in at the wrong point on part of the chorus. Bruce wanted to wipe that but Alan asked him not to so it remained part of the record.'

'We Don't Talk Any More' was released in July 1979 and its success meant that EMI felt it should be included on *Rock 'n' Roll Juvenile* which was scheduled to be released in September.

'Cliff and Terry didn't want it included,' says Welch. 'They said it was their album. EMI said, but this is a monster single. I think in the end they had to half force Cliff to put it on the album.'

'We Don't Talk Any More' went to number one and sold 2,750,000 copies. It was the best-selling single of his career, and Alan Tarney was brought in to produce his next album, *I'm No Hero*, which was recorded at Riverside Studios during May and June 1980.

It was a Tarney *tour-de-force*. No longer limited to being session bass player or occasional songwriter he dominated the whole project, playing and arranging almost all the music, writing or co-writing all but two of the songs and producing everything.

From his love of the Eagles' harmonies, Todd Rundgren's synthesizer wizardry and the chord changes of Steely Dan, Tarney was creating Cliff's first identifiable 'sound' since his days with the Shadows when the twang of Hank's Stratocaster announced the arrival of a Cliff disc.

One of his great strengths was that he could produce demo tapes that were so polished that Cliff could instantly imagine the finished result. The margin for error was reduced drastically because all that was normally required was for the engineer to remove Tarney's vocals and replace them with Cliff's. The backing tracks never needed re-recording.

'He was a dream to produce,' says Tarney. 'The first thing I noticed was his voice which sounded so huge. Then I noticed that he had a good sense of the person who would be listening to the song. He doesn't need to put on a great performance, he just needs to sing the song. He'll try it out two or three times and then that's it.'

Five weeks after completing the album Cliff went to Buckingham Palace to receive an OBE, the first time a pop star had been recognized in this way since the Beatles were awarded MBEs in 1965. He arrived in his Rolls Royce, and was dressed in a black suit, red tie and red shoes.

'I've been to the palace before,' he explained. 'I know there's a lot of red about the place.'

I'm No Hero was released in September 1980 and the next month, during a five-concert run at the Apollo Theatre in London, Cliff turned forty. Just as has happened when he turned twenty and twenty-one and thirty, and when he'd been in the business for ten years and twenty years, a media hoopla ensued. How long could he go on? Did he ever think at eighteen that he would still be around at forty? Was he planning to retire?

What was extraordinary about this milestone, as he slipped into middle age, was that his career was in better shape than at any other time since the very early sixties.

Sitting in his dressing room at the Apollo the night before his birthday he said he was 'grateful and amazed' to arrive at middle age. His telephone had been ringing so much all day that he'd eventually had to take it off the hook.

'The two things that determine how well I will carry on are the quality of my voice and my own taste in music,' he said.

'If my taste in music continues to coincide with public taste then there's no reason why I shouldn't have a hit when I'm fifty. No reason at all. I've had my biggest ever single at thirty-nine!'

'I never thought I'd top "The Young Ones", "Living Doll" and "Bachelor Boy" but I have. So age has nothing to do with it. I've just got to use my integrity and hope that my voice stays intact. If it breaks down, I'll have to think of doing something else.'

The success of 'We Don't Talk Any More' around the world raised the prospect of another assault on North America and so it was that in January 1981 Cliff went on a ten-day promotional tour to Los Angeles, Toronto and New York, appearing on the Merv Griffin and Dionne Warwick shows and facing two solid days of magazine and newspaper interviews.

Interest in America was still high. 'Suddenly', his duet with Olivia Newton-John, was at number twenty in the *Billboard* charts. Publications requesting interviews with him ranged from *People* magazine and the *New York Times* to rock magazines such as *Circus*, *Rock* and *New York Rocker*. He did a live interview on NBC's five o'clock news. He even found he was being played on some New Wave stations alongside the Police and Joe Jackson.

Cliff now had one of his most enduring bands. Backing singers Tony Rivers and John Perry had recorded with him since 'Miss You Nights' and they were joined by Stu Calver. Drummer Graham Jarvis was musical director. There were two keyboard players, Alan Park and Graham Todd, lead guitarist John Clark, bass player Mark

Griffiths and rhythm guitarist Mart Jenner.

Part of the tour was filmed by a television crew putting together a four-part documentary series for BBC2. Cliff had been approached by the light entertainment department, who were keen on an eighties follow-up to 'It's Cliff Richard', but he wanted to do something other than a song-and-dance show with special guests and so suggested the documentary appoach.

Nineteen years since his last American tour, Cliff flew back. It was an unambitious tour of 2,000–3,000 capacity theatres in cities where his singles had been getting heavy airplay, but the idea was to gain a foothold.

The opening night of the tour was in Seattle but that weekend before the Monday show, while the band were still in Los Angeles, the trailer containing all their equipment was stolen from outside their motel. They were left with no lighting, no sound and no instruments.

'It was horrific,' remembers David Bryce, Cliff's professional manager. 'I just had to call all the music stores around LA and ask them to stay open late for us, which they did. It was hard for the musicians because they'd lost instruments that they were familiar with and which they'd modified in little ways.'

The tour arrived in New York on 2 April to play the opening night at a new club, the Ritz, with Jack Good and Olivia Newton-John in attendance. Cliff was still expressing his disappointment at the loss of equipment.

'At the moment we're only showing half of what we can do,' he explained. 'I came here to give them our current show but we haven't been able to do it. The fact that the fans like it means that when we come back they won't know what's hit them.'

The next day there was a smaller disaster when the tour bus arrived in Baltimore and it was realized that no one knew where the venue was.

'When we got to Baltimore the tour manager realized he had left his briefcase back in the hotel in New York and that the schedule was in it,' remembers Graham Todd.

'We were driving around looking for posters to find out where we were supposed to be and when we finally got there, half an hour before show time, we discovered that the revolving stage wasn't working.'

His longest-ever American tour finished on 20 April with much the same result as the others. He had been well received but by a very small group of people and, judging by the Union Jack flags waved in some of the auditoriums, a good proportion of these may have been Brits anyway.

Once back in London he started rehearsing for a rock 'n' roll special which was to form the basis of one of the documentary programmes. The idea was to fit him up with a pink jacket, get him to sing his favourite songs from the fifties and reunite him with one of his musical heroes.

Cliff's choice of heroes for the Hammersmith Odeon concert was either Elvis' original guitarist Scotty Moore, Ricky Nelson's guitarist James Burton or Phil Everly of the Everly Brothers.

James Burton asked for too much money and Scotty Moore, who hadn't picked up a guitar since playing on Elvis' comeback TV special in 1968, couldn't be coaxed from his tape-duplicating plant in Nashville, but Phil Everly, who had become familiar with Cliff's work when touring Britain in 1959, jumped at the opportunity.

'To step on a stage and sing with Cliff reminded me so much of singing with my brother,' he said. 'It was great to be able to sing Everly Brothers songs with someone I had tremendous respect for. That was really the reason I came over.'

The concert took place on 1 May and was a precursor of the 'Oh Boy!' section of The Event in that Cliff sang rock 'n' roll songs, dressed in period costume, employed a troupe of dancers and sang duets with a star of the period. In the audience was John Foster, now a rotund man with spectacles, back home living with his mother, and the three original Drifters—Sammy Samwell, Norman Mitham and Terry Smart. They hadn't been together since Smart left to join the Navy in 1959.

At the end of the month he returned to the studios to record *Wired For Sound*, again with Alan Tarney producing and arranging. The title track was the most contemporary sounding single of his renaissance, showing that he was every bit a contender in the battle of the new techno-pop artists like Soft Cell and Human League.

The lyric, written by B.A. Robertson, was a departure from his romantic subject matter. It was a love song but this time expressing his love for the Sony Walkman and the new portable music that was revolutionizing listening habits.

'I'd never written with Alan Tarney but he called me up one night and asked me if I'd like to write a song with him,' says Robertson. 'Mickey Dolenz, who used to be in the Monkees, was coming for a meal that night so I stayed in for the starters and then drove down to Hammersmith to listen to the backing track during the main course and then arrived back home with a cassette in time for the dessert.

'I got up the next morning, put the kettle on, put the cassette in and the title came to me straight away as I listened to it. A couple of hours later, I had written the whole song and I just read the lyrics to him down the phone.'

Cliff had for some time attempted to use his position to raise the profile of various British gospel artists but although he had been able to give them exposure by producing them and inviting them on his tours, none of the acts had ever achieved general market success. The most positive outcome of his involvement was reflected in his use, for the first time, of gospel writers on a secular album.

'Better Than I Know Myself', a gospel song disguised as a love song, was written by Dave Cooke and his songwriting partner Judy McKenzie, who had been one of the pioneer Christian folk singers in the late sixties.

'Lost In A Lonely World' and 'Summer Rain' were both by Chris Eaton, a twenty-year-old writer Cliff had met at a Christian convention in 1979 when Eaton was playing in a band for Dave

Pope, an evangelist and singer whose album *Sail Away* Cliff had produced.

'I'd written the title track for Dave's album and Cliff said he liked it and would like to hear more,' says Eaton. 'I sent him five songs on a tape but didn't hear anything for eighteen months. Then I got a call from Gill Snow at his office saying that Cliff wanted to do four of the songs, two of them on *Wired For Sound*.'

Wired For Sound went on to be Cliff's best-selling album since *I'm Nearly Famous*, with sales of over one million. Chris Eaton was able to give up driving taxis and beer lorries and was signed up as a songwriter to Patch Music, a music publishing company run from the Cliff Richard Organization by Stuart Ongley.

Cliff was particularly pleased with his inclusion of Christian writers in this way. In 1965, even if he had decided it was possible, there were no Christian writers of high calibre who could have contributed to his albums or singles. Now there were, and it had a lot to do with the change in attitude which Cliff and his generation had created in the church, that young people were growing up considering commercial songwriting as a career possibility.

He had never felt that his faith was something stuck on to his life although, at times, his two-tier career seemed to suggest that.

'Interviewers tend to ask me certain questions and then suddenly switch to discussing Christianity,' he said. 'They don't realize that the first part of the interview was also coloured by my Christian faith. I can't separate me from me.'

22

'We're the new Charles and Di'

S ince becoming a Christian in 1966 there had been no obvious romantic interest in Cliff's life. There had been girls who had adorned his arms when he arrived at film premières and charity functions but there had been no girlfriends.

The fact that this apparently abstemious period had coincided with his close relationship with Bill Latham didn't go unnoticed by the press.

Roderick Gilchrist, Entertainments Editor of the *Daily Mail*, observing that Jackie Irving had been his last serious date noted that: 'He now lives with a male friend in the show business shelter of Weybridge, with his friend's mother. Inevitably this has led to suggestions that he is "gay"—a word that had not been used in this way when he first entered show business.'

Cliff denied that he was homosexual and explained that his reasons for not bed-hopping with women were spiritual rather than psycho-sexual.

'As a Christian I don't believe in extramarital sex because God says it's wrong and I have to assume that he knows better,' he said. 'I don't sleep with women at all now. Not since my Christian conversion.'

Three years earlier he'd broken this news to pop writer John Blake, then of the *Evening News*, who commented: 'Since Cliff became an ardent Christian more than ten years ago, I am slightly stunned by this revelation.'

The story was headlined 'My Ten Years Without Sex... by Cliff Richard', as though sexual restraint because of religious conviction was a perversion in itself.

Cliff's fidelity to Christian teaching seemed beyond doubt. The deeper question was whether his celibacy was solely a matter of obedience or whether he was a celibate by nature.

If he was unmoved by sex his chastity was more an acceptance of his natural condition than a victory over seething desires. In the days before religion his lack of interest appeared eccentric but, as a Christian, there was an explanation which non-believers could understand even if they didn't approve.

'I don't particularly have any great sexual urges or needs,' he confessed to David Wigg of the *Daily Express*. 'I don't feel I have to spend my life with someone special for sexual favours. But that's my good fortune, isn't it, really?'

The implied good fortune is that he is free to devote his energies to his career. There are no distractions. There are no emotional entanglements. He is responsible to nobody but himself. His only marriage, as anyone who knows him well will say, is to his work.

This is why it was so out of character to see Cliff Richard going out with tennis star Sue Barker in the autumn of 1982. Ever since entering show business he had avoided being seen with the girls he took out.

Jackie Irving, his longest-standing girlfriend, was rarely photographed with Cliff. Delia Wicks was sworn to secrecy. His romance with Una Stubbs was unknown even to his closest friends and colleagues. But on 23 March 1982 Cliff flew out to Denmark with Sue Barker to see her play an exhibition match and the next day's tabloids were full of it: 'Sue and Cliff in Love Riddle' (*The Sun*), 'Sue and Cliff Set Up a Love Riddle' (*Daily Mirror*) 'Cliff and Sue Take Off and Say There's No Love Match Blooming' (*Daily Mail*) 'Cliff, Love and Me by Sue Barker' (*Daily Star*).

The bare bones of the story were that Cliff had been spotted with Sue in a departure lounge at Heathrow Airport awaiting a flight to Copenhagen. What the press immediately wanted to know was whether this was love and whether a wedding was in the offing.

'I think he's a super person but to talk of marriage is wrong,' Sue told James Whitaker of the *Daily Star*. 'There's nothing nasty in the rumour. It just isn't accurate.'

When the couple flew back after an overnight stay Cliff was asked whether he loved her. 'I'm not going to say that,' he said. 'I don't want to embarrass her. She says she doesn't mind, but it's not fair. I've only met her four times. We'll be seeing a lot more of each other, but it's early days. Who knows what we'll feel in a year's time?'

Within three months they were a hot item. Neither of them was now pretending it was still a case of 'just good friends'. They were spotted at Wimbledon where Sue openly nibbled his ear, kissed his neck and stroked his hair while watching a game. At a pre-Wimbledon party thrown by veteran tennis designer Teddy Tinling they allowed themselves to be photographed cuddling and holding hands.

Cliff even proudly announced to reporters that he and Sue were the new Charles and Di. 'There had to be someone to take over once they got married,' he boasted. Asked if they would be following the royal example Cliff said, 'I don't know. It's early days yet. We are taking it from day to day. If we decide to get married there will be an announcement.'

Cliff and Sue's relationship had all started with Alan Godson, a Church of England vicar with a parish in Liverpool who had helped found an organization called Christians in Sport to bring together sports people with a shared faith and to help evangelize their peers.

Godson himself was a tough-looking ex-Rugby-football player renowned for his fearlessness in presenting the Christian message in dressing rooms and on playing fields. It was not unknown for him to suddenly pull up in his car and start preaching to someone in the street if he so felt the call.

He had been introduced to Sue Barker by sports commentator Gerald Williams, a personal friend of his and also a supporter of Christians in Sport. At twenty-five Sue was Britain's rising female tennis star and although she had been baptized at the age of twenty-one her Christian faith had been dormant until she met Godson. For the past few years she had been involved in two intense relationships with fellow sportsmen. Now she wanted to re-dedicate her life as a Christian.

Alan Godson was aware that life as a Christian was going to be tough for her on the tennis court. Not only would she find it hard to be in regular contact with a church but there would be ridicule from fellow players and grillings from the press. The only person that he could think of who had triumphed in a similar situation was Cliff. So he called him and gave him Sue's telephone number.

'I thought that because they lived in the same area and faced similar problems he could coach her into handling the gospel publicly without getting destroyed,' says Godson. 'I thought that he was the only one with the nous to be useful as a servant to her.'

While this was happening (September 1981) Sue was playing in the Brighton Indoor tournament and coincidentally had met the Shadows who were staying at the same hotel while playing concerts on the south coast.

'Hank was the tennis nut and came and watched me playing doubles with Virginia Wade,' says Sue. 'The next day I was due to play against Tracey Austin in the finals and Hank, Bruce and Brian came and they all got hooked. Cliff was apparently watching the match on his television at home and when I won I went straight over and hugged Hank. Cliff wondered what on earth was going on!

'That night, when I got home to Wimbledon, he called me. At first I thought it was a joke. I had been having this running joke with some engineers from British Telecom and I thought it was one of them playing a prank. So I just played along. I said, "Oh really!" I didn't think it was him. But then he told me that Alan had given him my number and he thought it would be a good idea if we got together to chat.

'I was flying off to Japan at the end of that week and we had to get together on the only free night I had which was when I was actually going to see the Shadows in London.'

Sue was going to the concert at the Dominion Theatre with fellow tennis player Sue Mappin and they were joined in their box on the night by Cliff and Bill Latham. After the show they all went out to eat together and discussion turned to the problems of British tennis. Cliff wanted to know why tennis was such a privileged sport in this country and what needed to be done to find the tennis stars of tomorrow. Out of this first meeting grew the idea of what, in ten years' time, would be the Cliff Richard Tennis Trail—a charity which helps school-age children to develop a love for the game.

At the time Cliff was not noted for his love of tennis. He was what Sue now refers to as a 'pat-a-cake' tennis player, someone who liked to knock a ball around a court but for whom 'the ball wasn't coming back very much and it wasn't much fun'.

It was Sue who stimulated his interest in playing tennis. 'He used to come and watch me train,' she says. 'I gave him a hit and he found he was getting absolutely exhausted in half an hour and he saw that if he learned to play well it would be a means of keeping fit. I think he'd played with his friends for hours but with me he was getting tired. He saw tennis as a challenge.'

From Japan Sue went down to Australia and then on to America where she lived as a tax exile. It was while she was away that the *Daily Star* broke the story that had been successfully kept a secret for over twenty-one years. Beneath the headline 'Cliff My Secret Lover' Carol Costa told all about her brief affair in the first of a three-part series.

The tone of the story was set in the first paragraphs. 'I loved Cliff Richard, and I suppose I always will. But over the years I have come to realise that he isn't perfect.

'And that's why I have decided to tell the truth ... after keeping quiet for so long.

On tour in the Far East at the time, Cliff had already got wind of the imminent publication because he had been called and asked for his

▲ 1973: Cliff visiting Bangladesh with the relief agency Tear Fund

▲ 1978: At home in Weybridge— (clockwise) Cliff, Cliff's mother Dorothy, Bill Latham, Bill's mother Mamie, Derek Bodkin (Dorothy's husband)

◀ 1981: Baltimore, US— Cliff at a soundcheck

May 1981,
Hammersmith
Odeon: Cliff with
Phil Everly at the
Rock 'n' Roll special
which was filmed for
BBC TV ▶

Same concert. The
first time the Drifters
had met since Terry
Smart left at the end
of the fifties: (left to
right) Ian Samwell,
Norman Mitham,
Terry Smart, Cliff ▼

◀ 23 July, 1980: Cliff with his mother Dorothy after receiving his OBE

Cliff with Alan Tarney, songwriter and producer of albums such as Stronger and Always Guaranteed ▼

▲ 5 July, 1982: Cliff with Sue Barker at Wimbledon during the height of their romance

▲ The holiday gang in Portugal in the seventies—(left to right) David Rivett, Graham Disbrey, Glyn MacAuley, Bill Latham, Cliff

◄ Cliff at his villa in Portugal

◄ February 1989: Cliff and Sue Barker at a celebrity tennis match in London

August 1985: On holiday in Portugal—(left to right) Cliff, Bill Latham, Glyn MacAuley, Graham Disbrey, David Rivett ▼

▲ July 1989: Cliff's uniforms
and gowns party—(left to right)
Jill Clarke, Graham Disbrey,
John and Carol Davey, Cliff

1986: Cliff as the rock star,
Chris, in Time, with (left to right)
Dawn Hope, Jodie Wilson,
Maria Ventura ▶

▲ Elton John's Rocket Records gave Cliff his first US top ten hit when it released 'Devil Woman' in 1976

▲ June 1989: The Event—Cliff on stage with the Dallas Boys and Vernons Girls

Thirty years separate these two photographs but Cliff is now a bigger live attraction than he has ever been

comment on the story. He would say only that, 'Carol must have her reasons for publicizing what was very personal. She has the freedom to do that. But I also have my freedom and I don't wish to publicize anything that personal.'

He never discussed the relationship with Sue, but he did get together with Stu Calver and John Perry to pray about the situation and then he called his mother in Broxbourne and warned her what was about to happen.

'I'm sensitive about anything bad that is written in the papers,' says Cliff's mother, Dorothy Marie. 'Cliff told me not to worry. He said that if she wants to write that's entirely up to her. I was quite upset but he wasn't.'

The story had come about because Carol, going through a lean time, had written to Cliff asking for financial help. Cliff had replied with a handwritten letter saying that he was already heavily involved with charity work. 'I'm telling you this,' he wrote, 'so that you'll realize my position and therefore understand more easily when I say that I just can't help you.'

Feeling that she had been snubbed, Carol determined to sell the one thing that she knew was of value, the untold story of her time with Cliff.

Unfamiliar with the world of newspapers, she told some friends in the music industry that she was interested in talking. One of these friends, Adrian Rudge, knew a freelance book editor, Carol Illingworth, who he thought might be able to interview Carol—in the presence of a tabloid journalist—and put her story into writing.

'Adrian called me up and suggested I could give Carol Costa some help and advice about telling her story,' says Carol Illingworth. 'So I got in touch. The only real help I gave her was to help her put her thoughts into some sort of order. I found her an extremely articulate, intelligent woman. Adrian then got into the newspapers through his contacts in the music world.'

According to Jet Harris, Carol was paid £8,000 for her story. According to other friends she said that she had spiced up the story to make it sound more sensational than it really was by saying that Cliff had been a great and passionate lover when in fact he'd been a reluctant participant.

With Cliff still touring the Far East and Sue in America, they exchanged a couple of letters and then, in February 1982, while playing in the Dallas Tournament, Sue received a phone call from him.

'It was totally out of the blue,' she says. 'He asked me what I was doing and I told him that I was only due back in England for a long weekend and I was going to Denmark with my brother to play an exhibition match. He said, "Well, I'm not doing anything. Do you mind if I come along?" I said, "No. Of course not." We met up in London in March and flew off to Copenhagen together, and I couldn't believe what happened after that.

'It was only the second time we had met. When we got off the plane people were asking us when we were going to get married and I thought this was absolutely bizarre.

'As far as I was concerned we had been to a concert, had a dinner, written two letters . . . and I was thinking, blimey, I don't think we're even going out! I didn't count it as a date. I thought, gosh, I'm going to put my foot in it so badly. By saying nothing you make it worse. If you say, "Of course not", you insult the other person.

'In some ways it drew us closer together. Although the press tried to make out that we were upset, we just laughed at a lot of it. We used to phone each other up and say, "Did you read that article? I didn't say any of that. I haven't spoken to them."'

Press speculation increased over the following months. Sue was playing on the European circuit and Cliff was recording his new album *Now You See Me, Now You Don't* at Strawberry South Studios in Dorking. It was during this recording that the friendship changed into something recognizably different.

'After we returned from Denmark my parents stayed with me at my flat for the few days I was in England and Cliff was doing the album and he just phoned up and said, "Look, I'd really like to see you again. Will you come down to the studio tomorrow because

I'm stuck down here."

'It was then that I sussed that something was up because we had arranged to meet in a week's time when he'd finished and my parents were gone, but he was saying "I don't want to wait a week. I want to see you tomorrow." So we did meet then. I felt the same way but I certainly wasn't going to make the phone call. I was very pleased that he had called.'

Now You See Me, Now You Don't was a further attempt to introduce the writing of his Christian friends to a wider audience, this time with an album which although regarded by EMI as a gospel project would get the same commercial push as any other release.

His choice of producer was Craig Pruess, a young American who'd been a child prodigy as a musician and had studied physics, philosophy and comparative religion at the Massachusetts Institute of Technology before arriving in England in 1973.

'He wanted this album to be more heavyweight and to break away from the pop sound,' says Pruess. 'He approached it to prove a point and he did have a point to prove. He didn't want his gospel albums to be regarded as inferior to his other albums. He felt they could be as good as anything else he did. He wanted to fuse his beliefs and his enthusiasm with his professional life.'

Pruess also noticed that Cliff was remarkably content during the period of recording. 'Of all the time I spent with Cliff I felt closest to him around that period,' he says. 'It was balanced. He could relate to couples and with my wife Jenny we went out a lot for meals as a foursome.

'I remember mixing the album at the Townhouse and Sue and Cliff were cuddling on the couch behind us. It was great. It was the happiest I had ever seen him. It helped him to loosen up. Sometimes around his band and all the people he works with he has to keep a distance for professional reasons.'

During the summer they began spending every available moment together, visiting the theatre, seeing films, playing tennis, but more often than not staying at home in Weybridge where Sue would cook a meal and they'd both watch a video. They were affectionate towards each other, they laughed a lot and there was the bonding of their Christian faith.

What was particularly refreshing about the relationship was that it took Cliff temporarily away from show business and Sue away from sport. They found they could relax and drop their guards.

'She enjoyed being with him and I think she shook him up,' says Alan Godson. 'She brought the champagne back to his spiritual life.'

In August Cliff and his mother left England for a three-week holiday in Bermuda. Her marriage to Derek Bodkin had recently ended in divorce after he had found another woman. Bill Latham and his mother Mamie, Graham Disbrey, Glyn MacAulay and David Rivett accompanied them on the trip. MacAulay and Rivett, both accountants with Crusader backgrounds, were the latest additions to the summer holiday gang. They stayed in a private villa in a secluded bay.

Sue went off to Marbella and when she returned on 26 August she broke down in tears at Heathrow when reporters surrounded her and surprised her by informing her that in her absence Cliff had said it was now 'Marry or break up time'. When Cliff flew back two days later Sue was not at the airport to meet him.

It was these incidents that prompted the *Daily Star* to publish its front-page headline story challenging Cliff to make his mind up.

'Cliff Richard, you are fast becoming a CAD!', wrote Sandra White on 28 August. 'You flew back from your holidays yesterday and kept quiet about your intentions. As Britain's Number One Bachelor Boy, you are too old to be coy. Do the decent thing. Make your mind up: Do you want to marry Sue Barker? Or not?

The story went on in much the same vein and ended with a coupon 'What should Sue do?' with three boxes marked 'Marry Him Now!', 'Wait A While' and 'Give Him the Elbow'.

Cliff read the story and told Sue about it. She told him not to worry and a few days later left for the US Open and didn't return until late in

September. When they linked up again Sue realized that something was different. The physical affection was now gone. Whatever romance had been there had turned into friendship.

'We were still boyfriend and girlfriend but it wasn't the same,' says Sue. 'I think during that time away we had had a lot of time to sit back and think about what we wanted to do and I think we both realized that we were spending too much time together. It certainly still felt like a strong relationship but certainly not as fast and furious as it had been.

'I think that during the summer we had probably seen too much of each other. It certainly affected my tennis in that I was so busy working out how we could see each other that I wasn't getting on with what I should be doing. I don't think it was particularly good for him either because he was dashing out to watch tournament after tournament. It was what we wanted to do though.

'It may not have been good career-wise but we were having fun. Bill must have been tearing his hair out because Cliff just wasn't around that much.'

During this time it appeared to close friends that Cliff was still mulling over his options. He spoke to married friends about the decisions he was facing and clearly saw marriage as a possibility. It had been while he holidayed in Bermuda though that he had more or less decided that he wanted to put the brakes on.

'I spoke to Sue on the phone from Bermuda because it's when you're away from people that you really start to think things through,' he says. 'I was feeling that I should curb it a bit. I don't really know why I felt that way. I still found her attractive and still enjoyed being with her.'

In 1988, he told *Woman's Own* magazine that it had crossed his mind that 'marriage might be the outcome' but that one of the things that had decided him against it was an incident where Sue had become irritated when he had not told her where he was going one day.

'I suddenly realized that in the marriage relationship you no longer live for yourself,' he said. 'And, in the end, the love that I have for Sue was overshadowed by the fact that I love my lifestyle that much more.'

When Sue read this she was upset, not least because, as with Jackie Irving, during their time together he hadn't hinted that marriage was ever under consideration.

We had a very close relationship for a few months but I need to know someone for a couple of years before I thought of marrying them.

'I don't know whether he thought about marriage or whether he thought, "I've got quite close to this person—do I want it to continue? If it continues it's obviously going to involve making a decision."'

During a gospel tour of South Africa in 1981, which Cliff had played with Garth Hewitt and Nutshell (two British acts he had produced singles for), Bill Latham had struck up a relationship with an English woman who was a friend of the tour organizer. Her name was Jill Clarke, and her parents had emigrated to Johannesburg during her teens. The following year Latham was in Sun City with Cliff and Jill drove up to be with him, by which time it was obvious to friends that something serious was starting.

In the summer of 1983, with Cliff apparently contemplating the possibility of marriage to Sue, Jill flew back to England to be closer to Latham. For several months she stayed with Sue at her flat in Wimbledon and she and Latham would go out on double dates with Cliff and Sue.

Close friends of Cliff and Bill's felt that a double wedding in 1984 was definitely on the cards, during the same period if not on the same day. How things changed so drastically has never been adequately explained.

For Sue the most disappointing aspect was that it had seemed to change gear without warning. There were no explanations as to why the kissing had stopped and why the phone calls dried up.

'I had felt the need to put the brakes on but I certainly hadn't wanted it to fizzle out like this,' she says. 'I think Cliff felt it was all going too far although he wouldn't talk about it.

'It was almost as if he didn't want to front it. Without us ever having sat down and talked about it, our relationship had gone into a different stage. It slowed down to a halt where there was no romance at all.'

They kept seeing each other, mostly for meals, but Cliff no longer displayed open affection as he had done prior to Bermuda. As far as the public was concerned, Sue and Cliff were still an 'item' and as late as July 1984 Sue was speaking publicly as though it was thriving as a romance.

'I love him, he's great and I'm sure we love each other,' she told one interviewer. 'But as for being in love, I'm not so sure—it's such a funny phrase. I don't think I'm in love with him and I don't think he is with me . . . We're still getting to know each other. Sometimes we don't meet for weeks on end.'

The truth was that although Sue was hopeful that there might be a future she could see that Cliff was unwilling to share a lot of himself. It might have drifted on indefinitely had Sue not started dating a fellow tennis star.

'I don't remember a particular conversation with Cliff to say we've changed but we did have a conversation to say this is it,' she says. 'I remember we were in a restaurant in Sydney in October 1984. I had met someone over here who I wanted to see more of and who didn't like the attachment I had with Cliff even though by this time we were only friends.

'We went out for dinner and I told him I had met someone else. He was really pleased. He said, "I suppose that means I won't be able to see you quite so much." And that was that.'

The relationship had lasted almost two years, second only to his time with Jackie Irving although most of it was spent apart and only a fraction of it was truly passionate. It followed the same pattern of an early intensity followed up by a sudden cooling and a reluctance to progress towards commitment.

Those who only saw the public displays of affection tend to be dismissive of the relationship. They argue that it was just a convenient time for Cliff to be seen with a girl on his arm and that it boosted his image. But among his closest friends there was a genuine belief that something could have happened.

'I don't agree that Cliff has never found the right girl,' says Peter Graves. 'Sue Barker was the right girl. She was a Christian, she understood his show business commitments, she was madly in love with him and they looked fabulous together.' But again Cliff had weighed up his options and decided to stick with the decision that he'd first made in 1968, to put the career before the girl. Says Graves, 'Now he is married to his lifestyle and that has become more important to him than any woman could ever be.'

23

'Cliff likes anything that knocks an audience sideways'

D uring the first half of the eighties Cliff was on the road for anything up to four months of the year in Australia, the Far East, Europe, Scandinavia, South Africa and America, as well as carrying out his annual gospel tours of Britain.

In this schedule he found time to make two further field trips on behalf of Tear Fund—the first, in 1982, a week-long stay in Kenya and the second, in 1984, a fortnight in Haiti. The purpose was to stay in touch with the charity but also to act as narrator and interviewer in two films: *Cliff In Kenya* and *It's A Small World*.

The conditions, particularly in Haiti, were far removed from the five-star luxury Cliff was used to on his tours where hotel managements fell over themselves to give him the best possible treatment and local record companies showered him with gifts.

There was starvation, poverty, disease, political violence and the menace of voodoo. In Port au Prince, the capital of Haiti, they stayed in a small hotel. On the small island of La Gonave, which could only be reached by a boat, they slept in a missionary bungalow.

'He is a tremendously adaptable person,' said George Hoffman, who had already been with him in Bangladesh, India, Nepal and the Sudan. 'He never stands on ceremony. I've never heard him complain once, whatever the food we've been given and whatever places we've had to sleep in.'

In Kenya he reduced a group of Masai tribesmen to giggles by playing rock 'n' roll to them on his acoustic guitar.

'Their previous experience of white people was of development workers and missionaries who were all rather serious,' says documentary film director John Muggleton. 'To have this guy playing wildly on a guitar and rolling on the ground was quite amusing for them.'

Having revamped his approach to recording in the seventies Cliff was starting in the eighties to develop his stage show. The new band were not expected to dress in black or hide behind their musical scores. He began to develop a more theatrical approach to performing: working out dance routines, acting out songs like 'Devil Woman' and incorporating ideas from science fiction films (especially *Close Encounters Of The Third Kind*) and West End musicals (especially *Starlight Express*).

Until the mid seventies he had relied exclusively on light and sound equipment available at each venue which meant that he lagged noticeably behind the major touring acts of the day who were each trying to out-dazzle the other with the spectacular nature of their shows. Now he was investigating state-of-the-art systems: overhead trusses, motorized lights and lasers.

'Cliff liked anything that knocked the audience sideways,' says lighting engineer Bob Hellyer. 'He started to want to choreograph numbers, to have effects linked to particular lines in the songs, and so the show became part rock 'n' roll and part theatre.'

The tours abroad were almost always to countries where Cliff was established, with the exception of North America, where there were a couple of last flings, and the Far East, which was sometimes fitted in for convenience en route to Australia. Japan, once a good market, had inexplicably gone off him since his comeback with 'Devil Woman'.

In his career he had played in every significant commercial territory in the world. He'd even played in places where there was little chance of selling records, such as Jerusalem, Beirut, Bangkok, Moscow, Calcutta, New Delhi and Belgrade.

The places where he was most successful were Britain, Europe (especially France, Holland and Germany), Scandinavia (especially Denmark), South Africa, Australia and New Zealand.

'It's all down to how much attention you give each territory,' says Peter Gormley. 'In the early days he would go anywhere, he would look forward to it and he would have fun. But as you get older you lose your enthusiasm for jumping on planes and switching all over the place.'

On tour Cliff maintained a proprietorial distance from the band and road crew, appearing for after-show meals but rarely hanging out with them and always travelling first class with his tour manager David Bryce.

Bryce had become an important part of the management team. Originally he worked on the road with Cliff on behalf of agent Leslie Grade and then, in the mid sixties, worked directly for Cliff.

He has been around show business since the end of the war when he began work as a 'call boy' in West End theatres, knocking on dressing room doors before the curtain went up.

His brother was Dickie Valentine, the most popular male vocalist in Britain before the rock 'n' roll era, who was killed in a car accident. Through him he got into the Grade agency, going out on the road with stars such as Bill Haley and Buddy Holly. Well-muscled and prematurely bald, he had the effect of intimidating people without having to resort to violence. On the road he became the liaison between Cliff and the members of the band; if there was ever any trouble it was ultimately Bryce who had to sort it out.

Although no code of conduct was imposed there was an unspoken understanding that no one would risk tainting Cliff's good name by indulging in Led Zeppelinesque on-the-road antics. If the tabloid press could get the words 'Cliff' and 'Orgy' into the same headline it wouldn't mind how tenuous the connection.

People switched on their best behaviour when they were around

Cliff anyway. 'A lot of the normal banter would stop when he came in the room,' admits guitarist Mark Griffiths. 'It was just out of respect for his views. I think the sort of humour that musicians enjoy would have been a bit too strong for Cliff. You just didn't want to involve him in it.'

If anyone blasphemed by saying 'Jesus Christ' or 'God', Cliff would brush it aside by saying, 'Right name. Wrong context', but obscenities made him feel uncomfortable. During recording sessions musicians would often retire to the bathroom for a quick five-minute swear before being able to carry on.

None of this was done through fear. His naïvety, particularly over sex, made them feel protective towards him. 'To swear in front of Cliff would be like swearing in front of your mother,' as one band member put it.

On tour in Hamburg, some of the band gathered in the foyer of the hotel in preparation for a visit to the Reeperbahn, the city's notorious commercial sex district. Cliff sauntered in, saw them about to leave, and asked if he could join them.

'We were all saying, "Well Cliff, I don't think you'll want to go where we're going",' says Graham Todd. 'There was a general feeling that we had to look after him which is a bit silly when you think he's a fully grown man. He's not at all worldly in that respect.'

In Japan in 1974 he was told by someone in the band that he would be fine to have as much sake as he wanted with his meal, as long as he didn't switch to another alcoholic drink. As a result he got drunk for the first time since his Italian experience in 1959.

'Naïve little me drank more than I should,' Cliff admits. 'The next day everyone said to me, "You were great! You were really one of the lads!" They were thrilled that I had got drunk. I felt dreadful. I hated it.'

Cliff was also kept in the dark about much of the practical joking that went on all around him on tour. It was assumed that he'd either disapprove or fail to see the humour.

He does have a good sense of humour—almost everyone comments on his readiness to laugh—but it was thought that some of their activities might be too much for his taste.

The bulk of the pranks centred on hotel rooms, and the priority of any touring band member was to keep his key with him at all times. Failure to do so could result either in a straightforward festooning with tea bags or the complete removal of all furniture.

Having your key didn't guarantee immunity. You could find yourself locked out by the simple trick of switching the plastic door numbers so that you tried the wrong door, or you could find yourself stuck in if a gang decided to apply adhesive 'gaffer tape' to the edges of your door.

When the management of an Edinburgh hotel released Alan Park from his gaffer-taped room it pulled away so much of the paintwork that they billed the Cliff Richard Organization for the damage and had the group banned from staying there again.

There was also no protection for those who were asleep. Dave Cooke woke one morning to find his room completely full of toilet paper and when Mart Jenner retired to his room after a heavy night of drinking the rest of the band took advantage of his comatose state to climb in through his window from a fire escape, strip him naked and cover him from the waist downwards with shaving foam.

'He didn't wake up until the middle of the night,' remembers Mark Griffiths. 'The window was open, he was frozen stiff and he had absolutely no idea what had happened to him.'

The undisputed master of the wind-up was tour manager Ron King, who'd first driven Cliff on the Kalins' tour. His practical jokes were legendary in the business because of their elaborateness. Once, while driving the coach for a British tour by American star Del Shannon, he arranged for two friends to dress up in uniforms as border guards and arrest Shannon by the roadside for attempting to enter Scotland without a visa.

His favourite joke with the Cliff band came when he discovered that Mart Jenner was involved in a dispute with his next-door neighbours and had one morning run over their son's bike with his car. Not wishing to be arrested for criminal damage, Jenner had cut the frame up and buried it in a field. His only mistake was to tell a member of the band.

While Cliff was on stage in London, King went outside the theatre and found an obliging policeman whom he brought to the side of the stage. When Jenner idly looked into the wings King pointed at him and mouthed the words 'That's him!' to the policeman who then left, his duty having been done.

At the end of the concert Jenner unplugged his guitar, leaped off the stage and ran terrified out of the theatre. He was so quick that no one could catch him. 'I couldn't get him on the phone at all,' says King, 'and then when I did get hold of him and told him what had happened he said, "Thanks a lot, Ron. You've just given me the worst weekend of my life!" '

Water bombing was the less elaborate prank the band members favoured. Plastic laundry bags were hoarded during a tour, then filled with water and released from hotel rooms. The resulting explosions were often loud enough to suggest a terrorist attack.

In fact, water bombing became something of an art form for the musicians. They started dangling a microphone from the window so that the noises could be recorded and compared. Later they compiled stereo recordings by placing another microphone at the point of impact. Cassettes of the top plops would be circulated among interested parties.

In New Zealand Dave Cooke decided that Cliff might be a repressed water bomber. 'All the others were trying to keep me quiet,' says Cooke, 'because they never wanted Cliff to know anything but I just asked him if he fancied doing a few water bombs that night and he said he'd love to. He thought it would be great fun.

'I'd collected about sixty bags and we started throwing them out of the window and Cliff just loved it. It was all very childish, but great fun.'

Nothing more was thought about this until an incident on a gospel tour with the singer Sheila Walsh, his latest gospel protégé, when a loud explosion was heard outside the hotel one night as the band congregated in Mark Griffiths' room.

Wanting to join in whatever fun was going on they began hurling bombs from the window with Sheila Walsh rapidly filling bags from the bathroom tap. One of the bombs, however, hit the roof of a van, creating an almighty noise which alerted the hotel management. Mark Griffiths, whose window had been noted as the source of the bombardment, was later questioned by local police.

The next day, in Manchester, David Bryce gave everyone a severe dressing down, threatening Sheila with the sack. 'Cliff's career could have gone right out the window,' he admonished them, as they tried to stifle their giggles over his inappropriate metaphor.

'Cliff was standing there being unusually quiet,' remembers Dave Cooke. 'Two or three months later we discovered why. He had been the one to throw the first bomb.'

Sheila Walsh had been brought to Bill Latham for management by her husband Norman Miller, an executive for the Christian record company Word (UK).

A television show—called Rock Gospel and screened by the BBC—was built around her. She became the support act on the Tear Fund tours and Cliff began to produce her with Craig Pruess. But success in the secular world proved elusive.

A hit record seemed assured in 1983 when Cliff agreed to record a duet with her for the DJM record label but the result, 'Drifting', became one of his least successful records ever, reaching a highest chart position of sixty-four.

'It was humiliating,' Sheila recalls. 'I was interviewed on Capital Radio just as the single was released and I was asked if I thought it would be a hit. I said of course it would be—Cliff could do a duet with Miss Piggy and it would be a hit. When it died a death I felt really stupid.'

Through knowing Sheila, Cliff came into contact with the Cobham Christian Fellowship, a non-denominational church led by Gerald Coates which practised a less formal style of worship and believed in such 'spiritual gifts' as speaking in tongues. Its meeting place was either a scout building or a school hall.

The Cobham Christian Fellowship was an example of a recent phenomenon in evangelical Christianity known as the 'house church' movement. It was the fastest growing sector of the church and had started with people literally meeting in front rooms but had been forced to expand into larger premises.

One 'house church' in South London, for example, has 2,100 members. Cobham Christian Fellowship, which had started in 1971 with five people, now has a congregation of 600 locally, with a further 900 in associated groups.

Sheila and her husband Norman, who had sold their house for the sake of her career, had moved in with Gerald Coates and his wife Anona in their eighteenth-century home in Esher (formerly a residence of Clive of India), and it was here that Cliff developed a friendship with Gerald.

Since leaving Guildford Baptist Church, following David Pawson's resignation in 1979, Cliff and Bill Latham had become irregular churchgoers. Initially they tried to fit in at Walton-on-Thames Baptist Church, but then tended to drift for long periods.

Cliff's attraction to the Cobham set highlighted a major difference between him and Latham. Whereas Cliff fits in naturally with uninhibited expressions of praise, believing that if it's alright to get visibly excited by rock'n'roll then it's alright to get visibly excited by God, Latham is by nature a traditionalist who prefers the prayer-book worship of the Church of England. It was noticeable that Cliff quite often made his visits to Cobham alone.

'There was a two or three-year period when Cliff clearly identified with us,' says Gerald Coates. 'He would come to our services, sometimes with Bill, sometimes without, and I know that he enjoyed our worship and teaching.

'Over that time Cliff and I would pray together. I think he was going through one or two things with those who were close to him and we were able to talk and I was able to advise. Bill encouraged these meetings.'

One of the hardest bits of news Cliff had to deal with during that period was the sudden death of Graham Jarvis, his drummer since 1978.

Unknown to Cliff, Jarvis had become a chronic alcoholic, sometimes polishing off a bottle of vodka before a show and another one back in his room late at night. On the last tour, which finished on 14 December 1985, the rest of the band were alarmed to notice that his skin and the whites of his eyes were turning yellow.

On 29 December he checked himself into a hospital detoxification programme in Croydon. Dave Cooke was the last group member to speak to him.

'I called him on the day before New Year's Eve and said I'd come along and play some backgammon with him,' he remembers. 'He sounded quite good. I told him I could either come that night or wait until the morning.

'I got a little Bible together for him as a present and at half past eight the next morning I called up to double check that it was OK to visit. The nurse answered and said, "Who's calling?" She then put me on to his wife Lorraine who was in tears. She said that he'd died half an hour ago.'

The shock to everyone came because they hadn't realized how seriously ill he had been. He hadn't lost his normal good humour throughout the tour and was never known to miss a beat. But, at thirty-five years of age, he was a victim of cirrhosis of the liver.

'The funeral was in North London and all the band except Mart Jenner were there,' remembers Graham Todd. 'Dave Cooke had a song called "Where You Are" which Graham had always liked and Cliff was going to perform it. But when it came to the time he said a few words but he was just too choked up to sing. I think he felt that if had known about it he could have done something to get Graham off the booze but I don't think anything would have done that.'

It marked the end of an era. Cliff was already planning to change the line-up. He intended to be involved in a West End musical which was planned by Dave Clark (formerly of the Dave Clark Five) and

Jarvis' death provided a convenient opportunity to break the news. John Perry, Mart Jenner and Dave Cooke were phoned by David Bryce and told that they would no longer be needed.

Taking part in a West End musical had been a long-term ambition of Cliff's. Since 1980 he had been specifically talking about a production which explored the possibilities of holographic technology.

'Having had a little experience in the acting world I would like to bring that together with the kind of singing I do to create the first real pop-rock musical,' Cliff said. 'In other words, get a really great story and pepper it with songs written by people like Terry Britten, John Farrar and Alan Tarney.

'Why shouldn't something like this happen? Why shouldn't the public go to a show and hear the top twenty live on stage, performed within the framework of a play? Why not? Why do we always have to have the traditional kind of musical? I'd like to do a show where every song gave me goose pimples, songs like "Miss You Nights", "Devil Woman" and "Dreamin'". I'd personally like to face that challenge.'

He had seen a lot of promise in a script sent to him by Chris Hutchins, a former publicist for Tom Jones and Engelbert Humperdinck, who was now a Fleet Street gossip columnist.

It was a brilliant idea of a pop star who begins to tire of his career while at his peak and who one day meets a petrol pump attendant who is his spitting image. The star realizes that he can relieve some of the pressure he's under by getting his lookalike to stand in for him by signing autographs at the stage door.

The story progresses with the lookalike taking over more and more areas of the star's life until he can perform his concerts. He then makes a move on the star's girlfriend. What excited Cliff about the idea was the possibility of having one of the characters played by himself in the form of a hologram. Unfortunately, a suitable ending was never found for the script and the project was abandoned.

The project which Dave Clark approached Cliff with in 1983 was a science fiction musical, *Time*, which Clark had not only had a hand in writing but which he was keen to produce, using his own money. He had already been recruiting stars to contribute tracks to an album which would precede the theatre opening, people such as Julian Lennon, Freddie Mercury, Dionne Warwick and Stevie Wonder. Freddie Mercury had a posthumous hit in 1992 with 'In My Defence', from the musical.

It was a simplistic moral tale of the earth's judgment, by the Time Lord Melchizidek, for the usual crimes of war and pollution, the fight for a reprieve organized by earthling pop star Chris and the wise sayings of the inscrutable Akash who although apparently not meant to represent God looked as though he'd have a hard time bowing down to anyone.

Its origins were in a musical called *The Time Lord*, with book and lyrics by David Soames and music by Jeff Daniels, which was put on at the Overground Theatre in Kingston Upon Thames in 1978. Dave Clark didn't see it but he read the script and heard a tape of the songs, and thought he could do something with it.

Clark met with the two writers in 1980 and they began to forge something new. The story was altered, the songs were re-written with Clark as an additional songwriter and a collection of new songs by outside writers was added into the mix.

The gist of the musical's message was that we'd all get on a lot better if we started being kind to the earth and kind to each other. The more profound philosophical and theological issues raised by this homespun wisdom were ignored.

'It was a musical about caring,' says Dave Clark. 'Most of the bad things in life are caused through envy, bitterness and greed and unless you get yourself in order you are in no position to put the world in order.'

'I believe all gods are one and that's what I tried to convey through the musical. I believe that everyone should have the right to believe in the way that they feel is right for them. As the song says, "It's in every one of us to be wise".'

In this respect Cliff's personal beliefs were at odds with the intention of the writers but he was able to justify his role by claiming that while the musical fell short of presenting the whole truth, as he understood it, what it did say was true as far as it went.

When Akash, represented by a hologram of Sir Laurence Olivier's head, declared that love was everlasting and death was defeated Cliff felt he could add, under his breath, that this was so with Jesus. There was a sense in which it was 'in everyone of us to be wise', as the final song said, but only if we were 'born again of the Spirit'.

Some church people felt that the omissions constituted heresy rather than partial truth. The teaching that wisdom is to be found within, they pointed out, was uncomfortably close to the New Age doctrine that we need no outside saviour to reconcile us with God because God, or the energy source, is within us all.

There was a line in the original version which referred to a 'Time Lord' who went to Nazareth two thousand years ago. Cliff had this changed to 'a guiding light'.

'I respect Cliff for his religious beliefs and there was always a fine line to be walked,' admits Dave Clark. 'We had a lot of discussions about it and we ended up with no references to God at all. The challenge for Cliff was to play a part. I didn't want people to think that it was Cliff.'

Time, despite the involvement of top musical director Larry Fuller and top choreographer Arlene Philips, opened on 9 April 1986 to scathing reviews. The *Sunday Times* called it 'a spectacular load of bilge' and claimed that Cliff couldn't act his way into a deserted railway station.

Theatre critic Sheridan Morley considered it one of the century's worst musicals and Milton Shulman thought it could only really be enjoyed by children. The only aspect of the production to be universally applauded were the sets created by John Napier.

Yet no amount of condemnation heaped on the musical, for its one-dimensional characters, its lack of drama and its unmemorable score, could prevent it from being a hit. Cliff fans were faithful to the extreme, treating it as if it was a twelve-month concert run, streaming to the front of the stage during the finale and waving their Cliff scarves in the air. When Cliff's term finished there had been over 700,000 tickets sold.

Time was a big commitment for a pop star in Cliff's position to make. It not only restricted him to one city for a year and a half but it meant being tied to a daily routine. He was on stage eight times a week, a total of over a thousand hours in a twelve-month run.

He would drive up to London each day in his Volkswagen Golf and got into the habit of eating his main meal after the show, often in the company of other members of the cast. He became particularly close to Roger Bruce, the production manager, and the dancers Wayne Aspinal, Jodie Wilson and Rosemarie Ford.

'We all found it terribly difficult to wind down after a show and we liked to do something different,' says Jodie. 'Sometimes we'd even play tennis. We'd go down to the David Lloyd Tennis Centre near Heathrow and would start a game at around midnight.'

Because Sunday was his only day off, Cliff would spend the time at home rather than attend church. It marked the beginning of a withdrawal from regular church-going, a move which worried his friends who could envisage the prospect of him drifting along without the affiliations which he himself had always recommended in his books as being essential to Christian growth.

His final night in *Time* came on 11 April 1987. Cliff was congratulated on stage by Dave Clark and then said a few words himself, some of them to the critics who had panned the show. 'You should write now that this is the greatest thing that has ever hit theatre,' he said.

Without Cliff, *Time* lost the focus of its commercial appeal. He was replaced by David Cassidy but six months later the show was taken off only to return for one night in 1988 to raise money for AIDS charities. It was never to open in any other country.

24

A man of today and tomorrow

C liff had been without a smash hit album of original material since Alan Tarney worked the magic on *Wired For Sound* five years before. *Now You See Me, Now You Don't* (1982), a gospel album in disguise, had reached number four in the album charts but of the singles released from the album, 'The Only Way Out' just edged into the top ten and 'Where Do We Go From Here?', only reached number sixty.

Dressed For The Occasion (1983), which was recorded at the Royal Albert Hall with the London Philharmonic Orchestra, consisted mostly of back catalogue songs. *Silver* and *Rock 'n' Roll Silver* (1983), designed to mark Cliff's twenty-five years in show business, were a mixture of new material and old rock 'n' roll classics.

The Rock Connection (1984), was another of Cliff's 'co-productions', this time with his former engineer Keith Bessey. It only reached number forty-three in the charts, his worst position since the *I'm Nearly Famous* comeback. The singles picked from it did no better. 'Heart User' made number forty-six while 'Shooting From The Heart' didn't even enter the top fifty.

It was David Bryce's suggestion to bring Tarney back as producer to arrest the slide.

Ever since hearing Michael Jackson's *Thriller*, which yielded five hit singles on both sides of the Atlantic, Cliff had nursed the idea of recording an album chock-full of hits—the ultimate Cliff Richard collection.

'I had dinner with David Bryce and I said to him that I felt I had never done the definitive Cliff Richard album,' says Tarney. ' "We Don't Talk Any More" should really have been on *I'm No Hero* and *Wired For Sound* was a hodge-podge of all sorts of writers. I felt I had never produced the album I could have done.'

Tarney's opportunity to do this came with *Always Guaranteed*. Recorded in September 1986 at R.G. Jones Studios while Cliff was still appearing in *Time*, it was one of his best albums ever, providing all his hit singles for the next year and the first of 1988. It was also one of his most commercial albums with sales of over 1.3 million copies.

It had been written in the studio. Tarney, who again played almost all the instruments, would arrive early in the morning to write and then Cliff would spend four hours each afternoon adding his vocals to the new backing track before disappearing to the Dominion Theatre.

'Alan liked to work on his own,' remembers engineer Gerry Kitchingham. 'He would start the day wandering around strumming the guitar and then he'd come up with a tune and he'd call me in and we'd get something on tape. That's the way he wrote "Some People". He came in with nothing and by the next day he'd got a hit song.'

Always Guaranteed illustrated Cliff's enduring ability to come back with commercial cutting-edge pop. Almost thirty years after his first hit he was still coming up with material that was effective competition for the chart acts of the day.

It has been this contemporariness that has set him apart from his peers and it's partly explained by his undiminished urge to be a chart contender. Although he's justly proud of his past achievements and will gladly recite chart positions and record sales, his main motivation is to do things of significance now.

His most animated conversation is always about the music he's currently making, not about glory days gone by. He has never basked in nostalgia, never reads books about himself and only reluctantly takes part in reunions with the Shadows.

'He doesn't keep cuttings,' says Bill Latham. 'He has no interest in old photographs. He's just not interested in talking about the past. You would expect him to have all sorts of mementoes but he only has a few things hanging up on the walls because they happened to be there. If he lost them all overnight he wouldn't care two hoots.'

It's an appropriate attitude for Britain's most consistent chart artist to have. Too much attention to his own past and he'd find himself as a golden oldie, affectionately remembered but unranked. Part of his achievement has been never to focus on a small part of his career and sell it back to the public.

There have been times when that would have been the easiest thing to do. Just as Little Richard recreates the American fifties and Gerry and the Pacemakers celebrate the Mersey boom, so Cliff could have made a handsome living out of presenting himself from the time of *The Young Ones*.

Because his commitment was to rock 'n' roll as a style of music rather than as an attitude he has never been one of those longing for a return of the excitement that surrounded the innovations of Elvis and Bill Haley. It genuinely bemuses him when old Teddy boys come up to him and wail about the death of rock 'n' roll.

'There is a new excitement today,' he says. 'If I'm asked whether I prefer singing "Move It" or my latest hit I say my latest hit because it will have a different kind of excitement. I would prefer to be excited by today's noise than yesterday's.'

He would never have been fulfilled by simply arousing memories. He needs to feel that he is a force to be reckoned with and he still regards the singles charts as a battleground where reputations are won and lost and where newcomers need to be seen off.

The stories are legion of Cliff's obsession with chart placings. When 'Devil Woman' entered the *Billboard* charts Bruce Welch walked across the stage during a concert in Hong Kong and whispered the news in his ear. In the summer of 1989, when the holiday gang were sailing off the coast of Croatia (then Yugoslavia), Cliff had his chart placings faxed to him on the boat despite the fact that all normal business was ignored during this period.

In 1990 he was delighted to have surpassed Elvis Presley's record of fifty-five British top ten hits, an achievement which meant that he was now the supreme top ten artist of all time in his own country.

The singles' market is less significant today than it was when he launched his career. Having a hit single no longer means making a fortune. Yet the top thirty remains an effective shop window for any pop artist. It ensures radio and newspaper coverage, it establishes the artist in the public consciousness and it acts as a trailer for the album.

'He really wants to remain a contemporary artist,' says Alan Tarney. 'I think he sees any newcomer as a threat to him and it's really good for him to see things in this way. He responds immediately.

'Most people stop fighting but Cliff wants to get up there and be better. If Jason Donovan is the latest heart-throb then Cliff would like nothing better than to get up there and show him how it should be done. That's what keeps him going.'

Throughout the eighties he found himself in demand by major artists wanting him to duet with them. Andrew Lloyd-Webber asked him to record a single of 'All I Ask Of You' with his then-wife Sarah Brightman which would draw attention to his new musical, *Phantom of the Opera*.

A&M Records approached him to duet with Janet Jackson, Dave Clark had his vocals added to a track from *Time* recorded by Stevie Wonder in California and Elton John invited Cliff to join him in singing 'Slow Rivers'.

It marked the rehabilitation of an artist who although hugely popular with the public had never been taken to the bosom of the rock aristocracy and had received a torrent of critical abuse over the years.

His beliefs were no more popular than they had been in 1966 but he had proved that he was a man of his word, unafraid to take the 'road less travelled', and integrity has its own reward. His music hadn't become more hard-edged and rebellious but there was no shame in being an unadulterated hit maker, especially if you had never made claims to be anything else.

'I think it takes a lot of strength of character to have Cliff's choices,' says Tony King, who is able to compare Cliff with his knowledge of working closely with stars like Elton John, Freddie Mercury, John Lennon and Mick Jagger.

'In a way his choices are more daring because they are out of step with what everyone thinks you have to be in order to be a rock 'n' roll artist. They are braver choices in that respect. Mick Jagger's choices are certainly a lot easier for young people to identify with.'

The anarchic cult comedy show of the mid eighties, 'The Young Ones', cast one of its main characters, played by Rik Mayall, as an ardent Cliff fan (hence the tribute in the title). When the cast came to record a single for the charity Comic Aid they chose to do a send-up of 'Living Doll' and asked Cliff to join in the joke. The record sold one million copies, almost as many as the original, and reached number one.

It was a useful part of the process of keeping Cliff's name linked with contemporary pop cultural figures and also of showing him to be someone who could laugh at himself.

The only time he has been enraged by the mockery directed at him was in 1984 when the NME (13 October), carried a 'review' of his gospel concert at Hammersmith Odeon. It was little more than a piece of hate mail written in the style of a conversation between the reviewer and Satan.

It made no mention of the music but directed a vitriolic attack on Cliff, his fans and Christianity. It referred to Cliff as a 'Nazi', ridiculed his celibacy and described his fans as 'two-dimensional masochists'. The final paragraph was a nasty obscene insult.

Cliff responded by suing the paper for libel. He won and was awarded £5000 damages which he immediately gave to the Arts Centre Group.

The most unlikely recording combination was that of Cliff and

Van Morrison: the beaming pop star and the glowering rock idol. Where Cliff was smooth, Van was rough. Where Cliff was adored, Van was admired. Physically, temperamentally and artistically they were polar opposites, each revered for totally different reasons by totally different audiences.

Yet what they shared was stronger than these differences. They had both started out in the skiffle era, both were interested in spiritual issues and both were men who doggedly followed their chosen paths regardless of the fashionability of their concerns. It was on this level that they had first met at an Arts Centre Group supper party and a strong mutual respect built up.

When Van came to record his album *Avalon Sunset* he thought it would be a good experiment to contrast his tough soulful vocals against Cliff's sweet mellifluous voice. The song, 'Whenever God Shines His Light', was not one of Van's best, but it was one of his more clearly Christian songs in that it linked God to Christ, rather than to an anonymous natural force. It became his first top ten hit in Britain since, as a member of Them, he reached number two in 1965 with 'Here Comes The Night'.

Some purists thought that an artist of Van's stature should never have deigned to record with a mere show business creature such as Cliff. For them it was a like a member of the aristocracy sharing his sandwiches with a coal miner.

'Why did you choose to record a duet with Cliff Richard?' asked an incredulous *NME* reporter. 'Are you an admirer of his work?'

'Cliff Richard?' asked Morrison, making sure he'd heard the question correctly. 'You're joking, aren't you? You're kidding? I grew up with Cliff. He'd be on "Saturday Club". I was a teenager, you know...'

The same year that Cliff increased his credibility with the rock audience by helping Van back into the charts he had his first dance-floor hit with 'I Just Don't Have The Heart', a record produced and written by the Mike Stock, Matt Aitken and Peter Waterman team, which did wonders for Cliff-awareness among the *Smash Hits* generation.

Stock, Aitken and Waterman had been dominating the charts with danceable pop tunes with programmed drum beats and vocals by singers such as Kylie Minogue, Jason Donovan and Rick Astley. For a while they seemed invincible. The music critics hated their formula-laden music and dippy lyrics but they sold by the truck load. By 1991 they had produced or written 106 titles and seen fifty-two of them enter the top ten, making them the most successful team of producer-songwriters in British chart history.

As chart-orientated people the SAW team and Cliff understood one another. Whereas Cliff couldn't see himself replicated in Mick Hucknall (from Simply Red) or Michael Hutchence (from INXS), he could see himself in Jason Donovan who presented a cheerful image, had an interest in musical theatre and made hit singles.

Stock, Aitken and Waterman met Cliff for the first time at the Ivor Novello Awards in April 1989 where they had won an award for writing Rick Astley's 'Never Gonna Give You Up'. Cliff was at the next table and he leaned over and said, 'If you ever come up with another song like that—give me a call.' They told him they'd love to work with him and took it from there.

'Usually we know the singers we work with very well but we didn't know Cliff and there wasn't time to find out what made him tick,' says Peter Waterman. 'We had to imagine we were Cliff and dream up an appropriate story.

'I came up with the title. I said, just imagine Cliff had fallen in love with this girl and then met someone else. What would he do? We thought, well, he's such a spiffing chap he wouldn't have the heart to tell her and that's where it came from. That's what the song was all about.

'I Just Don't Have The Heart' proved, if anything, that Cliff was the consummate British pop singer, able to surf any trend. The technology had changed but pop music, at heart, remained the same: it was melodic, rhythmic music, usually about love and usually with good harmonies. One sign of the new technology was that for 'I Just Don't Have The Heart' Cliff was taped doing his warm-up vocal exercises, then a sample of it was used effectively at the beginning of the single. 'When Cliff heard it,' says Waterman, 'he had no idea whose voice it was.'

Cliff has always produced his best work when surrounded by brilliant talent brimming with new ideas. If he had been a singer-songwriter he would undoubtedly have run out of ideas by now but being an interpreter of other people's ideas means that he is constantly able to recharge his career with the fire of someone else's youth. His best songs throughout his career have been written by young men (and one woman) in their twenties or thirties.

His office is deluged by cassettes from songwriters because he is one of the few top-selling artists today who hardly ever records his own material. Stuart Ongley of Patch Music reckoned that around one thousand songs a year are sent in. These songs are now weeded out by David Bryce who then passes on what he thinks is the best to Cliff. Sometimes an outside friend, like DJ Mike Read, is called in for a second opinion.

The songwriters who've proved most successful with Cliff—people such as Hank Marvin, Bruce Welch, Alan Tarney, Terry Britten and Chris Eaton—are those who've worked with him as musicians and have been able to pass songs on to him directly. They're also the first to find out what music he's currently fascinated with.

Terry Britten used to arouse Cliff's interest by playing his latest riffs through during band soundchecks. 'Cliff would then come over and say, "That's nice, Terry," and Terry would shrug and say, "Oh, it's just something I'm working on",' remembers Graham Todd. 'Then Cliff would say, "That would make a nice song." Terry was very smart in that respect.'

Cliff prides himself on being able to spot potential hits, and argues that it's this instinct, even more than his voice, which has enabled him to stay on top for so long.

Chris Eaton wrote 'Saviour's Day' in October 1989. He brought a demo of the song to the office Christmas party despite having been told by Gill Snow, Cliff's secretary, that the whole of 1990 was already mapped out with 'From A Distance' planned as the next year's Christmas single.

'I told Cliff that I wanted him to hear this song,' says Eaton, 'so we left the party and went to sit in his Rolls where we played the tape. He loved it straight away. He said, "This is a number one song." You've got to hand it to him—he does have a feeling for what's going to make it.'

His latest collaborator is Paul Moessl who at twenty-six is half Cliff's age. He was spotted playing in the house band at Blazers club in Windsor when David Bryce went along to see Jimmy Tarbuck. He thought he sounded innovative and arranged for him to deputize during *Time*.

When Cliff formed a new band in 1987 for his 'Beyond Time' tour he retained Alan Park as his musical director, Mark Griffiths on bass and John Clark on guitar but recruited the rest of the musicians from the ranks of the *Time* musicians, including Paul Moessl on keyboards.

A year later Moessl was suddenly summoned to David Bryce's office in Esher 'for a little talk' and assumed that he was about to be 'let go' in the time-honoured fashion. He just couldn't think what he'd done wrong.

'Then they said, "We've got this song. Have a listen to it",' he remembers. 'It was "Mistletoe and Wine". I said, "Yeh, it's very Christmassy isn't it?" They said, "We want to record it and Cliff wants to give you the chance of doing it." I was completely taken aback.

'I don't know why they chose me. I put it down to youth. Cliff will always take a chance. I think he susses out young people and if he trusts that they've got an idea about what's going on he'll try and tap into that.'

'Mistletoe and Wine' went to number one and became the best-selling British single of 1988 and Paul Moessl had become the new blue-eyed boy who could carry on bringing new life to Cliff's recording career.

For *Stronger*, Cliff's follow-up to *Always Guaranteed*, Moessl was introduced as 'guest arranger' on two tracks—'Joanna' and 'The Best Of Me'—with Cliff credited as producer. 'The Best Of Me', the first release from the album, went to number two and sold over 750,000 copies.

Because of the success, Moessl became arranger and co-producer for Cliff's 1991 Christmas album, *Together With Cliff Richard*, a UK-only release capitalizing on his unprecedented run of Christmas number ones, which included his part in the re-recorded 'Do They Know It's Christmas?' for Band Aid.

Instead of a great follow-up to *Always Guaranteed* and *Stronger*, his last two studio albums, he produced an uninspired collection of 'Christmas favourites' including 'Scarlet Ribbons', 'Silent Night' and 'White Christmas'. It was as if the seventies and eighties had never happened.

In 1992 Paul Moessl began writing with Cliff for *Cliff Richard: The Album*, which he would again co-produce.

'In fact the original title was *Access All Areas* (taken from the badges worn backstage by those granted unlimited access to stage, arena and dressing rooms), and reflected the idea that we have tried to get different song styles onto the album,' says Moessl.

'Cliff's always looking ahead. He's into fresh ideas, fresh turnover and he's always trying to do something someone else hasn't done. He had a bad throat when we were recording and he started singing in a completely different way.

'It sounded so good that we recorded the album while it was in this lapsed state. When he got better he couldn't sing in exactly the same way again. It's a bizarre way of doing things but it worked and it shows his openness towards doing things in different ways.'

The biggest worry among those working with Cliff was that he was now feeling the full effect of Peter Gormley's retirement which had taken place in the early eighties, even though Gormley continued to offer advice. Although he was already well-established by the time Gormley took over his career, there's no doubting the effect of this quietly spoken but rock-solid Australian in guiding him steadily through the ups and downs.

Talk to Gormley about how it's done and he shrugs his shoulders. He says he never did market research ('it's all bull'), never went out to create an image for Cliff ('image creation is a term that annoys me considerably') and has no philosophy of management that he could ever pass on to anyone else.

'You did what you had to do,' he says simply. 'You worked according to your own judgment. It was purely a matter of instinct and judgment. There were no methods whatsoever. We never had any arguments about it. I presume we all thought alike.'

As a manager he was more than a negotiator, promoter and protector. He was a friend and father-figure to Cliff, and his instinct for what was right extended to the choice of singles.

'He has an incredible intuition about what is right and wrong for Cliff,' says Cliff's former producer Dave Mackay.

'Sometimes you'd be slaving away over something for Cliff, trying to get exactly the right feel, and he'd just walk in and stand at the back and say, "Hate those drums, son." You'd listen to it back again and he would always be right although he's not musical. He just knows Cliff and his audience.'

With Peter Gormley gone the management was divided between David Bryce (professional), Malcolm Smith (business) and Bill Latham (charity, Christian and media). None of them had the overall control that Gormley had exercised. The fear being expressed by those within the inner circle was that Cliff would now make more unchallenged decisions, and that this wasn't always a good thing.

'Peter was the rock on which it was all built,' says one member of the inner circle who has worked with all three. 'Cliff and Peter Gormley are the greatest double act of all time. People always underestimate Peter but Cliff knows. He provided him with the ultimate platform. There is something wonderful about Cliff and Peter preserved that for thirty years. He kept it pure.

'Now he's lost that guiding figure. The next phase will be interesting to watch.'

25

'My Kinda Life'

T hirty-five years after his first (£200) tour Cliff Richard is a very wealthy man. In 1991 *The Sunday Times* valued his fortune at £50 million, ranking him at number 182 in a list of Britain's 200 richest people. In 1992, with his fortune apparently undiminished, he moved up to 158th position. The magazine estimated that the *From A Distance* album and tour had generated over £22 million.

There were only three other British pop stars on the list: Paul McCartney with £380 million, Elton John with £100 million and Mick Jagger with £75 million, each of whom have had shorter careers than Cliff but who have made more from publishing royalties and from sales in America.

Cliff denies that he's worth as much as that: 'When that story came out I got a note from Malcolm Smith, my business manager, which said, "Don't spend it because I haven't found it!" '

Cliff's revenue is based primarily on ticket sales, mechanical royalties on albums and singles (he has made very little from songwriting), merchandizing and videos. In the early part of his career he also made money from films and television.

His singles sales have been phenomenal. Thirty-two of them have sold over one million copies each and his total world sales now approach eighty million. His albums consistently made the top twenty from 1958–66, and again from 1976 onwards. Today a modest effort will sell at least 500,000 and a hit album as many as 1,500,000.

But it has been his live shows that have shown the most rapid growth over the last decade. Since moving out of the Empires and Odeons which characterized his touring throughout the sixties and seventies, he has been regularly filling the country's largest exhibition centres for extended runs.

Mel Bush, who has promoted all Cliff's British tours since The Event in 1989, believes that as a live entertainer Cliff could outsell any other act in the world. He is already one of only six acts which have filled Wembley Stadium for two or more nights on the strength of their name alone. (The others are Michael Jackson, Madonna, Bruce Springsteen, the Rolling Stones and Genesis.)

'If Cliff had the time and wanted to do it, I think he would have absolutely no problem in playing to a million people in this country on one tour,' says Bush. 'To play to over 400,000 in 1990 we only played in four centres.'

In 1990 he played at the Wembley Arena for eighteen nights, reaching a total of 216,000 people and breaking all previous records for the Arena. His 'Access All Areas' tour in 1992 played fourteen nights at Birmingham's NEC (capacity 12,378), five nights at the Sheffield Arena (cap. 12,000), three nights at the Scottish Exhibition Centre in Glasgow (cap. 10,000), fifteen nights at Wembley Arena (cap. 12,000), four nights at Kings Hall, Belfast, (cap. 6,000) and three nights at the Point Depot in Dublin (cap. 4,500).

Simple calculations reveal that on that tour he played to 480,792 people and that with seats selling for £19.50 and £17.50 this means (presuming at least a third of the audience bought the higher-priced tickets) that the gross revenue from the box office must be approaching £9 million. Production costs, which included a specially constructed stage and rehearsals at the Docklands Arena, were rumoured to be approaching £2 million but much of that will have been covered by the smart practice of taking paid bookings for the tour almost a year in advance so that interest could accrue.

This doesn't take into account the income from merchandizing (sweat shirts, programmes, mugs, caps, badges, keyrings, torches, brooches) and the rejuvenation of his back catalogue.

All Cliff's finances are handled by Malcolm Smith, a 41-year-old chartered accountant who joined the Cliff Richard Organization as managing director in 1987 from the City firm of Touche Ross, having worked on Cliff's accounts from outside since 1985. He is a director of fifteen companies, including those which absorb the money generated by Cliff's career.

His fellow directors on these companies are the same; Cliff's mother, Michael Simkins who has been Cliff's lawyer since 1960 and his colleague David Franks, Cliff's accountant Philip Parker and Peter Gormley. All financial decisions are made jointly.

The turnover of these companies combined has steadily climbed over the last decade. In 1985 it was less than £2 million but by 1988 it had doubled and in 1991 it was almost £8 million.

Yet Cliff appears to be detached from his fortune. He genuinely has little idea of what he's worth, has never been a profligate spender and his pocket money is set at forty pounds a week which is brought to him by Bill Latham each Thursday evening in a brown envelope made up by Gill Snow.

The Cliff Richard Organization, in Claygate, Surrey, has a staff of twelve but Cliff himself only employs two people: his full-time gardener Mick and housekeeper Megan who comes in three mornings a week. He owns no valuable works of art, doesn't jet-set or gamble and has no expensive habits other than tennis.

His main assets appear to be his home in Weybridge, bought for £1.4 million in August 1987, his new Portugese holiday home and vineyard bought in 1992, a cottage in North Wales with 125 acres of land, the Claygate office building and his three cars—a 1980 Rolls Royce, a 1989 Range Rover and a 1990 Mercedes Benz 500 SL.

Since March 1966 he has followed the Christian practice of 'tithing', giving away at least a tenth of his income to charity. This is usually done through the Cliff Richard (Charitable Trust) Ltd. which in 1991 benefited from over one million pounds and has almost no administration costs. On top of this he donates more than a tenth of his working time to charity and church events: making personal appearances, video tapes, books and Bible cassettes.

Since leaving Tear Fund in 1978, Bill Latham has managed Cliff's Christian and charity affairs, and more recently has handled the press. Together they make frequent public appearances in church situations where Cliff is interviewed about his faith and about Third World concerns.

Cliff is now so readily associated with charity work that it's easy to assume that it's second nature for him to give in this way.

Bill Latham believes that by nature he wouldn't choose to involve himself in the troubles and turmoils of the Third World and that if he hadn't been transformed by his response to the Christian gospel he would probably be an insular person.

'I think Cliff's concern for others has come about largely as a result of Christian self-discipline,' he says. 'I think the nature of the Christian faith demands that one looks outside oneself. I think he's forced himself to be aware of others. I don't think it's necessarily easy for him to do it because I think he is by nature more self-absorbed.'

The profit from all his gospel tours is automatically put into the trust as is the income from some of his religious books. The trust then gives fifty per cent of the income to Tear Fund and the rest is spread around other charities.

He feels particularly close to the Arts Centre Group because it had grown out of the group with Nigel Goodwin and David Winter that he'd been a part of starting in 1965. In 1971 he bought a mansion in Great Dunmow, Essex, which he then allowed the ACG full use of as a retreat and conference centre. (It has since been sold.)

'We get a lot of letters from people asking for money,' says Gill Snow. 'The answer we give is that we don't help individuals because all of Cliff's giving goes through his trust and that is authorized only to give to registered charities.

'A lot of the stories are heart-breaking but if you give to one person then you're stymied. At the moment, in the middle of a recession, ninety per cent of the requests we get are mortgage-related. People are losing their businesses or their homes. I write back to them all individually and try to be as sympathetic as possible.'

Cliff is generous to family and friends but never impulsive in the way that Elvis used to buy Cadillacs for passing strangers or Elton John has been known to hand out jewellery. He set Donna's first husband up in business and bought homes for his sisters and mother.

'It's not in Cliff's nature to throw his money around,' says Bill Latham. 'He's more cautious. He doesn't give his money away on impulse although he has always looked after his family.'

When he does spend his money it tends to be on the house and garden. When he was living at Rookswood he discovered that Latham and Graham Disbrey were keen tennis players, so he had a tennis court built, even though they only had a chance to play on it twice before the house was sold.

In Totteridge and at Feather Green he spent money building extensions and then promptly moved out when there seemed nowhere left to extend. At his new home in Weybridge, which needs no enlarging, he has extended the garages.

He recently saw a painting in an art gallery catalogue which he liked and was thinking of buying for his home but when he found out it cost £25,000—peanuts for a multi-millionaire however small the multi might be—he threw up his hands in horror. 'But I could decorate my house for £25,000,' he said.

The amount represents less than 0.27 per cent of what he is likely to have grossed in 1992 but he still thinks more in terms of the forty pounds in the brown envelope than of the invisible millions that are processed in Claygate.

It's often a point of annoyance to the musicians that he fails to realize the cost of living in Britain today because all his major expenses are sorted out by other people and the cash in his pocket is mainly there for tipping.

Once at a band meal he started to say that he didn't see why people had such a hard time on Social Security because he seemed to manage well enough on what was in his brown envelope. 'But you don't have to pay your mortgage out of that,' Tony Rivers argued. 'You don't pay your bills and buy your meals with that.'

He doesn't live a typically showbizzy life. His closest friends are not drawn from entertainment but from accountancy, teaching, sport, church and charity. He's not often spotted at openings and first nights and never goes clubbing.

He rarely entertains at home and if he does it will often be with a group of old and trusted friends from the Crusader days. He enjoys cooking pool-side barbecues and for bigger parties he'll hire caterers.

He loves organizing theme parties. For his fiftieth birthday in 1990 he had a marquee erected on the lawn and everyone had to come as they were in 1958. Recently he's held a woodland party under the trees at the bottom of his garden, an 'over the top' party where guests dressed in anything from Arab robes to space suits, and a 'ball gowns and uniforms' party.

His holidays follow the pattern that was set in 1966, which means two or three weeks in the sunshine with the 'holiday gang' where he'll swim, play tennis or sunbathe while listening to music on a Sony Walkman.

Most often these holidays have been in Portugal but there have been trips to California (1968), Israel (1972), Madeira (1973), South Africa, Bermuda (1983) and Florida. In 1987 and 1989 a London art dealer, David Mason, gave them the free use of his ocean-going yachts *Lindsay Jane* and *Lindsay Jane II*. On the first trip they toured the Greek islands and on the second the coast of Croatia (then Yugoslavia).

'The problem on the cruises was that Cliff had difficulty finding access to tennis courts,' says Graham Disbrey, the only person other than Bill Latham and Cliff who has been on all the 'gang' holidays.

'We managed in the end but sometimes it was half a day's venture to actually find one. In Portugal he has his own court and so after sunbathing and swimming he would be coached for one to two hours.'

Tennis has become for him little short of an obsession. Ever since playing badminton as a boy he has enjoyed racquet games but after meeting Sue Barker he changed from being a casual performer to a deadly serious contender with all the grit and determination he once displayed on the rugger field.

He started playing regularly at the David Lloyd Tennis Centre and receiving lessons. Soon he was becoming a fixture on the social circuit of the British tennis scene, turning up at Wimbledon, organizing pro-celebrity tennis tournaments and injecting much-needed money into schemes to improve Britain's standing on the world tennis scene.

Today, he tries to ensure that he is booked into hotels that have tennis courts and on some tours he travels with a tennis pro. He plays doubles against the likes of Chris Evert Lloyd, Steffi Graf and Ilie Nastase and friends suggest that although he professes to play only as a hobby he secretly believes that, even in his fifties, he can go on improving.

'He became infatuated with the game,' says Sue Barker. 'He can't accept not doing it well. I kept telling him that children mimic and can pick things up quite quickly but that he had no hope at his age. I think he then approached it in the spirit of trying to prove that I was wrong.

'He still doesn't look like a natural player, like someone who has been playing all his life. There is always a distinction between someone who has played as a kid and someone who has taken it up much later in life. You can see it in the flowing motion of the shots. The result is still the same, but you can feel that it's manufactured rather than natural.'

Tennis commentator Gerald Williams believes he is better than a good club player and that he could well sneak into a minor county team.

'He's very fit and competitive and plays a good game,' he says. 'He really understands tennis. When he talks about it on radio and TV he makes more sense than a lot of people who earn a living from talking about it.'

In 1992 he and Bill Latham went on holiday to Lech in Austria with tennis partner Charles Haswell, his wife and two female friends, and here he tried skiing for the first time. He was on the beginners' slope for just two days, graduated to the blue runs and by the end of the fortnight was confident enough to come down red runs and do parallel turns.

His involvement with skiing again shows the depth of his determination. He is never content to dabble. He has to attain complete mastery, confounding those who say it can never be done. He needs a fresh supply of challenges, however apparently insignificant they may be.

One former producer, when asked why Cliff had never married, reputedly said, 'How can someone so in love with himself ever fall in love with anyone else?' The remark is quite cruel but there is a kernel of truth. How could someone so in love with their present lifestyle ever make room for the needs of another individual?

Bill Latham puts it like this: 'There is no way Cliff could have lived the life he has lived, contributed what he has contributed and achieved what he has achieved if he had been married. There is no question of that. Although he loves his home he doesn't feel tied to it and that freedom has meant that he has been able to do much, much more than if he had a family.

'It's also partly to do with the enthusiastic approach he has towards everything he touches. He always goes the extra mile. If he was to have a relationship he would give it everything. There would be no half measures.

'So because his commitments have been his career, his faith, and, more latterly, tennis, he has given himself wholeheartedly to those three activities. There hasn't been room for anything else.'

There have been no girlfriends since Sue Barker, although there has never been a shortage of women wanting to be Mrs Cliff Richard. Some of them get very close. They have even been to his house and cooked him meals, accompanied him to the cinema and eaten out at restaurants.

Cliff will be extremely charming and pleasant to them but there is a limit to how close he'll allow them to come. As soon as he senses that they are wanting more from him than he'll ever be able to give, he cuts them off.

It's back to that scene in *Summer Holiday* where Cliff says: 'Girls are all very well, but date them once and then run. Date them twice and they get serious ... Next thing you know, you're hooked and wondering what's hit you. No. No girl is going to own me.'

He enjoys female company, though. In the seventies he became friendly with the beautiful daughter of a wealthy landowner, who, somewhat naturally, misinterpreted the signals and assumed Cliff was falling in love with her.

She went on holiday to France where she was hospitalized after a car accident. The mother, who by now assumed Cliff was her daughter's boyfriend, immediately called the office and requested that Cliff look after her and have her brought back to England. It was only then that Cliff realized the depth of the misunderstanding.

More recently he became friendly with Marietta Parfitt, the divorced wife of Status Quo guitarist Rick Parfitt. A committed Roman Catholic and a gracious hostess, she would often accompany him on double dates with Bill Latham and Jill Clarke. She was also a regular guest at Weybridge and went into print saying that Cliff had helped her through a particularly bad time in her life.

For years he has said that he's just waiting for the right girl to come along but, at fifty-two, he has concluded that he is not the marrying sort.

'Maybe I have lived through all the things I needed to live through to find myself and what I want out of life,' he says. 'I don't think marriage is one of those things. I don't feel I'll ever get married now. I don't think I'm unique. I still have enough female company and it's fine.

'At the moment I prefer not having a romantic attachment. I find myself really free. I can do whatever I want. I don't have to look for babysitters. I shot off to Austria recently and I'd like to go again soon and I can just do things like that.

'Life for me is really quite nice and I like it the way it is. The only reason it's not selfish is because no one has to tie themselves to anyone else if they don't want to. It's a positive step in that I don't actually owe anyone anything. I don't have to be tied to anybody and I like that.'

The absence of serious romantic relationships with women and the long, close live-in friendship with Bill Latham lead many people to conclude that something homosexual is going on, despite the vigorous denials issued by both Latham and Cliff over the years.

'I have denied being gay since the idea was first mooted when I was eighteen,' says Cliff. 'I've never even contemplated the possibility that I might be gay. There's not much I can do to stop the rumours. Ultimately all that counts is what my friends and family know and they all trust and respect me.'

In 1991, while Cliff was rehearsing for a gospel tour at Bray film studios near Windsor, a group of extras working on Derek Jarman's film *Edward II* invaded the band's sound stage. They waved gay rights placards and urged Cliff to 'come out of the closet'.

It's not an altogether outrageous assumption to make simply because it is almost impossible to name another unmarried man of Cliff's age in show business who lives with a male friend, doesn't date girls and isn't homosexual. In other words, Cliff doesn't fit any model that people know of. He doesn't appear to be the 'confirmed bachelor' of the old-fashioned type, because most of these fellows don't dress in skin-tight cycling shorts and diamanté jackets. Cliff's image is not one of fusty bachelorhood but of glamour, style and romance.

The truth seems to be that Cliff doesn't fit the clearly defined models we are used to, where if you're not Rod Stewart or Bill Wyman then you must be Liberace. It's clear that from his mid-teens until his mid-twenties he did endeavour to form relationships with women but the desire for sexual commitment was never great enough to move beyond the stage of a fifties high school date. Also, the more attached he became to his lifestyle the harder it became to embark on a relationship which might threaten it.

After his relationships with Jackie Irving and Una Stubbs he seems to have become reconciled to bachelorhood, admitting (sometimes) that he wasn't bothered by strong sexual passions and seemingly impervious to temptation.

He had always had a very high view of marriage, and his conversion to Christianity can only have enhanced this. He believed he was called to live a celibate life while single and a faithful life should he marry.

This inevitably increased the significance of marriage both in his eyes and in the eyes of his fans, because there could be no euphemistic 'close friendships' or 'inseparable companions'. Serious courtship could only be conducted with marriage in mind.

At the same time, as a Christian, Cliff's single life could be looked at in a positive light, because both Jesus and the apostle Paul taught that some people are better prepared for Christian service because they are untroubled by the 'fires of passion'. It's almost certainly this that Cliff was referring to when he said that not having 'any great sexual urges' was 'my good fortune'.

When he met Bill Latham in 1964 the relationship provided him with the emotional succour that most men receive from a marriage. This 'brotherly affection', as Latham describes it, no doubt filled the natural emptiness that can result from living without close dependants.

But rather than being something homosexual, it confirmed his belief that he didn't need a marriage to fulfil him. His friendship with Latham and his career effectively replaced wife and children. There had never really been any need for sexual gratification and so that didn't constitute a lack.

If he hadn't met Latham it seems likely that Cliff would have remained single but it's unlikely that Latham would have remained unmarried if he hadn't met Cliff. Latham had steady girlfriends in the sixties and seventies (Cindy Kent among them) and now his long-term girlfriend Jill Clarke shares the Weybridge house with him and Cliff.

'I had never set my mind on being single,' Latham admits. 'I've had relationships in the past, am with a long-term girlfriend and am under constant pressure to marry but I don't feel that at my stage of life I would want the upheaval.

'In one sense I would have liked to have had a family but because my life has been so fulfilled in so many other ways it's not something I lose sleep over or become depressed about.'

The relationship between the two men is close but not suffocatingly so. A lot of the time they spend together is because of work, but when Cliff is recording or touring Latham carves out his own independent life.

Their interests are quite different. Latham has never been a big fan of rock 'n' roll, prefers cricket to tennis and can't stand the video games which Cliff so loves to play at home. He also has no interest in skiing. When Cliff first went to Austria Latham sat out the skiing sessions in local coffee bars. When the next trip was set up he chose not to go.

Among close friends they often allow these tensions to come to the surface. 'I've been at meals in the last few years where there have almost been fights between him and Bill,' says one friend. 'Bill talks a lot of common sense but Cliff will come out with comments about the unemployed and homeless, and I think it drives Bill to despair. I don't think Cliff understands.'

Cliff is unashamedly right wing in his political views. In his time he has advocated birching, called for wider censorship and suggested that the unemployed should help out in hospitals. He was a big supporter of Margaret Thatcher. He also dismayed many of his music business colleagues by continuing to play in South Africa during the apartheid regime, a move which earned him a United Nations blacklisting and a bomb threat while touring Scandanavia.

His attitudes are a mix of those he inherited as a child of the Raj and those he developed as a poor boy made good in England.

Thatcherism appealed to him because he had started with nothing and, through determination and talent, had become a multi-millionaire. His assumption was that anyone else with similar single-mindedness could make something of themself.

He is notably hard on people he regards as 'slackers', or who don't seem to 'pull their weight'. Seemingly oblivious to his own privileged position, he complains about those who work only for money.

His background in India forged a strong, almost uncritical, allegiance to those in power. Where other pop stars have questioned police behaviour, been critical of royalty, or protested against British foreign policy, Cliff has remained unstintingly loyal to the establishment.

Colleagues are often shocked by his ignorance of the harsher side of British life. Although he has witnessed the effects of Third World poverty, he knows little about the underclass of his own country.

This is not entirely his fault. Since 1958 he has lived a separate life. His encounters with the public and with officialdom are untypical because they are always in controlled situations and he is always treated with a respect not offered to the ordinary citizen. It's hard to come up with informed views about the world when the only world you experience is so protected.

'One of the causes for our disagreements is the blind spot I feel he has over the pressures in society today for people just to exist,' Bill Latham admits. 'He doesn't really understand the pressure of a mortgage, interest rates, unemployment and so on. I often feel he doesn't have enough empathy with people. I would like him actually to go to some inner-city areas in Britain to see just what the people there face.'

Yet Cliff needs Latham to shield him from the world and guard his diary. Latham plays the role of the often stern parent trying to control a naïve but talented and adventurous child who has no real perception of the adult world, no sense of time and no concept of what can and can't be done.

He admonishes him about his dress sense, reminds him of promises he has made to people and is almost always around as the looming presence which brings conversations to an end.

'Cliff is the "Let's do everything" one and Bill is the "No, you can't do that" one,' says Gill Snow, who has worked with Cliff and Bill in different capacities for over twenty years. 'They balance each other out in that respect. Bill is very organized and Cliff, like so many artists, isn't. But, underneath it all, there's a high degree of mutual respect and they are very close friends.'

The great triumph of their relationship has been that it works. Cliff has, over a period of years, been able to integrate his professional work with his spiritual faith to the point where he has become perhaps the best-known advocate for Christianity in Britain.

'It's hard to understand Cliff without Bill,' says Graham Disbrey. 'The overriding thing is that Bill has been the most generous, kindly person and he really has made his mark on the kind of person Cliff is today.'

Initially Cliff's proclamation of faith sat uneasily with his Talk Of The Town lifestyle, but it no longer seems out of place for him to speak about his love for Jesus in the middle of a show. No journalist can now write a profile of him without mentioning the fact of his Christianity because it informs everything he does.

Today, when it is quite common for rock musicians to display a passion for religion, it may not seem such an act of courage, but when Cliff did it in 1966, before the Beatles made known their allegiance to Maharishi Mahesh Yogi, it was stepping into unknown territory.

It's even more courageous for Cliff because he is essentially a people pleaser. His musical career has been based on satisfying the public taste. Yet with the stand he has taken as a Christian he has often had to fly in the face of public opinion and this has made him the target of abuse.

'He likes to be liked professionally, because if he's not liked, the career ends,' Bill Latham explains. 'He's hurt by professional criticism but he's not really hurt or upset if he's criticized for his opinions. He may get irritated but he's not offended or hurt. Regardless of the company he's in he'll be very outspoken about the things he believes in. There will be no holds barred.'

Some of Bill and Cliff's friends feel that Latham has sacrificed his own life for the sake of Cliff, that by remaining so close he has denied himself the opportunity of pursuing a career in his own right or of marrying and raising a family. They point out that his own gifts as as a communicator are no longer fully used and that he has to spend much of his time as an unacknowledged figure in the background while his famous friend grabs all the attention.

Latham denies this. 'It's not been a sacrifice at all,' he says. 'Quite the reverse. It's opened up areas of experience that have been very rewarding and fulfilling. I've seen it all as a privilege.

'Cliff and I just get on together. We work together well. Spiritually the team has been fruitful and my gut feeling is that it's right. There is a job to be done and we go out and do it.'

26

The bubble that didn't burst

I f Cliff had been asked in 1958 what he would have liked to have been doing in his fifties he would probably have said, 'singing'. But he could never have dreamt that his wish would come true.

That year his father was fifty-three, a gaunt, balding man with an austere Victorian demeanour. It would have been impossible then to have imagined someone of this age shaking a leg and singing 'Move It'.

Realistically, Cliff thought of a career that might see him through his teens before his young audience deserted him and he was forced to get a sensible job. By the time he was twenty he openly admitted that he was saving up for that inevitable day when 'the bubble burst'.

The bubble didn't burst. He has been through trying times though. He has put out records beneath his capabilities. But never in thirty-five years has he been less than a major star in Britain and every time he has seemed to be slipping he has come back with something bigger and better.

What makes his career doubly remarkable is the fact that he is not simply a survivor but someone who is constantly scaling new heights.

His first decade was largely spent establishing himself as a singles artist and as a film star. During his second decade, which ended in 1978, he emerged as a star of his own television shows and, for the first time, as a serious album artist.

But even by then he hadn't done everything. In his third decade, while producing his biggest-selling single ever with 'We Don't Talk Any More', he developed his stage show to new and spectacular dimensions.

By 1988 you would have thought that there was nowhere left to go. But he surprised everyone with The Event, his first stadium show, which was quickly followed by his longest run at Wembley Arena.

How has he survived so many changes in musical fashion? It would be easy to attribute it all to superior talent but if that were so then acts such as the Rolling Stones and Paul McCartney would have had equally consistent careers.

Part of the answer lies in the fact that most of the performers who became established in the sixties were songwriters as well as singers. Their fate has been tied up with their ability to create fresh material. Broadly speaking, they produced their best work in their twenties and early thirties. Cliff, who has always been an interpreter of other writers' songs, has not been affected in the same way.

Another part of the answer is that Cliff, because he is single, has been able to devote almost all of his energy to his work. He has been able to retain his youthful enthusiasm because he hasn't taken on the baggage of adulthood.

He is one of the most fiercely determined singers in the business, although this is often overlooked by observers because of his easygoing manner. The fighting skills he once established in the playground have been sublimated into his career.

This devotion has been supplemented by the help of good colleagues. In a business noted for sharp practice he has been extremely fortunate with those who have influenced his career. Very early on he fell in with good, honest men such as Peter Gormley and Norrie Paramor, who gave him strong fatherly direction as well as much room as possible to be himself.

Undoubtably his greatest talent has been his pure and well-rounded singing voice. It is distinctive (you can tell a Cliff record within a few notes), he has maintained it well (he took voice lessons in 1991 and now tunes up for twenty minutes before each concert) and is in perfect keeping with what the public know of his character—warm, smooth, compassionate, reassuring.

He knows what he wants. Although he has been supported by good musicians, song writers and producers, he must take credit for seeing the potential in these people. He has an eye for talent just as he has an ear for hit songs. But more than even the music itself, his continued success is due to his warm personality and to the unique relationship he has built up with his fans.

Many performers are content to churn out singles on a 'take it or leave it' basis and refuse to do anything more than the minimum of publicity. Cliff has always unashamedly given the public what it wants and has allowed himself to 'belong' to his fans.

Because he recognizes that he is an entertainer rather than an artist, he has never taken the attitude that if he liked a song it is then up to the audience to learn to like it. Entertainers are not there to confound expectations and alter perceptions. They are there to provide pleasant distractions.

Right from the early days Cliff was talking of 'doing what the fans want me to'. In 1960 he actually brought a group of fans together at Abbey Road studios to chose his next single from a collection of twenty-one recorded songs (they chose 'Please Don't Tease').

Asked in 1977 what he would do if he was faced with a choice between personal artistic satisfaction and pleasing the public, he said he would compromise. 'I would compromise with quality songs though,' he said. 'I don't want to cut the parents and grandparents out.'

Although he values his privacy he makes himself available to his fans, both in person and through chat shows and press interviews. Many performers view their dealings with the media as a chore, but Cliff approaches it all with the zest with which he records his singles.

The result has been that those who follow him hold him in great affection. This is obvious to anyone who has attended his concerts where the rapport between stage and audience is the rapport of friends rather than that of salesman and customer.

Given Cliff's huge following in the UK and many other parts of the world, his failure to crack America is surprising. His relative lack of success there must be due, in part, to the fact that the American public knows nothing of Cliff's personality in this way. He comes to them each time with no legend attached. They hear the songs in isolation and buy them when they're particularly strong and ignore them when they're mediocre. In Britain there are those who buy the singles whatever the quality because of their allegiance to Cliff.

But even if Cliff had become well known in the States, it's likely that the American public would have considered him too soft for their taste anyway. Elvis could look like a mummy's boy in his colourful jackets but he could also look like a hoodlum. Cliff never looked convincing as a hoodlum.

Softer performers have normally had to compensate by being extravagent in other ways. It was when he went to America that Elton John developed his outrageous costumes and flying leaps at the piano. You have to shout really loud in America to get noticed. It's not enough simply to make 'good' records.

Cliff's image in Britain is well defined and well known. However, interestingly enough, he has only ever employed a publicist for particular albums or film campaigns and he was not manufactured at the hands of a public relations consultant. There is no Svengali in the background.

The two strongest characteristics of this well-known image are his decency and his youthfulness. Most of that which is revered or reviled about Cliff can be filed beneath these two headings.

His decency was established right from the start. Here was someone who was kind, polite, honest and caring. He didn't swear, didn't drink, wasn't seen groping girls, dressed smartly and was frequently used as proof that not all teenagers are bad.

All this wasn't too unusual at the time because even the worst behaved pop singers projected themselves as mother-loving milk-drinkers. It would have been folly in 1959 to brag about being drunk or to use obscenities in interviews. A hint of anti-social behaviour could end a career.

The difference with Cliff was that the image was largely true. By nature he was that dream boy who admired his mother, looked after his sisters, hated to see animals in pain, respected policemen and went to bed early.

What is amazing is that not only is the image the same thirty-five years later, but so is the reality. All who meet him seem impressed with his genuine 'niceness'. He makes people feel comfortable in his presence, he never gossips or bitches and he always appears cheerful and optimistic. 'You feel you are a much better person after having met him,' says actor Anthony Andrews. 'His outlook on life is so positive it always has an effect on you.'

No one interviewed for this book, even those fully aware of his weaknesses, suggested that there was any sham involved in his public image. Years of scrutiny by the tabloid press has unearthed no hypocritical behaviour and he is remarkable in having created no enemies in the music business.

'He really is an ordinary guy who got caught up in extraordinary circumstances,' says Sammy Samwell. 'What you see is what you get.'

When he is criticized it is not for being phoney, but for being 'too good to be true'. His decency is sometimes perceived as a character weakness, as though it must signify a dull and unadventurous personality.

The truth is that, although he has obviously inherited an even temperament, much of what is perceived as his 'niceness' is the result of determination rather than of spinelessness. He believes it is important to love others even when you don't feel like loving. He struggles to be gracious, even when it would be more convenient to be rude.

'In the Bible, Saint Paul says that there is an "evil me" that is constantly trying to override the "good me",' Cliff explains. 'If I can let the "good me" win in front of the public as often as possible, I consider that a success rather than a fault.

'The fault is that I can't always control my thoughts, and I can't stop thinking that I'd rather be doing other things. I'd rather smash some people in the face because they really annoy me, but it's a success that I don't smash them in the face!' His Christian faith affects his thinking about everything, and there is no doubt that his greatest ambition is to express the values of Jesus in all that he does.

It's often said that the clean living that has resulted from his Christian conversion has enabled him to stay younger for longer, by protecting him from traditional show business excesses. It's also probably true to say that his face reflects his personal contentment. He doesn't appear to carry any baggage either of guilt or resentment, and the enthusiasm he exudes comes largely from a sense that he is working out God's purposes in his life.

Certainly his involvement in the Christian world has preserved his innocence by allowing him to remain unaffected by recent social upheavals. Whereas his contemporaries bear the marks of having lived through the decades of revolution in sex, drugs and politics, Cliff still appears to emerge from the Blytonesque world of the fifties, where jolly policemen push their bicycles down country lanes and people still say 'crikey' and 'gosh', while drinking fizzy pop.

His single status is a key element of this impression of eternal teenage. It remains important that he is available, that he can still be thought of as someone looking for the right girl.

If he had a wife, two children and a grandchild, his appeal would alter because he would no longer be seen as unshackled and able to give himself totally. In his most popular songs he allows himself to be perceived as lonely and vulnerable, a man still searching for love.

Yet the fantasy he offers remains romantic rather than sexual. He is not Tom Jones or Engelbert Humperdinck come to offer broad shoulders and a wealth of sexual experience, but a teenager from earlier times who wants nothing more than to hold his girl tight and tell her that he'll love her for ever. A night with Cliff, every fan knows, will end with a kiss on the doorstep.

As a consequence his followers don't respond to his overtures by throwing hotel keys and underwear on stage as they did for Elvis. The letters that come in to the office show that very few of them imagine doing naughty things with him. If they fantasize at all it's about being cared for by him. They see him as someone who, unlike their present partner, would be gentle and understanding.

None of this could have been carried off convincingly if he had looked old and grizzly. The fact that he looks and acts young has become an integral part of his image. 'I wish somehow I could be Peter Pan, the boy who never grew up,' he said in 1960. 'I'm going to stay young for as long as I can.'

Yet despite all his unparalleled achievements it still irks Cliff that he hasn't had the critical accolades he feels he deserves.

That a sizeable proportion of the record-buying public likes what he does is beyond doubt, but he realizes that he has never won the respect of those who will decide his place in rock 'n' roll history and he remains surprisingly sensitive to the way in which his contribution is often dismissed.

For American rock historians he may as well never have existed. *The Rolling Stone Illustrated History of Rock 'n' Roll*, for example, gives him only three passing mentions, none of which evaluates his music.

A typical career summary from a US perspective is given by rock critic Dave Marsh in the *Rolling Stone Record Guide*.

'Before the Beatles, Cliff Richard was England's answer to American rock,' he writes. 'He began as a sort of mini-Elvis, with a back-up group called the Shadows, who included a guitarist, Hank Marvin, an important influence on many British guitarists of the Sixties.

'But Richard converted to England's variety of fundamentalist Christianity, and whatever spark of spunk had been in his music was snuffed, though he continued to make the British charts throughout the Sixties.'

British critics are frequently as harsh. A review of his CD back catalogue in Q magazine concluded, '. . .these are 24 albums of limp-wristed tosh . . . Maybe he should have quit after "Move It".'

Overlooked in these summaries is the importance of his role in British rock between 1958 and 1962. During this time Cliff and the Shadows were *the* British rock 'n' roll outfit and together helped create the climate out of which the beat group phenomenon developed.

With their self-written songs and reliance on British craftsmanship, they sent out the message to Liverpool, London and Newcastle that a home-grown brand of rock 'n' roll was possible.

Cliff did imitate Elvis, but then so did almost everyone else at the time. For most aspiring rockers Elvis *was* rock 'n' roll and so to copy his style, intonation and movements was to follow the maker's instructions.

Cliff was also the first British singer to create scenes of mass hysteria—public expressions of teenage delight which were to climax in Beatlemania.

Also overlooked is his mastery of the pop ballad. His inclusion of slower, softer material is often dismissed as a betrayal of the promise put forward in 'Move It', whereas the Beatles' recordings of 'Yesterday' and 'Hey Jude' were greeted as being artistically adventurous departures which proved that rock 'n' roll had an expanding vocabulary.

Undoubtably the decade following his Christian conversion damaged his reputation because it seemed devoid of passion and innovation. For a while it looked as though he had settled for being an exalted end-of-the-pier entertainer providing something for everyone. That altered in 1976 when his renaissance began. Today he is more inspirational than he is influential. There are no mini-Cliffs trailing behind him ready to take his crown, but he remains a tremendous inspiration because of his professionalism, his consistency as a hit-maker and the weight of his history.

Artists as far apart on the musical spectrum as Van Morrison and Kylie Minogue's songwriter/producer Pete Waterman have respect for someone who has stayed on top for so long by following his tastes and his instincts.

Yet while Cliff may not be an idol for teenage musicians today he has become a role model for many Christians. It's not that they want to emulate his lifestyle, but he has become the most visible 'layman' in the country and probably the best public example of someone struggling to integrate the traditional Christian faith with work.

His books, talks, videos and gospel albums have been instrumental in bringing thousands of people to the Christian faith. Band members and record company executives have also been affected in the same way.

At a time when church leaders have become notably mealy-mouthed when explaining the nature of the faith they are supposedly defending, Cliff has triumphed as an articulate spokesman whom people respect, even when disagreeing with him, because they know that his beliefs have been tested in the real world.

During his 'Access All Areas' tour he spoke about his first hero, Elvis Presley, and then he talked about the hero of all heroes, Jesus Christ. The tough task that Cliff has set himself has been to be a disciple of Jesus in an industry that was given its modern kick-start by Elvis.

On the wall of his poolside bar in Weybridge he has a framed stained glass plaque. It hangs to the left of his AMI Continental juke box which is stacked with his favourite singles from the fifties. The plaque's prominent position suggests that its message has become something of a motto for him. It's easy to imagine him offering it up if ever asked what he would like his epitaph to be.

'Rock 'n' roll and God work together,' it reads, 'in the hands of someone who loves them both.'

Appendix Contents

Sources

Most of this book was researched from original sources. I conducted over 230 interviews with 195 people, the majority of whom had never been interviewed about Cliff before.

The research from interviews was supplemented by archive material from the following organizations:
BBC Written Archives, *Billboard*, British Film Institute, British Library, Broxbourne Borough Council, Butlin's Holiday Camps, Cheshunt Public Library, Chiswick Public Library, Companies House, Diocese of Calcutta, EMI Archives, Equity, Eurovangelism, Ferguson Ltd, Granada Television, Indian Tourist Board, India Office Library, Musicians Union, National Newspaper Library, National Maritime Museum, National Sound Archives, Office of Population and Censuses, Peninsular and Oriental Steam Navigation Company, Performing Rights Society, Press Association, Public Record Office Screen, Actors Guild, SOCAN, Spotlight, Sutton Public Library, Tear Fund.

There have been over thirty books written about Cliff so far although only a handful have been biographies. During research I made use of the following:

Driftin' With Cliff, Jet Harris, (Charles Buchan, 1959)
Cliff Richard, (Fan Star Library, 1959)
It's Great To Be Young, Cliff Richard (Souvenir Press, 1960)
Cliff Richard: Baron Of Beat, Jack Sutter (Valex Products, 1960)
Me And My Shadows, Cliff Richard (*Daily Mirror* Publications, 1961)
Cliff Around The Clock, Bob Ferrier (*Daily Mirror* Publications, 1962)
The Wonderful World Of Cliff, Bob Ferrier (Peter Davies, 1964)
New Singer, New Song, David Winter (Hodder & Stoughton, 1966)
The Way I See It, Cliff Richard (Hodder & Stoughton, 1968)
The Cliff Richard Story, George Tremlett (Futura, 1975)
Which One's Cliff?, Cliff Richard (Hodder & Stoughton, 1977 and 1990)
Cliff, Tony Jasper and Patrick Doncaster (Sidgwick & Jackson 1981 and 1992)
Cliff Richard and the Shadows, Dezo Hoffman (Virgin, 1985)
Cliff Richard In His Own Words, Kevin St John (Omnibus Press, 1991)
You, Me and Jesus, Cliff Richard (Hodder & Stoughton, 1983)
Jesus, Me and You, Cliff Richard (Hodder & Stoughton, 1985)
The Cliff Richard File, Mike Read (Roger Houghton, 1986)
Single-Minded, Cliff Richard (Hodder & Stoughton 1988)
Cliff Richard: The Complete Recording Sessions, Peter Lewry and Nigel Goodall Blandford).

Other books which mentioned Cliff were useful in their observations. Among these were:

Big Beat Scene, Royston Ellis (Four Square, 1961)
The Shadows By Themselves, ed. Royston Ellis (Consul, 1961)
Love Me Do: The Beatles' Progress, Michael Braun (Penguin, 1964)
Crusade '66, John Pollock (Hodder & Stoughton, 1966)
Awopbopaloobop Alopbamboom, Nik Cohn (Weidenfeld & Nicholson, 1969)
Revolt Into Style, George Melly (Allen Lane, 1970)
Land Aflame, Flo Dobbie (Hodder & Stoughton, 1972)
Spre-e'73, David Coomes (Coverdale House, 1973)
Rock 'n' Roll, Chris May (Socion, 1974)
The Guitar Greats, John Tobler and Stuart Grundy (BBC Publications, 1983)
The Story Of The Shadows, Mike Read (Elm Tree Books, 1983)
Days In The Life, Jonathan Green (Heinemann, 1988)
Rock 'n' Roll—I Gave You the Best Years of My Life, Bruce Welch (Viking, 1989)
Music Collector magazine no. 21 (January 1991)
Funny Old World: John Henry Rostill, Rob Bradford (Rob Bradford, 1992).

Articles about and interviews with Cliff are legion. Other than all the British national newspapers I consulted the following periodicals during my research:

Billboard, Boyfriend, Cheshunt Weekly Telegraph, Disc, Lucknow Pioneer, Marty, Melody Maker, New Musical Express, Newsweek, Radio Times, Record Mail, Ripley and Heanor News, Rolling Stone, Shepherd's Bush Gazette, Sutton Herald, The Stage, Tear Times, Valentine, Wallington and Carshalton Times, West Lancashire Evening Gazette.

Interviewee sources

Following is a list of my main interview sources for each chapter. Some sources have been left unattributed at the request of the interviewees.

CHAPTER 1
Roger Bruce, David Bryce, Mel Bush, Jimmy Henney, Sonya Jones, Hal Kalin, Linda Kay, Maggie Streader, Bruce Welch

CHAPTER 2
Vincent Bridgwater, Pete Bush, Joyce Clarkson, Rodger Cooke, Elsie Dazely, Joyce Dobra, Olive Gregory, Edna van Haeften, Gertrude Woodfall

CHAPTER 3
Dorothy Bodkin, Vincent Bridgwater, Olive Gregory

CHAPTER 4
Dorothy Bodkin, Pete Bush, Ivy Clare, Brian Cooke, Patricia Cookson, Ted Davy, Vincent Dickson, John Harris, Jacqui Harrison, Bob Henrit, Richard Holmes, Linda Lazarri, Norman Mitham, Jay Norris, Gladys Pearcy, Christine Poynter, Frances Slade, Mrs Slade, Mrs Tonks, Dorothy Willis

CHAPTER 5
Ruth Dickson, Jacqui Harrison, Betty Longhurst, Christine March, Marie Mitchell, Norman Mitham, Rev. M.J. Bannister, Jay Norris, Terry Smart, John Vince

CHAPTER 6
Sheila Bateman, Jimmy Grant, Chas McDevitt, Brian Parker, June Pearce, Frances Slade, Terry Smart, Dick Teague, Kathleen Teague, Mick Teague, Walter Teague, Wally Whyton

CHAPTER 7
Janice Berry, Dorothy Bodkin, Brian Cooke, Terry Dene, John Foster, Jacqui Harrison, Paul Lincoln, Norman Mitham, Steve Nichols, Ian Samwell, Terry Smart, Jan Vane

CHAPTER 8
Malcolm Addey, Janice Berry, Peter Bown, Franklyn Boyd, Frank Clarke, Stan Edwards, Mark Forster, John Foster, George Ganjou, Georgine Ganjou, Jack Good, Margit Good, Derek Johnson, Chas McDevitt, Norman Mitham, Caroline Paramor, Joan Paramor, Carl Perkins, Ian Samwell, Ernie Shear, Terry Smart, Tulah Tuke

CHAPTER 9
John Foster, Rita Gillespie, Jack Good, Jet Harris, Wee Willie Harris, Hal Kalin, Ron King, Hank Marvin, Paul McCartney, Mickie Most, Ian Samwell, Terry Smart, Maggie Streader, Bruce Welch, Wally Whyton, Marty Wilde,

CHAPTER 10
Franklyn Boyd, Jess Conrad, Stan Edwards, John Foster, David Lilley, Ray Mackender, Tony Meehan, Sammy Samwell, Tulah Tuke, Marty Wilde

CHAPTER 11
Lionel Bart, Janice Berry, Dorothy Bodkin, Franklyn Boyd, Tito Burns, Jess Conrad, Ronnie Ernstone, John Foster, Jet Harris, Wee Willie Harris, Andrew Ray, Maggie Streader, Jimmy Tarbuck, Cherry Wainer, Marty Wilde, Terence Young

CHAPTER 12
Lionel Bart, Roy Bennett, Tito Burns, Freddie Cannon, Jess Conrad, Yolande Donlan, Royston Ellis, Val Guest, Father John Oates, David Lilley, Ray Mackender, Wolf Mankowitz, Josie Pollock, Ian Samwell, Father Shergold, Maggie Streader, Sid Tepper, Bruce Welch, Mark Wynter

CHAPTER 13
Sheila Bateman, Tito Burns, Mike Conlin, Royston Ellis, Ronnie Ernstone, Jacqui Harrison, David Kossoff, Jerry Lordan, Tony Meehan, Steve Race, Cherry Wainer

CHAPTER 14
Roy Bennett, Stanley Black, Tito Burns, Ron Cass, Brian Crompton, Peter Gormley, Kenneth Harper, Jet Harris, Melvyn Hayes, Derek Johnson, Hank Marvin, Barry Ronger, Herb Ross, Cyril Simons, Sid Tepper, Bruce Welch, Delia Wicks

CHAPTER 15
Dorothy Bodkin, Vincent Bridgwater, Ron Cass, Mike Conlin, Royston Ellis, Adam Faith, Peter Gormley, Kenneth Harper, Jet Harris, Melvyn Hayes, Brian Locking, Ray Mackender, Hank Marvin, Tony Meehan, Lauri Peters, Victor Peterson, Una Stubbs, Bruce Welch

CHAPTER 16
Brian Bennett, Dorothy Bodkin, Ron Cass, Mike Conlin, Graham Disbrey, Royston Ellis, Kenneth Harper, Bill Latham, Hank Marvin, Jay Norris, Bruce Welch, David Winter

CHAPTER 17
Pete Bush, Mike Conlin, John Davey, Graham Disbrey, Nigel Goodwin, Peter Gormley, Peter Graves, Olive Gregory, Paul Jones, Bill Latham, Tony Meehan, Jay Norris, David Winter

CHAPTER 18
John Davey, Graham Disbrey, Dave Foster, Peter Graves, Cindy Kent, Bill Latham, Bill Martin, Tony Meehan, Olivia Newton-John, Larry Norman, Bruce Welch, David Winter

CHAPTER 19
Anthony Andrews, Terry Britten, Barrie Guard, Eric Hall, Kenneth Harper, George Hoffman, Bill Latham, Dave Mackay, Olivia Newton-John, David Pawson, Trevor Spencer, Alan Tarney, Liz Hutchison

CHAPTER 20
Terry Britten, Tony Clarke, Eric Hall, Christine Holmes, Tony King, Dave Mackay, Larry Norman, Trevor Spencer, Dave Townsend, Bruce Welch

CHAPTER 21
David Bryce, Tony Clarke, Chris Eaton, Phil Everly, George Hoffman, B.A. Robertson, Trevor Spencer, Graham Todd, Alan Tarney, Bruce Welch

CHAPTER 22
Sue Barker, Terry Britten, David Bryce, Stu Calver, Jill Clarke, Dave Cooke, Chris Eaton, Paul Field, Alan Godson, Nigel Goodwin, Don Grierson, Mark Griffiths, Jet Harris, Garth Hewitt, Carol Illingworth, Bill Latham, Phil Lloyd, Hank Marvin, Norman Miller, John Perry, Craig Pruess, Mike Read, B.A. Robertson, Dan Slater, Gill Snow, Alan Tarney, Bruce Welch, Muriel Young

CHAPTER 23
Dave Clark, Gerald Coates, Dave Cooke, Mark Griffiths, Bob Hellyer, George Hoffman, Ron King, Norman Miller, John Muggleton, David Soames, Graham Todd, Sheila Walsh, Jodie Wilson

CHAPTER 24
David Bryce, Peter Gormley, Tony King, Gerry Kitchingham, Bill Latham, Paul Moessl, Alan Tarney, Graham Todd, Peter Waterman

CHAPTER 25
Sue Barker, Gerald Coates, Graham Disbrey, Charles Haswell, Bill Latham, Gill Snow, Gerald Williams

CHAPTER 26
Dorothy Bodkin, Peter Gormley, Bill Latham

Where are they now?

Malcolm Addey, 58, engineered most of Cliff's sessions until 1968 when he left EMI Abbey Road. He now lives in New York where he runs a production company and produces classical and jazz albums.

Sue Barker, 36, retired from professional tennis in 1984 and four years later she married Detective-Sergeant Lance Tankard. She lives in Walton-on-Thames, Surrey, and is a presenter for SKY TV's sports programmes.

Lionel Bart, 62, went on to write the musicals *Fings Ain't Wot They Used T'be*, *Oliver!*, *Blitz!* and *Maggie May*. He lives in Acton, West London.

Brian Bennett, 53, lives in Hertfordshire with his wife Margaret (whom he met at the 2 I's in 1957) and they have three children. When not involved in being a Shadow he concentrates on recording music for film and television. He has written theme or background music for the television series 'The Ruth Rendell Mysteries', 'Dallas' and 'Knots Landing' and the films *The American Way* and *Terminal Choice*. He has recorded several albums under his own name and produced Hank Marvin's last solo album.

Roy Bennett, 75, with his partner Sid Tepper, wrote forty-three songs for Elvis Presley. He is now retired and lives in Flushing, New York.

Janice Berry, 52, married her husband Mike in 1962 and they have had three children—two daughters and a son. Cliff is godfather to the youngest daughter. Janice teaches physically handicapped children at a school in Stevenage.

Derek Bodkin, 51, remarried after divorcing Cliff's mother, and had a daughter. He has since divorced for the second time, and now works for the Post Office.

Franklyn Boyd, 65, moved to Canada with his wife Daphne. He is retired and lives outside Toronto.

Vincent Bridgwater settled in south-east London in the fifties where he worked for the Post Office. He died in 1992 at the age of 79.

Terry Britten began writing for the American market and is currently teamed up with Graham Lyle, once part of the duo Gallagher & Lyle. They wrote 'What's Love Got To Do With It?', a top ten hit for Tina Turner in 1984, and 'Just Good Friends', a track on Michael Jackson's 1987 album *Bad*. He lives and works near Richmond in Surrey.

Roger Bruce, 47, was Company Manager for *Time* and left the theatre after working on *Journey's End* with Jason Connery. He has been Cliff's Personal Assistant since 1988.

David Bryce, 60, is Cliff's professional and recording manager.

Tito Burns, 70, is now almost retired after a long career in show business as performer, agent and manager. He represents French singer Sasha Distel in every territory but France and pianist Victor Borgia in every territory but America and Canada. He lives in St John's Wood with his wife.

Mel Bush, 50, has been promoting concerts since 1960, working with acts such as the Eagles, Queen, the Beach Boys, Paul McCartney and Led Zeppelin. The Event was his first promotion involving Cliff and he has done all his British tours since then.

Pete Bush, 52, was a roadie for Adam Faith's group the Roulettes in the early

1960s. He married in 1968 and has three children. He still lives near Cheshunt and runs his own business making window blinds.

Stu Calver, 46, suffers from cystic fibrosis and has been unable to work since 1986. He lives with his wife by the sea in Devon.

Ron Cass, 70, has composed for television, film and stage as well as writing the novels *True Blue* and *Fringe Benefits*. He was musical director for the religious TV programme 'Highway' and lives in North London.

Betty Clarke, 52, married in 1961 (to a boy she met at Trinity Youth Club) and has two grown-up children. She works as a typing instructor in Enfield and lives in Goff's Oak near Cheshunt.

Frank Clarke, 69, played bass on numerous Abbey Road sessions including one for the Beatles single 'Penny Lane', and many more for Cliff. He retired in 1989 and lives near Cambridge.

Tony Clark, 47, began as a tape operator at Abbey Road in 1964 and went on to engineer several of Cliff's albums as well as those of the Beatles. He became Senior Engineer/Producer and left EMI in 1986 to become Technical Supervisor at the British Record Industry Trust Performing Arts and Technology School (better known as BRITS).

Joyce Clarkson, 78, is the last surviving member of Frederick William Webb's children. She lives in Cheshunt.

Gerald Coates, 48, is director of Pioneer People (the new name for Cobham Christian Fellowship) and an active Christian speaker. He is the author of many books.

Jim Collier made many more films for Worldwide including *The Hiding Place*, *Joni*, *Caught* and *The Prodigal*. He died in 1991 at the age of 62 after falling from a ledge beside a lake on his mountainside property outside Los Angeles. His last film was *China Cry* which he made for the Trinity Broadcasting Network.

Mike Conlin, 55, worked with Frank Ifield after leaving Cliff around 1964 and then went to Australia to manage Terry Britten's group the Twilights. He left the music business in 1970 and worked in merchant banking until the Big Bang in 1987. He married his wife Mary in 1976, and is now Senior Finance Officer for a Family Housing Association in West London.

Jess Conrad, 57, made four singles as a pop singer before concentrating on acting and singing in musicals. He was the original Joseph in *Joseph And The Amazing Technicolor Dreamcoat*, a role which he toured with for ten years, played Jesus in *Godspell* and recently acted in Mike Sarne's film *The Punk*. He now takes part in rock 'n' roll revival shows, works for various charities and is proud to have made what many consider to have been the worst single of all time, 'My Pullover' (in 1961).

Russ Conway, 67, had his last top thirty hit in 1962. He continued to play but was then forced into early retirement after a nervous breakdown. In 1989 he was diagnosed as having cancer and began to perform to raise money for charities, in particular his own fund which helps cancer patients.

Brian Cook, 52, became a trainee draughtsman on leaving school and is now Managing Director of his own company C.D.K. Electronics which specializes in refrigeration for major supermarket chains. He married in 1970, lives in Cheshire and has two children.

Dave Cooke, 40, is married to former 'Blue Peter' presenter Tina Heath and they have two daughters. He works as a composer and arranger.

Carol Costa, 51, divorced from Jet Harris and went on to have three children with musician Rod Slade from whom she has since separated. She was living in West London and running a market stall but her present whereabouts are unknown.

John Davey, 54, went on to become Headmaster of St Brandon's School near Bristol and is now examinations officer for Trinity Collge of Music in London. He is married with one grown-up daughter.

Olive Dazely, 70, married her first cousin and had two sons. Her husband has now died and she lives alone in Felixstowe.

William Edward Dazely died in Birmingham in 1969. He had five sons, one of whom has died. He is survived by his second wife Maizie who is 86.

Dorothy Dickson, Cliff's grandmother, died in Carshalton in 1980 at the age of 77. Her husband, Richard Dickson, died in 1952.

Vincent Dickson, 64, still lives with his wife Ruth in Carshalton.

Graham Disbrey, 55, is head of Art and Design at Chauncy School in Ware, Hertfordshire.

Joyce Dobra, 67, moved to England in 1947. She married Istvan Dobra, a Hungarian refugee who died in 1975. She has two sons and four granddaughters.

Chris Eaton, 33, divides his time between Stourbridge and Nashville. He recorded his own album *The Vision* in 1986 and has since been writing for American artists such as Russ Taff, Michael W. Smith and Amy Grant. He was part of Amy Grant's band on her last world tour.

Stan Edwards, 61, became an entertainer and then joined the Gas Board in East London before retiring in 1992.

Royston Ellis, 51, stayed on in the Canary Islands after arriving for the filming of *Wonderful Life* and left in 1966 to live in the Carribean where he wrote a number of best selling plantation novels under the pen name Richard Tressilian. He now lives in Sri Lanka and works as a travel writer.

Ronnie Ernstone, 55, has worked in the car trade all his life; as a fuel injection engineer, as the owner of a tuning business and now as a prestige car dealer. He lives with his wife in West London.

Adam Faith, 52, retired as a singer in 1967 to become an actor. He worked in repertory and then, in 1971, took the title role in the TV series 'Budgie'. He later returned to the music business as manager for Leo Sayer and producer for Roger Daltry. He appeared in the films *Stardust* and *McVicar* and authors a newspaper column which offers advice on business investments. He has recently starred with Zoë Wanamaker in the popular TV drama 'Love Hurts'. He is married to Jackie Irving, and they have one daughter.

Paul Field, 38, works as a solo artist and has released several albums including *Restless Heart* and *Building Bridges*.

Dave Foster, 59, is still International Director of Eurovangelism and lives in Switzerland.

John Foster, 54, worked in public relations for Walt Disney in London for twelve years. He then became an agent and now organizes promotional and corporate entertainment from his home in Northumberland where he lives with his mother. He has one daughter from a marriage which ended in divorce.

Sidney J. Furie, 60, directed the films *The Ipcress File*, *Lady Sings The Blues* and *Superman 4*.

Billy Fury continued performing and recording until his death in 1983, at the age of 42, of a heart attack.

George Ganjou continued to manage variety acts until 1982. His first wife, Adela, died in 1978 and he married Georgine in 1979. He contracted Parkinson's Disease and died, aged 87, in 1988.

William Gaunt, 56, has acted and directed in most major UK repertory companies, and for two years he was artistic director at the Liverpool

Playhouse. He became well known on television as Arthur Crabtree in 'No Place Like Home', and Richard Barratt in 'The Champions'.

Rita Gillespie, 60, works for a television writer in Los Angeles.

Alan Godson, 60, is vicar of St Mary's, Edgehill, in Liverpool and is Chairman of the Trustees for Christians in Sport. He is married with two teenage sons.

Jack Good, 61, lives in New Mexico where he spends most of his time painting religious icons. His autobiographical musical *Good Rockin' Tonight*, which featured actors playing the roles of Cliff, Billy Fury, Tommy Steele and others, was launched in 1991. He has a daughter and is divorced from his wife Margit. He converted to Roman Catholicism in 1962 and plans to join an order of Carmelite monks.

Nigel Goodwin, 55, travels the world encouraging Christian artists and is supported by the Genesis Trust. He lives in Windsor with his wife Gillian and has three daughters.

Peter Gormley, 73, now spends his summers in Weybridge and his winters in Sydney, Australia. He is married to Audrey and he has a child from a previous marriage.

Peter Graves, 50, is head of the German Department at Leicester University. He is married with three young daughters.

Harry Greatorex died in 1989 at the age of 63 after a lifetime spent managing entertainment facilities in Ripley, Derbyshire, including the Rolarena, the Hippodrome Cinema and Sunset Boulevard. He was a great collector of theatrical memorabilia, owning Harry Lauder's walking stick and a pair of George Formby's shoes.

Mark Griffiths, 44, plays with the Shadows whenever they record or tour, is a member of Plainsong, a group formed by Ian Matthews formerly of Matthews

Southern Comfort, and plays regular sessions with them. He lives in Northampton with his wife and two daughters.

Val Guest, 82, lives in Palm Springs with his wife Yolande Donlan. He went on to direct the films *Casino Royale, When Dinosaurs Ruled The World, Confessions Of A Window Cleaner* and *The Boys In Blue*.

Kenneth Harper, 70, married Pamela Hart, one of the dancers who acted in *Summer Holiday*. He went on to direct *The Virgin and the Gypsy* and is still involved in film production.

Jet Harris, 53, lives near Gloucester with his mother. He teaches occasional guitar lessons and plays in rock 'n' roll revival groups. His son Ricky, from his marriage to Carol Costa, lives in Weymouth and works as a tiler.

John Harvey, 57, is Professor of Aeronautics at Imperial College in London.

Melvyn Hayes, 58, became a familiar face in the situation comedy series 'It Ain't Half Hot Mum'. He continues to work in theatre and television.

Bob Henrit, 48, was drummer for the Roulettes (1963–67), Unit Four Plus Two (1967–68), Argent (1969–76). He currently drums for the Kinks.

George Hoffman was tragically killed in a road accident in October 1992 at the age of 59. He had been director of Tear Fund from 1968 until 1989 and from then until his death was executive chairman of Samaritan International.

Christine Holmes, 42, was once known as Christine Sparkle and worked as a presenter on the children's TV programme 'Crackerjack', with Leslie Crowther. She has also had hit singles as a singer in Canada and Germany. She now lives in Los Angeles and has been writing jingles.

Liz Hutchison, 45, had to leave Bangladesh after falling ill with glandular fever but returned for another year before finally coming back to England and working as a health visitor. She is now married with two sons.

Jackie Irving, 50, went on to become one of Lionel Blair's Dancers before marrying Adam Faith in 1967. They have one daughter.

Paul Jones, 51, is an actor, singer and broadcaster. He plays with the Blues Band, has a blues and gospel programmes on Jazz FM and BBC Radio 2, acts in the children's television series 'Uncle Jack' and is married to actress Fiona Hendley.

Herb and Hal Kalin, 59, live near Washington DC. They both got married at the end of the sixties and went to Maryland University. Herb became a probation officer and Hal worked for the criminal justice courts. Hal retired in January 1992, Herb in June. They now plan to sing together again.

Cindy Kent, 47, became a broadcaster and consultant in media and communication skills after the break-up of the Settlers in 1973. She has a son.

Tony King, 50, left Rocket Records and went to work with Mick Jagger in New York as his personal assistant. He is now working for financier Prince Rupert Loewenstein in London, managing Lulu.

Ron King, 71, retired as Cliff's Personal Assistant in July 1988. He is now enjoying a prank-free retirement in Orpington, Kent.

Gerry Kitchingham, 43, is Studio Manager and chief recording engineer at R.G. Jones where he has worked since 1966.

Paul Lincoln, 60, went on to manage the fashionable sixties' night club The Cromwellian and then in 1973 went to Australia where he dealt in the 'second-hand business'. He returned to England in 1987 and managed Charlies' nightclub in Southampton. He continued wrestling, as 'Doctor Death', until 1977. He is now retired.

Tom Littlewood ended up managing a sandwich bar in Great Windmill Street, not too far from the 2 I's. He died in 1988.

Brian 'Licorice' Locking, 54, has been an unpaid Jehovah's Witness pastor since 1963. For fourteen years he ran his own band in South East London, playing in pubs and clubs. He now lives near Rhyl in North Wales where he works as a cleaner in a psychiatric hospital.

Jerry Lordan, 58, had seventeen chart entries as songwriter. These include 'A Girl Like You' for Cliff and 'A Place In The Sun', 'Atlantis' and 'Wonderful Land' for the Shadows, and 'Diamonds' and 'Scarlett O'Hara' for Jet Harris and Tony Meehan. Tax problems, a divorce and a mental breakdown later put him out of the music business for ten years. He came back as a manager and producer and is now back writing 'less but better'. He lives in mid Wales.

Glyn MacAulay, 56, is the senior partner of the accountancy firm Neville Russell & Co.

Dave Mackay, 49, lives in England and writes music for television. He wrote the theme music for 'Bread' (which earned him an Ivor Novello Award), 'Making Out' and 'Auf Wiedersehen Pet'. He has also written an opera, *Paris*, which was voted best cast album by a panel of critics in Australia.

Ray Mackender, 60, successfully managed Mark Wynter in the sixties. He moved to Canada in 1973 as a freelance tour guide, a job that entailed frequent world travel, and has recently retired.

Wolf Mankowitz, 68, has written musicals, plays, novels, screenplays, short stories, poems and histories. He was a Professor of English at the University of New Mexico 1982–86 and Professor of Theatre 1987–88. He lives in County Cork, Ireland.

Bill Martin went on to write all the Bay City Rollers' hits with Phil Coulter, 'Surround Yourself With Sorrow' for Cilla

Black and 'Fancy Pants' for Kenny. The partnership ended in 1982 after sixteen years. He is now a music publisher.

Hank Marvin, 51, lives in Perth, Western Australia, with his second wife Carol, who he met in 1968, and three of his children. He became a Jehovah's Witness in 1973. His most recent solo album is *Into The Light*.

Chas McDevitt, 58, closed the Freight Train club in 1968. He sang with Shirley Douglas until 1975 when he went solo. The original Chas McDevitt Skiffle Group, minus the washboard player who has died, re-form around ten times a year. He has an album on President, *It Takes You Back Don't It*, and Rollercoaster plan to release a CD of a 1957 concert at the Royal Festival Hall.

Tony Meehan, 50, had several hits with Jet Harris before becoming an A&R man at Decca Records. He went on to become a prominent producer and musician, working with the likes of Eric Clapton and Paul MacCartney, before becoming involved in leisure industry projects in Australia. He is married to Sue and they have two children. He also has five children from his first marriage.

Norman Miller, 50, manages gospel musicians in America where his wife Sheila Walsh has become a popular chat show hostess on the CBN Network.

Norman Mitham, 52, joined Mark Four on leaving the Drifters and now works as a Sales Rep for United Biscuits. He married in 1964 and has two children.

Mickie Most, 53, moved to South Africa in 1958 and became a big pop star by covering US rock 'n' roll hits. After eleven number one hits in a row he moved back to England and became a producer, working with Donovan, Herman's Hermits, the Animals and the Yardbirds. In 1970 he formed RAK Records which signed Susie Quatro, Mud, Hot Chocolate and the group Kenny. In the 1980s RAK had great success with Kim Wilde and then, in 1986, the record company closed allowing Most to concentrate on Rak Recording Studios and Rak Music (publishing). He lives in Totteridge, North London with his wife and they have three children.

Olivia Newton-John, 44, had a string of hits in America and starred in the films *Grease* and *Xanadu*. She is married to dancer Matt Lattanzi and they have one child.

Larry Norman, 46, has persisted as a solo artist, touring the world and now selling most of his records through mail order. His most recent album is *Stranded In Babylon*

Jay Norris, 67, took early retirement from teaching in 1982 and now lives in York from where she still works as a drama examiner for the University of London. She is author of *Drama Resources Cards* and co-author, with Giles Bird, of *Worlds Of English and Drama, Dead On Time* and *In On The Act*. Her husband died in 1992 and she has two grown-up sons.

David Pawson, 63, has been travelling the world speaking at seminars for church leaders since he left the Millmead Centre, Guildford, in 1979.

Norrie Paramor left EMI in 1968 and set up three companies of his own, although he continued to produce Cliff. In 1973 he moved to Birmingham to be principal conductor of the Midland Radio Orchestra. He died in September 1979 at the age of 65.

Brian Parker, 52, played with the Parker Royal Four and Unit Four Plus Two. He left the music business and went into computers where he stayed for 26 years. He's now back 'playing keyboards and guitars and absolutely loving it'.

Larry Parnes stopped managing rock 'n' roll singers in 1965 and returned to his initial interests of clothing and theatre. He died in 1989 at the age of 59.

Lauri Peters, 50, left films to study classical theatre. After working as a stage actress she became a journalist, a photographer and a novelist. Then, in 1988, she took a job teaching drama in New York. She is divorced from John Voight.

Craig Pruess, 41, lives in Skelmersdale and has built his own studio where he writes music for television. He recently worked on *Hear My Song*, the drama about Joseph Locke, and *Assassin of The Tsar* which starred Malcolm McDowell. He has also recorded his own album, *The Eye Of Jupiter*, and lectures regularly on Indian classical music. He is married with two children.

Andrew Ray, 52, continues to work in theatre, television and film. His television credits include 'Crown Matrimonial', 'Edward and Mrs Simpson', 'Tales Of The Unexpected' and 'Vandervalk'.

B.A. Robertson, 42, has written lyrics for many of Mike and the Mechanics' songs, including the monster hit 'The Living Years'. He lives in Los Angeles and has been working on projects for the Disney organization including a 'revisualizing and re-recording' of the classic moments from Disney features for an album and a video called *Something Mad About The Mouse*.

Herbert Ross, 66, left theatrical choreography to become a film director. Among his films are *Play It Again Sam*, *Funny Lady*, *The Sunshine Boys*, *The Turning Point*, *The Goodbye Girl*, *Pennies From Heaven*, *Flashdance* and *Footloose*.

John Rostill joined Tom Jones' band in 1969 and worked extensively in America where he also began writing for Olivia Newton-John. He died in England in November 1973 having been electrocuted in his studio. He was 31. Three months after his death Olivia had her first US top ten hit with his song 'Let Me Be There'.

Ian 'Sammy' Samwell, 54, wrote 'Whatcha Gonna Do About It?' for the Small Faces and later became an A&R man for WEA records in London. For the past twelve years he has lived in Sacramento, California, where he helps develop local artists. He has two sons, Ralph and Tyson. In 1991, after suffering a viral infection of the heart, he underwent a successful heart transplant operation.

Ernie Shear, 65, worked on many more sessions for Cliff and is still playing. For the past thirty-four years he has been a member of the Jack Emblow Quartet which can be heard on the radio programme 'Sing Something Simple'.

Francis 'Frankie' Slade, 52, works as a painter and lives with her husband in Brighton.

Terry Smart, 51, joined the Merchant Navy in 1959 and is still serving. He lives in Harwich with his wife Cindy.

David Soames, 45, recently wrote the play *Teething Troubles*, the musical *Big Apple* and, with Jeff Daniels, the musical *Marriage, An Endangered Species*

Trevor Spencer, 45, lives in Perth, Western Australia. He runs the music production company Sh-Boom! with Gary Taylor, formerly of the Herd.

Maggie Streader, 53, became a member of the backing vocal group the Ladybirds in 1961, and went on to work with everyone from Bing Crosby to the Beatles. She is now involved in booking singers for recording sessions and performing with a re-formed Vernons Girls.

Una Stubbs, 56, joined the Young Vic in 1970 and has become a nationally-known stage actress. On television she has been in 'Till Death Us Do Part' and 'Worzel Gummidge', as well as being a regular guest on 'Give Us A Clue'. She has been married twice, first to Peter Gilmore and then to Nicky Henson.

Alan Tarney, 47, has written for Leo Sayer and Barbara Dickson. Recently he has been producing Voice of the Beehive and the Moody Blues.

Dick Teague, 57, is an accountant living in Lincolnshire. His mother and father are still alive (Walter is 91) and they live near their daughter Sheila in the West County. Mick Teague is 56.

Sid Tepper, 75, is retired and lives in Miami Beach, Florida. (See **Roy Bennett**)

Graham Todd, 50, has composed eight albums of library music (one recorded by the Royal Philarmonic Orchestra) and has been involved in the orchestration and production of soundtrack music for American television specials such as 'Voice Of The Heart' and 'To Be The Best'.

Mrs Tonks, 78, is retired and lives in Waltham Cross.

Dave Townsend, 41, has his own antique furniture restoration business. He only ever had two other songs covered, 'Far Side Of The Bay' by Elaine Paige, and 'That's When My Loving Begins' by Jimmy Ruffin. He has recently started writing again.

Tulah Tuke, 60, has worked as a make-up artist for the BBC in London and Glasgow before going freelance in 1980. She also paints portraits.

Jan Vane, 51, married in 1961 and had her first child in 1962. She now has three children, is divorced and works for an agency which supplies temporary reps.

John Vince, 52, worked in a bank for a year and a half after leaving school before joining the elctronics industry. In 1966 he began to lecture on computers at Enfield College of Technology and now he is a research consultant for Rediffusion. He has written books on the application of computer technology to areas of design. He is married with two teenage children and lives in Sussex.

Cherry Wainer, 61, lives in Las Vegas where she is Fashion Director for the Mirage and Golden Nugget hotel-casinos. She still shares a home with drummer Don Storer with whom she arrived in England in 1957.

Donna Webb, 50, lives in Ware, Hertfordshire with her husband Terry Goulden and her two adopted children Ty and Emma. She had two previous marriages to Paul Stevens and Tim Brandon.

Dorothy Marie Webb, 72, has a 'granny house' connected to her daughter Joan's property. She is now divorced, but still goes under the name of Bodkin.

Joan Webb, 42, lives in Broxbourne, Hertfordshire, with her husband David Pilgrim. She had two previous marriages to Colin Phipps and Peter Archer which produced three children.

Jacqui Webb, 45, lives in Norfolk with her husband Peter Harrison. She has five children, the youngest of whom is four, and became a grandmother in 1992 with the birth of Joseph, the first child of her eldest son Rodger.

Bruce Welch, 51, is involved in music publishing and production as well as being a Shadow. He has been married twice and has one son, Dwayne. He published his autobiography, *Rock 'n' Roll—I Gave You the Best Years of My Life*, in 1989.

Wally Whyton, 54, finished with the Vipers in 1959 and has since become an accomplished broadcaster creating such puppet characters as Ollie Beak and Spike McPike for television and presenting country music programmes on BBC Radio and the British Forces Broadcasting Service (BFBS) for over twenty years. He has also recorded a number of albums under his own name.

Delia Wicks, 54, did a lot of television advertising in the early sixties for Signal, Quality Street and Martini. She then went on to be part of the Black and White Minstrel Show until she married a builder in 1970 and settled in the Midlands. She is now divorced and lives alone in a Cotswolds village.

Marty Wilde, 54, married Joyce Baker of the Vernons Girls in December 1959 and daughter Kim was born in 1960. He continued to perform and record but was to make more of an impact as a producer and songwriter, with his son Ricky, when Kim Wilde took up a music career in the eighties.

Jodie Wilson, 26, acted in *Memphis Belle* and is now recording her own songs.

David Winter, 63, went on to become the BBC's head of religious broadcasting and the author of a number of books. He retired from broadcasting to become a vicar in Oxfordshire.

Peter Yates, 64, went on to make the films *One Way Pendulum*, *Bullitt*, *The Deep* and *The Dresser*

Muriel Young, 65, who was the first female announcer on commercial television in Britain (1955), now lives in County Durham, and paints. Her first exhibition of paintings was in Liberty's of London.

Terence Young, 78, directed the films *Dr No*, *From Russia With Love*, *Thunderball*, *The Valachi Papers* and *Sweet Revenge*.

Discography (UK)

1	Move It/Schoolboy Crush	Aug 1958
2	High Class Baby/My Feet Hit The Ground	Nov 1958
3	Livin' Lovin' Doll/Steady With You	Jan 1959
4	Mean Streak/Never Mind	Apr 1959
5	Living Doll/Apron Strings	Jul 1959
6	Travellin' Light/Dynamite	Oct 1959
7	A Voice in the Wilderness/Don't Be Mad At Me	Jan 1960
8	Fall In Love With You/Willie and the Hand Jive	Mar 1960
9	Please Don't Tease/Where Is My Heart?	Jun 1960
10	Nine Times Out Of Ten/Thinking Of Our Love	Sep 1960
11	I Love You/'D' In Love	Nov 1960
12	Theme For A Dream/Mumblin' Mosie	Feb 1961
13	Gee Whizz It's You/I Cannot Find A True Love	Mar 1961
14	A Girl Like You/Now's The Time To Fall In Love	Jun 1961
15	When The Girl In Your Arms Is The Girl In Your Heart/Got A Funny Feeling	Oct 1961
16	The Young Ones/We Say Yeah	Jan 1962
17	I'm Looking Out The Window/Do You Want To Dance	May 1962
18	It'll Be Me/Since I Lost You	Aug 1962
19	The Next Time/Bachelor Boy	Nov 1962
20	Summer Holiday/Dancing Shoes	Feb 1963
21	Lucky Lips/I Wonder	May 1963
22	It's All In The Game/Your Eyes Tell On You	Aug 1963
23	Don't Talk To Him/Say You're Mine	Nov 1963
24	I'm The Lonely One/Watch What You Do With My Baby	Jan 1964
25	Constantly/True True Lovin'	Apr 1964
26	On The Beach/A Matter of Moments	Jun 1964
27	The Twelfth Of Never/I'm Afraid To Go Home	Oct 1964

28	I Could Easily Fall (In Love With You)/I'm In Love With You	Dec 1964
29	The Minute You're Gone/Just Another Guy	Mar 1965
30	Angel/Razzle Dazzle	May 1965
31	On My Word/Just A Little Bit Too Late	Jun 1965
32	The Time In Between/Look Before You Love	Aug 1965
33	Wind Me Up (Let Me Go)/The Night	Oct 1965
34	Blue Turns To Grey/Somebody Loses	Mar 1966
35	Visions/What Would I Do (For The Love Of A Girl)	Jul 1966
36	Time Drags By/The La La La Song	Oct 1966
37	In The Country/Finders Keepers	Dec 1966
38	It's All Over/Why Wasn't I Born Rich?	Mar 1967
39	I'll Come Running/I Got The Feelin'	Jun 1967
40	The Day I Met Marie/Our Story Book	Aug 1967
41	All My Love/Sweet Little Jesus Boy	Nov 1967
42	Congratulations/High 'n' Dry	Mar 1968
43	I'll Love You Forever Today/Girl, You'll Be A Woman Soon	Jun 1968
44	Marianne/Mr Nice	Sep 1968
45	Don't Forget To Catch Me/What's More (I Don't Need Her)	Nov 1968
46	Good Times (Better Times)/Occasional Rain	Feb 1969
47	Big Ship/She's Leaving You	May 1969
48	Throw Down A Line (Cliff & Hank)/Reflections	Sep 1969
49	With The Eyes Of A Child/So Long	Nov 1969
50	The Joy Of Living (Cliff & Hank)/Leave My Woman Alone/Boogitoo (Cliff & Hank)	Feb 1970
51	Goodbye Sam, Hello Samantha/You Can Never Tell	Jun 1970
52	I Ain't Got Time Anymore/Monday Comes Too Soon	Aug 1970
53	Sunny Honey Girl/Don't Move Away (with Olivia Newton-John)/I Was Only Fooling Myself	Jan 1971
54	Silvery Rain/Annabella Umbrella/Time Flies	Apr 1971
55	Flying Machine/Pigeon	Jul 1971
56	Sing A Song Of Freedom/A Thousand Conversations	Nov 1971

57	Jesus/Mr Cloud	Mar 1972
58	Living In Harmony/Empty Chairs	Aug 1972
59	A Brand New Song/The Old Accordian	Dec 1972
60	Power To All Our Friends/Come Back Billie Jo	Mar 1973
61	Help It Along/Tomorrow Rising/Days Of Love/ Ashes To Ashes	May 1973
62	Take Me High/Celestial Houses	Nov 1973
63	(You Keep Me) Hangin' On/Love Is Here	May 1974
64	It's Only Me You've Left Behind/You're The One	Mar 1975
65	(There's A) Honky Tonk Angel (Who Will Take Me Back In)/Wouldn't You Know It (Got Myself a Girl)	Sep 1975
66	Miss You Nights/Love Is Enough	Feb 1976
67	Devil Woman/Love On	May 1976
68	I Can't Ask For Anything More Than You, Babe/ Junior Cowboy	Aug 1976
69	Hey, Mr Dream Maker/No One Waits	Nov 1976
70	My Kinda Life/Nothing Left For Me To Say	Feb 1977
71	When Two Worlds Drift Apart/That's Why I Love You	Jun 1977
72	Yes! He Lives/Good On The Sally Army	Jan 1978
73	Please Remember Me/Please Don't Tease	Jul 1978
74	Can't Take The Hurt Anymore/Needing A Friend	Nov 1978
75	Green Light/Imagine Love	Mar 1979
76	We Don't Talk Anymore/Count Me Out	Jul 1979
77	Hot Shot/Walking In The Light	Nov 1979
78	Carrie/Moving In	Feb 1980
79	Dreamin'/Dynamite	Aug 1980
80	A Little In Love/Keep On Looking	Jan 1981
81	Wired For Sound/Hold On	Aug 1981
82	Daddy's Home/Shakin' All Over	Nov 1981
83	The Only Way Out/Under The Influence	Jul 1982
84	Where Do We Go From Here?/Discovering	Sep 1982
85	Little Town/Love And A Helping Hand/ You, Me and Jesus	Nov 1982

L P s

1	Cliff	Apr 1959
2	Cliff Sings	Nov 1959
3	Me And My Shadows	Oct 1960
4	Listen To Cliff	May 1961
5	21 Today	Oct 1961
6	The Young Ones	Dec 1961
7	32 Minutes And 17 Seconds With Cliff Richard	Oct 1962
8	Summer Holiday	Jan 1963
9	Cliff's Hit Album	Jul 1963
10	When In Spain	Sep 1963
11	Wonderful Life	Jul 1964
12	Aladdin And His Wonderful Lamp	Dec 1964
13	Cliff Richard	Apr 1965
14	More Hits By Cliff	Jul 1965
15	When In Rome	Aug 1965
16	Love Is Forever	Nov 1965
17	Kinda Latin	May 1966
18	Finders Keepers	Dec 1966
19	Cinderella	Jan 1967
20	Don't Stop Me Now	Apr 1967
21	Good News	Oct 1967
22	Cliff In Japan	May 1968
23	Two A Penny	Aug 1968
24	Established 1958	Sep 1968
25	The Best Of Cliff	Jun 1969
26	Sincerely	Oct 1969
27	It'll Be Me	Nov 1969
28	Cliff Live At The Talk Of The Town	Jul 1970
29	About That Man	Oct 1970
30	His Land	Nov 1970
31	Tracks 'n' Grooves	Nov 1970

32	The Best Of Cliff, Volume 2	Nov 1972
33	Take Me High	Dec 1973
34	Help It Along	Jun 1974
35	The 31st Of February Street	Nov 1974
36	I'm Nearly Famous	May 1976
37	Every Face Tells A Story	Mar 1977
38	40 Golden Greats	Sep 1977
39	Small Corners	Feb 1978
40	Green Light	Sep 1978
41	Thank You Very Much (Cliff And The Shadows)	Feb 1979
42	Rock 'n' Roll Juvenile	Sep 1979
43	I'm No Hero	Sep 1980
44	Love Songs	Jul 1981
45	Wired For Sound	Sep 1981
46	Now You See Me ... Now You Don't	Aug 1982
47	Dressed For The Occasion	May 1983
48	Silver	Oct 1983

(a second album—Rock 'n' Roll Silver—was included as part of a limited edition boxed set)

49	Cliff And The Shadows	Sep 1984
50	The Rock Connection	Nov 1984
51	Always Guaranteed	Sep 1987
52	Private Collection	Nov 1988
53	Stronger	Oct 1989
54	From A Distance—The Event	Nov 1990
55	Together (With Cliff Richard)	Nov 1991
56	Cliff Richard: The Album	Mar 1993

90

20/9/57

We, the undersigned (members of Dick Teagues Skiffle group) hereby agree not to leave the group to take an individual engagement with any other musical concern without previously discussing the matter with the full group and its controlling manager.

Signed :—

Dick Teague
T. Smart

M. Teague
Harry Webb

G. Harrison
A. Wand.
N. Drums

Cliff's first contract

1958: Cliff's first billing as
Cliff Richard

The *Sunday Pictorial* advertisement that inspired Lionel Bart's
writing of 'Living Doll'

Hippodrome Birmingham

Dear Dave,
We've decided to have the "Red" Fender Guitar
With   A Three pickups.
        B With Tremolo lever.
        C Gold plated Hardware

The guitar is a "Stratocaster"
Have marked in catalogue.
When you send for it please order spare set balanced strings and also a "Fender Case"
Well Dave, thanks a million.
All the Best
Cliff.

1959: Cliff's letter to David Lilley organizing the purchase of
Hank Marvin's first Fender Stratocaster

1960: Cliff's billing on his first
tour of America

David Smith—m.—?

Vitriano Rebeiro—m.—?

George David Smith—m.—Emiline Josephine Rebeiro
(m. Calcutta 1869)

Marie Beatrice Smith
(b. 1873/1874)

—m.—

W.B. Bridgwater
(b. Hampstead 1870)

William Bridgwater—m.—Martha Walker

Dorothy Edith Bridgwater
(b. 1902)

—m.—

William Edward Dazely
(b. Kirkee 1896)

Daisy Haines——m.——Edward Dazely

William Haines—m.—?

William Dazely—m.—?

Dorothy Marie Dazely
(b. Lahore 1920)

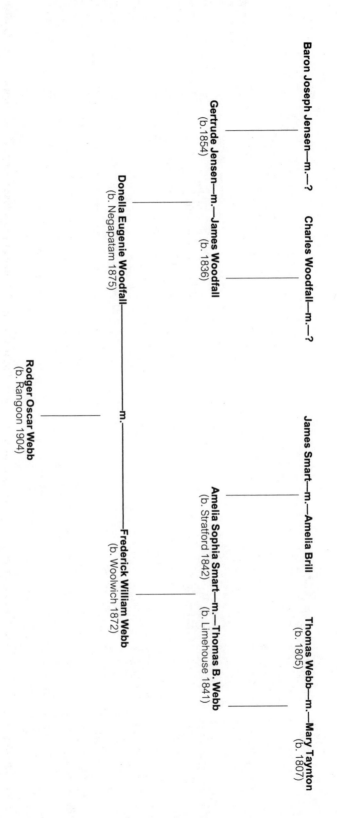

Baron Joseph Jensen—m.—?

Charles Woodfall—m.—?

James Smart—m.—Amelia Brill

Thomas Webb—m.—Mary Taynton
(b. 1805)   (b. 1807)

Gertrude Jensen—m.—James Woodfall
(b. 1854)   (b. 1836)

Amelia Sophia Smart—m.—Thomas B. Webb
(b. Stratford 1842)   (b. Limehouse 1841)

Donella Eugenie Woodfall—————m.——————Frederick William Webb
(b. Negapatam 1875)   (b. Woolwich 1872)

Rodger Oscar Webb
(b. Rangoon 1904)

Index

Y

Picture Acknowledgments

Every effort has been made to trace the copyright holders of the photographs in this book, but one or two were unreachable. We would be grateful if the photographers concerned would contact us.

SECTION 1
page 1: Vincent Bridgwater
page 2: (top & middle) Joyce Dobra; (bottom) Vincent Bridgwater
page 3: Joyce Dobra
page 4: (top) Dorothy Willis; (middle) Joyce Dobra; (bottom) *Waltham and Cheshunt Weekly Telegraph*
page 5: (top) John Vince; (middle & bottom) Jay Norris
page 6: Jan Goring
page 7: Jan Goring
page 8: (top) Terry Smart

SECTION 2
page 9: (top) Franklyn Boyd; (bottom) Ian Samwell
page 10: (middle) Popperfoto
page 11: (top) Ray Mackender; (bottom) Hulton Deutsch
page 12: (top) Royston Ellis; (middle) Ray Mackender; (bottom) Rex Features
page 13: (top three) Ron Ernstone; (bottom) Topham
page 14: (top) Rex Features; (middle) Ray Mackender; (bottom) David H. Hawley
page 15: (top left & right) Ian Samwell; (middle) Rex Features; (bottom) EMI Records

SECTION 3
page 16: (top) Delia Wicks; (bottom) Topham
page 17: (top) Popperfoto; (middle) Topham; (bottom) Rex Features
page 18: (top) Daily Express; (middle) Syndication International; (bottom) Camera Press
page 19: Graham Disbrey
page 20: (top) Daily Express; (bottom) Norrie Paramor
page 21: (top) Graham Disbrey; (middle) Rex Features; (bottom) Dave Foster
page 22: (top) London Features International; (bottom) Popperfoto
page 23: (top) Hulton Deutsch; (bottom) Rex Features
page 24: (top left) Joan Batten; (top right) Daily Express; (bottom) Rex Features

SECTION 4
page 25: (top) Tear Fund; (middle) Ray Mackender; (bottom) Steve Turner
page 26: Steve Turner
page 27: (top) Hulton Deutsch; (bottom) Retna
page 28: (top) Syndication International; (middle & bottom) Graham Disbrey
page 29: (top) Topham; (bottom) Graham Disbrey
page 30: (top) Graham Disbrey; (bottom) Topham
page 31: (top) Topham; (bottom) London Features International